THE DEVIL

IN

GOD'S OLD MAN

Sue Mayes Newhall

❀ ❀ ❀

THE DEVIL
IN
GOD'S OLD MAN

W · W · Norton & Company · Inc ·

NEW YORK

FOR Joe

Contents

	PROLOGUE	11
ONE	ARRIVAL	15
TWO	WHY NAMKHAM?	27
THREE	DIGGING IN	34
FOUR	NECESSITY AND INVENTION	72
FIVE	PATIENTS	93
SIX	HOUSEHOLD HELPERS	107
SEVEN	GATHERING CLOUDS	112
EIGHT	KUTKAI	121
NINE	FIRST DEPORTATION ORDERS	141
TEN	BROAD NATIONALIZATIONS	157
ELEVEN	RANGOON VACATION	172
TWELVE	THE OLD MAN'S DEATH	196
THIRTEEN	THE FUNERAL	217
FOURTEEN	FINAL DEPORTATION ORDERS	226
	EPILOGUE	247

Illustrations appear between pages 112 and 113

Acknowledgments

My deepest appreciation to Mr. Wyatt Blassingame for his invaluable advice in the preparation of this manuscript. Also, to Betty O'Dell and my other creative writing friends for their unfailing encouragement and help.

Prologue

In the summer of 1963 my husband decided, with my hesitant approval, to leave his medical practice in Florida for three years to aid in the work of a frontier hospital in northern Burma. We had three small sons, Tim, aged five, Philip, who was two, and Paul, ten months, when we embarked on our great adventure. The hospital to which we went had been founded and was still run at that time by Dr. Gordon S. Seagrave, known to many in America and throughout the world as the "Burma Surgeon."

Now the adventure is over, and I would like to share with others some of our experiences during the years in Burma. I want also to tell what kind of man Dr. Seagrave was in my opinion. Many who knew of Dr. Seagrave and his work have urged me to write a sequel to his books, describing the last months of his life, his final illness and death, and the fate of the hospital to which he devoted his life.

Most of all, I want to impart, if I can, what those years in Burma meant to me, and their impact on our family. During one's lifetime, there are a few incidents which markedly change the course of events and alter one's thinking. For some, these changes are for the worse; for others they are for the better. The changes I experienced as a result of our work in Burma were, without a doubt, for my betterment. Those years were a time for introspection, re-dedication, and spiritual rearmament.

The average person in America has heard of Burma but knows little about it. Neither did I before August, 1963. The following are some facts which may help to make the story clearer.

Burma is a small country in Southeast Asia about the size of Texas. The south-central section is often referred to as Burma Proper, and it is here that roughly thirteen million Burmese and two million Karens live. The strip along the coast of the Bay of Bengal on the west is known as the Arakan district and is often included in Burma Proper, for the Arakanese are closely related to the Burmese. This whole area was ruled by the Burmese kings before the three Burmese-British wars.

Around Burma Proper are the mountainous Frontier States, which touch on the borders of India, China, and Thailand. Proceeding clockwise around Burma Proper are the Chin Hills, the Naga Hills, the Kachin State, the Northern Shan States, the Southern Shan States, the Wa States, the Karen State, and the Tenasserim Division.

From these Frontier States come a wide variety of people. The Karens are kind and gentle as a rule, and Karen women make up most of the nursing profession. The Burmese have overlorded them for centuries and treated them as inferiors. The Karens took to Christianity eagerly when it was introduced into Burma and there are more Christians among the Karens than any other group. The Kachins are short, stocky, and strong, and are known as fierce fighters. They, too, have adopted Christianity in large numbers. The Shans migrated from southern China, where they had their own kings and walled cities centuries ago.

In addition to the Karens, Shans, and Kachins, there are the Chins, Wa, Lahu, Lisu, and many others, as well as large numbers of Chinese. To the inexperienced observer most of these peoples closely resemble one another. It is only after months of observation that the differences become apparent. They range in color from light brown and pale yellow to dark brown, and the black of some Indians. All have black hair and very dark eyes. Each group has its own social customs, type of dress, and language. They usually band together in isolated communities, and there has always been prejudice and animosity among them.

Such was the Burma we found in the summer of 1963.

THE DEVIL

IN

GOD'S OLD MAN

CHAPTER ONE

ARRIVAL

My eyes gradually became accustomed to the dimness of early dawn, and I surveyed the small room in which I had slept. Neither the room nor its contents were different from most bedrooms, but I felt strange and a little frightened. Outside, a steady rain beat on the windowpane.

I lay there trying to reconstruct the events of the previous week. Had it been only a week since we had left our home in Bradenton, Florida? I closed my eyes, and could visualize our family stepping from the great jet which had carried us 12,000 miles from New York to Rangoon, Burma. First off the plane had been Tim, our five-year-old son, followed by Philip, aged two, who clung to my hand to keep from falling down the steep steps. Then came my husband, Joseph Newhall, carrying Paul, who was only ten months old. Joe also held a box which had housed Huckleberry Hound, our dachshund, throughout the flight. With us was Mrs. Fanny Ellison from New York, a representative of the

American Medical Center for Burma, Inc.

At Mingaladon Airport in Rangoon we were met by a short Burmese with bristly graying hair and gold teeth. He introduced himself as Tun Shein, the administrator of the Namkham Hospital, and he immediately took charge of everything for us.

It would be many months before we knew the full worth of this man, Tun Shein. His small frame and agility made him appear much younger than his sixty years. We found him to be a man of unusual skill, courage, and integrity. He was a Karen, a staunch Christian, and a leader among his fellow believers, having held the high office of General Secretary of the Burma Baptist Convention. The Burmese called him U Tun Shein, the *U* corresponding to our English word *Mr.* The term is reserved for older men and actually means "uncle." To his fellow Karens, Tun Shein was known as Thra Tun Shein, meaning "teacher."

Tun Shein took us to the Baptist Guest House, where we were to stay for the next few days. According to protocol, we had to check in at the U.S. Embassy and make other contacts before leaving Rangoon for our ultimate destination, the small town of Namkham in the Northern Shan States, over 700 miles to the north. These arrangements had taken five days.

Ancient trucks and buses clattered down the streets of Rangoon, open bazaars dotted the curbs. The natives carried large black umbrellas as protection against the sun and the frequent summer rains as they ambled to their shops or to the pagodas for prayers to the Lord Buddha. Rangoon was hot and wet, but it wasn't an unfriendly city, and I might even have enjoyed my five days there if I had been able to relax and free my mind of the many anxieties which cluttered it.

The first part of our trip north from Rangoon was an overnight train ride to Mandalay. Our family and Fanny Ellison were crowded into a small compartment in the first-class car. The six of us—and Huckleberry—made quite a compartmentful, and before the night was over Fanny must have felt that she knew all of us pretty well. We took turns lying down, and alternately opened and closed the two small windows. Consequently, we either sweltered and or were eaten by mosquitoes and covered with cinders. It wasn't until we got off the train in the morning and I had a chance to observe the crowded third-class cars with their hard wooden benches that I appreciated the relative comfort of our car.

Tun Shein and his Shan driver, Hsu Aung, met us at the Mandalay station. They had driven the 250 bumpy treacherous miles from Rangoon in the black Rambler Station Wagon owned by the Namkham Hospital. We must have looked ridiculous as we drove away from the railroad station with trunks and suitcases stacked precariously on top, covered with a tarpaulin, and tied with ropes. In addition, the entire space behind the second seat of the station wagon was filled with baggage. The car looked as though its rear end might drag at any minute, as indeed it did later when we hit the numerous pot-holes along the road.

People were packed into the car almost as tightly as the baggage. Tun Shein was behind the wheel and next to him was Fanny, with the driver-mechanic, Hsu Aung, on her right. That left the back seat for our family. Joe gamely folded his six-foot frame into the small space allotted to him, while Tim squirmed all over his lap. Philip and Paul sat on the seat between Joe and me, and Huckleberry tried to find room to lie down on the floor.

Our first stop was in downtown Mandalay at the U.S. Consul's home, where we met Miss Ruth McClendon, Acting Consul. Then, back in the sardine can we called a car, we left Mandalay. Within a few miles the already overworked motor began to groan and strain as we left the lowlands of south Burma and started the trek into the hills of the Shan States.

By early evening we had reached Maymyo, where we had a delicious meal and a good night's sleep at the Guest House located on the Baptist Mission Compound.

The next day's travel was long and hard, beginning soon after dawn and lasting until dark. During that time we covered only 250 miles. The Burmese roads were not made for high speeds; I was sure they were the bumpiest and most winding roads anywhere, and filled with bottomless holes. To keep my mind off my tired and cramped muscles, I watched the scenery. We left the hot plains behind us and steadily climbed deeper into the Shan Hills. The air became cool and refreshing. As the rolling hills gave way to higher peaks, I was reminded of similar beautiful spots in the Smoky Mountains of North Carolina. . . .

I was brought back to the present by sounds of movement in other parts of the house. We had spent a comfortable night in Kutkai at the home of Baptist missionaries. It was time to rise and prepare for the final day of travel. I felt a surge of excitement just knowing we would soon arrive at the Namkham Hospital. I shook Joe. "Wake up, it's time to get on the road again!"

He groaned, "My legs can't take much more of that cramped car. What time did Tun Shein say we should get to Namkham?"

"We should be there before noon, but we have to get moving. Tun Shein is probably pacing the floor right now, wondering how we can sleep past dawn."

Fanny was dressed and waiting for breakfast when we walked into the kitchen. She looked excited and happy, for she, too, was anxious to arrive at Namkham. She was traveling under the auspices of the American Medical Center for Burma, Inc., the group which supported the work of the Namkham Hospital, and it was her prime objective to study the needs of the hospital for a few weeks and prepare a report for the board of directors in New York. She considered her assignment much more than a job: it was her share in a great humanitarian undertaking.

As I had guessed, Tun Shein was waiting for us somewhat impatiently, so we hurried with breakfast and got our things into the car. The rain was still falling as we left the town of Kutkai. The narrow winding road was level for a few miles, and then, once again, we began to climb into the mountains. The Rambler labored and groaned under its great load, and many times almost came to a stop on a steep grade.

"You folks ever heard of the Burma Road?" Tun Shein asked. "Well, this is it. Actually, we've been on it since we left Lashio yesterday afternoon. It runs from Lashio across the China border to Kunming. You may remember that it was built during the early days of World War II as a supply route for Chiang Kai-Shek's armies. Now it's the only road linking the Shan Hills area and points north with the southern part of Burma."

Of course I had heard of the Burma Road, but I expected more than a winding trail. It had been blacktopped at one time, but lack of maintenance had left the pot-holes with pot-holes, and the hard surface had worn off in many spots. The road was scarcely wider than our car, with sheer drops down the mountainside. Passing was difficult but traffic was exceptionally light. We met only an occasional oxcart with its tattooed Shan driver, and some-times an ancient, overloaded bus.

We drove through numerous villages, inhabited predominately by Shan, or Kachin, or Chinese. All had bamboo houses with thatched roofs. The men were tattooed, the women turbaned. It took real skill for Tun Shein to bypass the pigs and chickens, and the bare-bottomed children who arranged themselves along the road. A passing car such as ours obviously was a rarity.

Outside the villages, we passed endless rice paddies. Here and there were small streams where nearly naked boys wearing large coolie hats were scrubbing their water buffalo.

"These boys have to take good care of the buffalo because the families couldn't harvest their crops without them," Tun Shein explained. "The buffalo also pull the plows and carts, and serve many other purposes. To the Shan farmer the buffalo is the most important member of the family, next to himself, of course!"

By midmorning we reached the junction of the Burma and Ledo Roads. From this point on the Burma Road continued north a few miles and across the China border, and the Ledo Road wound on a northwesterly course through the Kachin State and into India. At the junction was a tiny village, Mongyu, where we had to stop for a customs check. Tun Shein had forewarned the customs officer that we would be passing through, and he was prepared and most cordial. Dressed in a long wraparound skirt called a *longyi,* the traditional dress of Burmese men and women, he glanced through our papers, but did not examine any of the baggage. Then he invited us to have tea with him. By this time we were surrounded by curious children who had never seen such strange-looking people before. They looked, touched, smiled, and wiped their runny noses on their shirts.

The local teahouse was a bamboo shack with a dirt floor and no doors or screened windows. My first thought was to pass up the tea, but I decided it would be best to make a pretense of drinking, at least. A large rat walked gingerly across one of the rafters overhead, and I held my breath for fear he would slip and fall on our table. This was our introduction to Shan tea, and it was not my favorite drink after the first taste, nor did it become so after many more. Grown in the Shan Hills, the leaves are dried and then used without any further curing or aging. That bitter brew, drunk plain except for an occasional pinch of salt, was too much for me. I learned later that every Shan interrupted his work many times a day for a cup of tea, whether at home or in the middle of a rice paddy.

A few miles past Mongyu we began to descend into a beautiful valley. "When I get here, I feel that I'm almost home," Tun Shein told us. "This is the beginning of the Shweli Valley, and that is the Shweli River running down the middle of it. Those green hills over on the other side of the valley are in China."

Near the town of Muse, Tun Shein pointed out a stone marker about five feet high which stood approximately fifty feet from the road. "This is the closest we ever come to the China border. That stone marks the boundary line."

There were no border guards, nothing to indicate that one could pass from one country to another by stepping beyond that stone. It was surrounded on all sides by rice paddies, and I wondered how some of the farmers knew whether their small plot of ground was in Burma or in China.

I noticed a white Jeep panel truck parked in the shade of a tree some distance ahead of us. Without warning, Tun Shein pulled up beside the truck and stopped. Completely puzzled, I looked at the vehicle and saw these words printed on the door:

A gift to the Namkham Hospital for the people of Burma from the people of the United States through C.A.R.E.

The door of the Jeep opened and out stepped a heavy-set elderly man and a dainty Burmese girl about seven years old. The man wore dark trousers and a white dress shirt open at the neck, with the sleeves rolled up past his elbows. He had a shock of white hair and a mustache to match. His massive head was cocked slightly to one side on his broad shoulders and he moved stiffly toward our car. His first words were a gruff statement to Tun Shein. "You're late."

Tun Shein smiled and replied, "Dr. Seagrave, this is Joe and Sue Newhall and their boys, and Fanny Ellison."

"So this is Dr. Gordon Seagrave, the Burma Surgeon," I thought. Joe and I had read his book *The Life of a Burma Surgeon* and had corresponded with him before leaving the States. Somehow, he had seemed more legend than reality to me, and yet, here he was, very real. I sat almost dumbfounded until I realized that everyone else had gotten out of the car and warm greetings were being exchanged. Dr. Seagrave and Fanny had been friends for years through correspondence, since she handled many business matters involving the hospital.

Dr. Seagrave turned to the little girl who hung shyly in the background. "Come on up here, Augusta. Folks, this is Augusta Star Po, my adopted granddaughter." He might have added, "and the apple of my eye," for he obviously loved the child very much.

Dr. Seagrave then said to our driver, "Hsu Aung, you come along and drive this toy for me. We'll get on back as quick as we can and alert the hospital staff that the rest of you are on the way."

Once more we got back into the car and drove the remaining few miles to the town of Namkham. As we approached, Tun Shein directed our attention to a group of stone buildings on the top of a hill to our left. "That's it," he said, "the Namkham Hospital." He made a sharp turn and the car labored and strained up one last hill.

I shall never forget the sight as we rounded the final curve and stopped beneath a huge banyan tree. There were hundreds of people of all sizes and descriptions, some standing and some squatting oriental fashion around a large stone building. Every eye was trained upon our car.

Tun Shein gave a tired sigh and threw up his hands. "You'll have to go the rest of the way by yourselves." So we opened the car doors and ventured forth.

By this time Dr. Seagrave had approached us once more and said, "Hsu Aung and I blasted the ambulance siren to tell everyone that you were near, and they've all turned out to welcome you to the Namkham Hospital."

It was a welcome to end all welcomes. The entire staff and all the student nurses were there in a long neat row, dressed in bright-colored *longyis* and smiling shyly. The compound school had been dismissed for the big occasion and children were milling about all over the place. Every patient who could possibly get out of bed was outside or leaning from the windows to get a first glimpse of the American doctor and his family. Even the townspeople had turned out in large numbers.

At the head of the line of welcomers was a short, thickset man with graying hair whose dark skin and features told of his Indian ancestry. He wore a stethoscope draped around his neck, and he looked very bored.

"This is Dr. Olwen Silgardo," said Dr. Seagrave. "He has been here at this hospital for over twelve years."

We shook hands with Dr. Silgardo, who smiled and mumbled a few words. Then Dr. Seagrave led us to four nurses who stood together. Each wore a sky-blue *longyi,* a short white blouse called an *engyi,* and a cap with a black band. There was no doubting the sincerity of their welcome. I have never seen such sweet smiles as theirs, as each of them handed us a bouquet of flowers bound together by a large white ribbon. Indicating the first nurse, a short, elderly woman with glasses, Dr. Seagrave said, "This is Grandma Naomi, our matron. She has been around here longer than anyone except me. Next is Esther, who runs our laboratory and X-ray. Next to her is her sister, Pansy, who is the dean of our nursing school and also my secretary. Incidentally, Pansy is Augusta's mother. Last in this group is Emily, the chief nurse-midwife. These are our senior nurses, and without these four gals I couldn't run my hospital."

Moving on, we passed by a line of staff nurses, stopping to shake hands as we were introduced. Some were described by Dr. Seagrave as "oldtimers" who had been with him since the war years. There was Ngwe Nyunt, Say Paw, Dorothy, Eleanor, and others. I remembered many of their names, having read about them in *The Life of a Burma Surgeon.*

The student nurses were next in line, all 140 of them. The fourth-year girls in midwife training wore pink *longyis.* The third-year girls wore green, the second bright red; the first-year girls wore dark blue, and as yet had no caps. I marveled that Dr. Seagrave knew the name of each one and the part of Burma from which she had come. There were Shan, Kachin, Karen, Lahu, Wa, Chin, Arakanese, Paloung, and Chinese girls. Some knew only a few words of English, but language was no barrier as we held their hands and saw their big smiles and twinkling dark eyes.

Upon reaching the end of the long line we were taken to our

house. The whole group followed in a giant parade as we walked on a narrow dirt road, down one hill and up another. Ahead of us was a large stone house with a gaily painted sign over the door: WELCOME HOME. Near the back door, standing very straight, was a neatly dressed Chinese with his hair parted in the middle and slicked back. "I am Wong Jack, cook," he said. Behind him were two Karen girls, Shirley and Nella, who were to do the housework and be nannies for the children.

So much was happening so quickly that I barely saw the interior of the house as we were led through it. The kitchen appeared adequate but quite rustic, with its wood-burning cookstove and unpainted walls and cabinets. It opened into a dining room and then a large living room, comfortably furnished and carpeted. Both living and dining room had large stone fireplaces. We hastily examined the three large bedrooms, and then, to my great relief, I discovered a bathroom, complete with a bathtub and a real flushing toilet. Stairs led up from the dining room to an attic which had been partially finished with walls made of woven bamboo strips. The attic looked perfect for children's games on a rainy day, and it proved to be even more valuable as a storage place and for drying laundry during the rainy season.

Our tour of the house was cut short as we were whisked away to Dr. Seagrave's house for lunch. By now we had gathered that almost everyone referred to him as "the Old Man." Tim accompanied Joe, Fanny, and me, but the two younger boys stayed behind with the nannies and rested.

Once again we met Pansy, for she and Augusta lived in Dr. Seagrave's home and were the only family he had in Burma. Pansy was a petite Karen with shining dark eyes and long black hair which she wore pulled back and tied in a knot in the traditional way. She had worked hard to prepare food she thought we would like, and, among other things, had made some ice cream for dessert. Unfortunately, their ancient and unpredictable refrigerator had only frozen it to the consistency of thin mush. Pansy's disappointment far exceeded our own, for we ate the soupy ice cream with pleasure.

It didn't take long to discover that Dr. Seagrave loved to talk. In his slow drawl he kept up a constant flow of stories about the hospital and the people in it. One of the first stories concerned Pansy's tragic marriage to a "good-for-nothing s.o.b.," which had lasted only a few months. I squirmed in my chair, feeling uncomfortable at hearing this very personal tale in Pansy's presence, but she didn't seem to notice.

When he was not eating, Dr. Seagrave always had a lighted cigarette in his hand. The first two joints of all four fingers on his left hand were stained brown from years of chain-smoking. When I asked him what his favorite brand of cigarettes was, he replied, "I like Camels best of all, and Chesterfields next, but I'll smoke anything."

"Can you buy American cigarettes here?" I asked.

"Hell, no. All we can buy here are these Burmese Capitains." He held up a round can from which he had just removed a cigarette. "They taste like burning rope. Whenever anyone makes a trip to Rangoon they beg, borrow, or steal some cigarettes from the U.S. Embassy Coop for me. I always start the day with a Camel if I have any just to get that good taste in my mouth. After that I smoke a can or two of these ropes before I allow myself the luxury of another good cigarette."

That evening a dinner was held in our honor in the nurses' dining room. Everyone on the compound was invited and the room was packed. Members of the staff had been working for days to make the room festive with paper streamers, balloons, and welcome signs.

Joe, Tim, and I sat at the table of honor with Dr. Seagrave, Fanny, Dr. and Mrs. Silgardo, and U Hkun Lu, a member of the local hospital committee in the town of Namkham. The dinner consisted of enough American dishes to please us and enough Burmese food to suit everyone else. Following the dinner the program began with a group of student nurses singing "Welcome Dear Doctor," to the tune of "Welcome Sweet Springtime." After that we were entertained with short songs in Burmese, Karen, Shan, Kachin, Chin, Chinese, Lahu, and Lisu by girls dressed in the appropriate native costumes.

Then, it was time for the speechmaking. U Hkun Lu and Tun Shein gave brief words of welcome and Fanny and Joe responded. I had hoped that I would be excused from this chore, but everyone insisted that I say a few words, too. I hardly knew where to begin or what to say. I was exhausted by the many days of hard travel, and yet thrilled by our welcome to Namkham. I felt a nagging loneliness for family, friends, and the familiar things we had left behind, and at the same time I looked forward to working with these new friends in the years to come. So I simply told the group that I wanted very much to do my best while working at the hospital, and that I knew they could help me as much as or more than I could help them.

When I sat down, Dr. Seagrave growled, "Congratulations. That's the best speech I ever heard. I'm so damned tired of people coming out here who think they know it all and the Burmese don't know anything. You'll get along fine here."

Before the party was over, two of the student nurses brought us gifts of welcome. One was a basket filled with tiny tomatoes, several papayas, and a live chicken. Timmy was thrilled with the chicken and wanted to hold it. It got loose as we were walking home and Huckleberry chased our chicken dinner off into the darkness.

CHAPTER TWO

WHY NAMKHAM?

Many people have asked me, "Why did you leave your home, a growing medical practice, and a comfortable life to go halfway around the world to a country filled with disease and uncertainty?"

I never did understand all the reasons. As I look back over the months and years before our trip to Burma, it is difficult to pick out the events and factors which led to our decision to go.

Joe graduated from Tulane University School of Medicine in 1955. We were married shortly after and spent four happy years in New Orleans while he took an internship and specialty training at Charity Hospital and I worked in the same institution as a medical technologist.

Finding a place in which to settle after Joe's residency was not particularly difficult. We knew we wanted to live in Florida, near the water and away from congested areas. Bradenton, on the Gulf Coast, had those advantages, plus promising practice opportunities. So we moved to Bradenton in the summer of 1959.

Joe began the practice of obstetrics and gynecology in association with Dr. Albert A. Simkus. Al was congenial and helpful and everything went smoothly. Within four years we were well on the way to the success of which we had dreamed. We had a new home, two automobiles, and a membership in the Country Club, and were well accepted in the community. Best of all, we had three fine sons.

Then one evening in February of 1963 Joe came home from the hospital unusually late. The children were in bed and I was washing dishes. As was his custom, he read one of his medical journals while eating. Finally he looked up and said, "Here's an interesting news item I read earlier. I've been turning it over in my mind all day. Let me read it to you."

> A search is under way for a young American GP with an interest in surgery who can work with the famed Burma Surgeon, Dr. Gordon S. Seagrave. Minimum appointment at Seagrave's 325-bed hospital in Namkham, Burma, will be for two years. The candidate should be 40 or under, married or single, and ready to leave for Burma as soon as his visa is approved. Appointment carries with it travel expenses, western-style housing accommodations and a modest yearly salary. Interested doctors are asked to write to the American Medical Center for Burma, Inc., 6 Penn Plaza, Philadelphia 3.

"This sounds very interesting to me, and I think I'd like to write and inquire about it. What do you think?"

I stood motionless at the sink for a few seconds. I had always prided myself on being calm most of the time and on being able to hear startling news with no outward show of concern, but this was a pretty hard test of my serenity. What should I say? Finally the words rolled out. "Okay, I give up, why this bolt out of the blue? Do you really mean it? Do you want to give up everything here and go to Burma? I don't even know where Burma is, and I never heard of the 'famed Burma Surgeon.'"

Joe's face was serious. "Haven't you ever read the book *The*

Life of a Burma Surgeon? Dr. Seagrave is an old fellow who's been running a hospital in northern Burma for years and years, and in that book he tells about his experiences. I wouldn't want to spend the rest of my life in Burma, but two or three years maybe, like this article says."

I forgot the dishes in the sink and dropped into a chair at the table. "If we were going to do something like that, we should have done it before getting so involved here."

"Well, those people really need care and there are so few doctors to help them. Now, don't get excited and start packing. I was mostly thinking out loud."

"No, you weren't either, Joe, I can tell. So, come on out with it and tell me what you've decided to do."

"Susie, you know I wouldn't decide to do anything without your okay. Don't you? But you wouldn't mind if I wrote and asked a few questions, would you?"

"No, I guess it wouldn't hurt, but, well, just well, that's all. I thought I was settled for life."

"And I'm sure you are. It's just that . . . I enjoy my practice here, but if a patient doesn't come to me, she can go to any number of qualified men and receive care. If she doesn't like the way I part my hair, some other doctor parts his on the other side so she goes there. In a place like Namkham I could do my best for a patient and know that if he hadn't come to me he probably would have done without. When I'm an old man I'd like the satisfaction of knowing that I've contributed something worthwhile to mankind, as well as making a good living for myself and my family. That's not bad, is it?"

"Of course not. It's a very worthwhile ambition, but assuming that we did go to Burma, what would happen to your practice here, and could you return later?"

"Those are just two of the many things that would have to be worked out. Now that Dr. Southerland has joined us, I think he and Al could take care of things. Maybe they would want to take in another doctor while I was away. I'm sure they'd be willing to let me return to the group later if I wanted to. If not, I'd have to make other arrangements."

"Don't say that so lightly. Starting a new practice takes a long time and a lot of work."

"But it's not impossible, and most likely it won't be necessary. Look, nearly everyone we know is so busy doing this thing and that, and most of it is silly nonsense. They're so tied down with mortgages they practically have to call the bank to see if it's all right to take a day off. That could happen to us, and I'd like to do my one good turn before I'm completely snowed."

"Okay, but what about the boys? Do you think it's fair to them? Those Asian countries have malaria, dysentery, and who knows what all. And what kind of schools do you think we'll find? Timmy starts school in September, you know."

"Susie, I'm sure that if there was a serious health hazard for the children the center wouldn't ask a married man to go. And if it comes down to all of Asia or my boys, of course I'm for my boys. We'll find out what we need to know later and work out the answers as we go along. All I propose to do now is write a short letter of inquiry. That won't commit us to a thing. Besides, I imagine a lot of doctors will write to find out the details and our chances of being selected are pretty slim."

That night I lay awake for hours. Should we, or shouldn't we? Was it worth the price? I knew that all I had to do was say flatly, "No, I won't go," and that would end it. But down deep I did want to go. It was the sort of opportunity that came to few people, and Joe seemed keen on it. I had seldom objected to any of Joe's ideas, for I knew him to be absolutely sincere, and whatever conclusions he reached came after deep thought. When faced with an important decision, he considered all the possibilities, arrived at what he honestly believed to be the best solution, and proceeded without a backward look. If things didn't work out he never brooded, but felt he had done what he thought best. Sometimes, when I was tense and worried, I had been annoyed by his calm and self-assurance, but over the years of our married life I had come to have a great deal of respect for his clear thinking and logic.

The next day Joe wrote a letter to the American Medical Center for Burma, Inc., usually abbreviated A.M.C.B., expressing interest in going to the Namkham Hospital and requesting more information. There was a quick reply, and I learned that if we were chosen I, as a Registered Medical Technologist, would be expected to work part-time in the hospital laboratory.

February came to a close, March and April passed. We sent and received many letters. By this time, the Board of Directors of the A.M.C.B. knew all about us, and we knew as much as possible about the Namkham Hospital, whose work they supported. It was obvious that we were being seriously considered and I still didn't know whether that was good or bad.

In May we received a letter from John Rich, Chairman of the Board of A.M.C.B. stating that he and the other directors were having a difficult time making a choice. Approximately 120 applications had been processed. Through the weeks the field had been narrowed to six couples who were being asked to fly to Philadelphia for personal interviews. Would we come?

A few days later we were in Philadelphia along with the other five couples. Two of the wives had M.D. degrees, two were registered nurses, and one was a registered medical technologist, as was I.

Eight members of the board interviewed each couple separately, and then the entire group had lunch together. Following that, we all stood around a hotel room making conversation.

At about two o'clock Mr. Rich asked the applicants to wait in the hotel lobby while the board deliberated, for they had to make a decision that day.

The next fifteen minutes were an eternity. By that time I was completely confused. I had answered all the questions as honestly as I could, but perhaps I should have told the board outright that I wasn't a hundred percent sold on the idea. I did feel it would be a great honor to be selected; on the other hand, I would have been terribly relieved to return to my home and forget all about Burma. I felt certain that the board would choose one of the two couples where the wife was an M.D. Why shouldn't they want two for the price of one?

When we were finally called back to the hotel room my legs were almost too weak to carry me. Mr. Rich announced that the vote was unanimous to ask the Newhalls to go to Namkham. I didn't know whether to shout for joy or burst into tears. I suppose I acted as nonchalant as though that sort of thing happened to me everyday. But later, when Joe and I were back in our own hotel room. I threw myself on the bed and cried. Between sobs I managed to blurt out, "I don't want to go to Burma or anywhere. I just want to go home and stay there!"

Joe sat down beside me and began to stroke my hair. "Now Susie, please don't cry. This is just the initial shock. It will pass and you'll be fine. I've never seen the time you couldn't take things in your stride. Wait and see. Everything will be okay, and this will be a wonderful experience for us and for the boys." I was comforted but only partially convinced.

When we checked out of the hotel an hour later the clerk asked, "Say, which one of you folks got picked to go to India?"

"Burma," Joe corrected him as he signed the room slip. "We did."

"Man, I wouldn't be in your shoes for anything." Then he turned to another clerk behind the desk and said, "These people have volunteered to go to Burma for three years to work in some two-bit hospital. That's about the last place I'd want to go. Give me the bright lights any day."

"Now, what would this boob know about why we want to go to Burma?" I thought as I eyed the clerk, with his sharply pressed dark suit, flashy tie, and well-oiled hair. Bright lights? What was so wonderful about bright lights?

Joe and I walked proudly out of that hotel lobby, hand in hand. I was convinced.

We returned to Bradenton and began the involved process of obtaining passports and other necessary travel documents. With the hope of leaving the United States in August, Joe terminated his practice partnership July 1st so that he could devote his entire time to packing, selling our house, and making the myriad necessary arrangements. If we had known that the Burmese government had practically discontinued issuing visas to foreigners we would have been too discouraged even to begin proceedings. Later, I was to shudder when I thought of the inconvenience and embarrassment we would have suffered if we had sold our house, Joe had discontinued his practice and the visa had not been granted, or even delayed for months. However, within a few weeks we were given a three-month visa, with the general understanding that it might be extended an additional nine months, and renewed yearly.

On August 8, 1963, we left Bradenton for New York, where we were joined by Mrs. Fanny Ellison, who was making a short visit to the Namkham Hospital in the interests of the A.M.C.B.

On Sunday night, August 13th, we left New York by jet, bound for Rangoon, Burma.

CHAPTER THREE

DIGGING IN

It was our first morning in Namkham. I could hear at least half a dozen roosters announcing the new day. Joe was sleeping soundly, emitting his familiar snore. I lay there quietly beside him for a few minutes and looked about me.

Our room was large and comfortable, if not very elegant. Against one wall stood a tall dresser with drawers askew, the only piece of furniture in the room except for our bed. Along one entire wall was a wardrobe which provided storage space and a place to hang clothes. The wooden floor was bare, and in the very center of the room a large, round pipe reached from floor to ceiling. I wondered if that was all that held up the ceiling. The walls had been constructed of a cheap plaster which was crumbling and needed paint, and the ceiling was a thin composition beaverboard. The four double windows opened outward. Inside them was a heavy wire mesh and also regular wire screen. "That should be protection enough from those hungry Anopheles mos-

quitoes," I thought, and at the same time I noticed the bedroom even had a screen door, in addition to the heavy wooden
one, to keep out any mosquitoes which might get into other parts
of the house. The most depressing thing about the room was the
baggage which cluttered the floor. I groaned, thinking of the
unpacking which lay before me.

I became aware of the soft padding of bare feet beyond our
room. Listening carefully, I could hear voices, two or three of
them. I got out of bed, put on my housecoat, and went to inves-
tigate. Wong Jack and the two nannies, Shirley and Nella, were
in the kitchen. Wong Jack had a roaring fire going in the cookstove, and as soon as I appeared the two girls began brushing the
dining room floor with a short straw broom.

"What are you doing here so early? It isn't even six o'clock yet."
In an attempt to make myself understood I spoke in a ridiculously
loud voice.

Wong Jack threw another small log into the stove and turned
up the damper. "I come start fire, cook bleakfast. Bleakfast at
seven o'clock. Today I go bazaar early, buy lice."

Shirley spoke English very well, and she said that she always
came to work early to have the house swept before breakfast.
Then she was free to help the children eat. Nella didn't understand a word of English, so she ducked her head, smiled, and
continued sweeping.

I found it a bit disconcerting to have people wandering about
my house at all hours, but I thought how nice it was going to be
to have "bleakfast" ready when I got up instead of having to fight
that old cookstove myself. I felt like a guest in Wong Jack's
house. Something in his manner intimidated me and I didn't like
that, but to have household helpers at work so early! I wasn't sure
what their salaries were to be, but I knew it was very little as
compared to maids in the United States who came at nine and
left at four.

Feeling unneeded and unwanted in the kitchen, I ambled back

to the bedroom and began trying to find some clothes to wear. It wasn't easy in that jumbled mass of suitcases and dirty laundry. During my search, Joe raised himself on one elbow and gave the room a quick once-over. "What happened? A cyclone come through here?"

"Looks like it. Where's the one bag that had some clean clothes in it?"

At that moment the screen door opened and in strolled Philip and Tim sleepily rubbing their eyes. "Hey Mom, where's the bathroom?" was Tim's greeting.

Fanny was staying with Dr. Seagrave and Pansy. Since she was at Namkham primarily for business reasons, the Old Man wanted her as near as possible so he could talk with her about the needs of the hospital at any hour of the day or night.

After we had eaten breakfast, Fanny and Pansy came to see us. They were on their way to bazaar and asked me to go with them, so I hastily put aside my unpacking, glad for the excuse to leave the littered rooms. Wong Jack went along with us, rather grumpily, for we had delayed him for over an hour. He was accustomed to doing all the shopping alone and leaving for bazaar much earlier, before the best fruits and vegetables were gone.

We drove in a battered brown 1948 DeSoto sedan which had been Dr. Seagrave's private car before the addition of the Rambler station wagon a few months before. Fifteen years plus the lack of spare parts and the atrocious roads had left the DeSoto very near the condition of the old one-horse shay. I shall never forget that ride down the hill from the hospital. The driver fought to control the unreliable steering mechanism, and since there were no brakes, he tried to slow our rapidly increasing descent with the grinding gears. As we bumped and bounced and sped around the curves, my anxiety mounted. Had I survived a twelve-thousand-mile plane flight only to be killed by plunging into a rice paddy? But seconds later we were safe and sound at the bottom of the hill and headed toward town. The narrow road was lined with houses of woven bamboo strips. On both sides of the road solid lines of people filed slowly along, either on their way to or from the bazaar. Most carried heavy burdens in two baskets which dangled from opposite ends of a long bamboo pole balanced on their shoulders. It was fascinating to watch them walk with that load. They could twist their hips in such a way that their shoulders never moved, and whatever was in their baskets never spilled out.

The bazaar was held every fifth day, no matter what day of the week it was. People from miles away brought their wares for sale. There were Kachins from the hills dressed in their wool skirts and silver-bedecked jackets. There were Paloungs in their rags and tatters, Shans, Lisu, Chinese, and others. Some came from across the Chinese border. There was only a river to divide the two countries in that section, and no border guards. Many of the people had walked for days from villages far back in the hills just to bring a basket of fruit, vegetables, or scrawny chickens to sell, and to buy cotton flannel for shirts, rubber slippers called *hpynats,* tobacco, tea, and hot spices.

Filth and confusion were everywhere. People milled about, mangy dogs covered with ticks snooped around picking up scraps of food, and children roamed the grounds. Mothers squatted on the ground nursing their babies while guarding their items for sale. Frequent rains had left the ground one large mud-hole. Numerous ditches filled with muddy water and garbage ran between the bamboo shacks with their thatched roofs. Rats scooted beneath the rotting shacks. Some people simply squatted and relieved themselves wherever they were. Ancient buses, trucks, and oxcarts filled the streets.

Wong Jack led the way. He went from one vendor to another, selecting a handful of small tomatoes here, a few potatoes there, a fresh pineapple, some strange-looking greens of a doubtful origin, three hungry live chickens, and the all-important "lice." When he thought one seller's price was too high or the produce inferior he moved on to another. Most of the sellers spoke only Shan, and Wong spoke to them in their native tongue. To others he spoke Burmese, and to us he spoke English. Perhaps he committed as many grammatical errors in Shan and Burmese as he did in English, but he made himself understood.

Finally he took us to the rear of the bazaar grounds, where there were two small houses. Beef was sold in one, pork in the other. All the beef had been sold and Wong mumbled under his breath about how late we had made him with his shopping. There was still some pork left and Wong asked for one *viss*. Pansy explained that a *viss* was a weight, originating in India, which equalled approximately three and a half pounds and was broken down into a hundred units called *ticals*. Without regard to the cut of the meat, the butcher walked over to a carcass which hung from the ceiling, took a large knife, and sliced off a piece. His scale was a balance with a basket on one end and a large stone on the other. When he had about the right amount of meat, he plopped the quivering mass on a large banana leaf and wrapped it up.

Our total grocery bill from this grand shopping tour was thirty-five *kyats*, about seven dollars in American money. We had enough to feed our whole family for the next five days.

After the bumpy ride back to the compound, Wong and I began taking the food from the baskets and placing it in the refrigerator. "Where are we going to find eggs, Wong? And the children need milk."

Wong always answered when spoken to, but he never bent over backwards to be solicitous. "I buy eggs in village. One *kyat*, four eggs. Gurkha milkman come every morning. I buy one *viss* milk from him tomorrow."

"Good." I moved about the kitchen, examining the cabinets, which I found to be filled with an assortment of dishes, cooking utensils, and cockroach droppings. The refrigerator was a fairly late model of a well-known brand made in the United States. In order for it to be connected to the electrical outlet a large transformer was necessary to cut down the 240 voltage to somewhere near 110. "Why is there so much water in the bottom of this refrigerator?" I asked Wong Jack.

"Hospital generator not running from 11 p.m. to 7 a.m., and off again from 1 p.m. to 5 p.m. No electricity, refrigerator defrost. All the time defrost, freeze, defrost, freeze."

"We're lucky to have any refrigeration at all," I thought. I knew that the only other refrigerator was at the Old Man's house and it usually wasn't working.

Our old wood stove was a relic, but Wong seemed to take pride in it. It was the only cookstove in Namkham. Everyone else did their cooking over an open fire in a small cookhouse in the rear of their home. The cookhouses were constructed of woven bamboo, with dirt floors and an open space between walls and roof so that smoke might find its way out. Wong felt that our stove was a vast improvement. It was obviously a status symbol for him.

A large earthenware jug sat on the counter in the corner of the kitchen. When I asked what it was for, Wong explained that all drinking water and water for cooking was kept in that jug. On the back porch he showed me a large drum which was kept filled with water from a well in town. A crew of Shan men filled several drums at the well each day and pulled them back up the hill in a trailer behind a jeep, splashing water with every bump. Wong boiled water from the drum on the porch and then placed it in the jug for our use.

I wanted to know about Wong Jack's background, and after a slow start he warmed up and talked readily. As he talked he began to speak rapidly and wave his hands for emphasis, stammering when he could not recall the proper English word. He told me that he was born on the island of Hainan, a few miles off the southernmost tip of China and across the Gulf of Tonkin from North Vietnam. When he was a young man, Japan took over the island and life was so difficult for him that he left home and became a cook on a British freighter. With the outbreak of World War II, he was put off the ship and interned in India along with hundreds of his fellow Chinese. Though they were not enemies, they were alien to both the British and the Indians and no one knew what to do with them. About that time, General Stilwell's army, of which Dr. Seagrave and his nurses were a part, was preparing for the long hard push back into Burma. They needed coolies to carry supplies, so many of the interned Chinese, Wong Jack among them, were pressed into service. Later it became known that Wong had had experience as a cook, and Dr. Seagrave put him to work cooking for his unit. After their group finally reached Namkham and the war ended, Wong stayed on as Dr. Seagrave's personal cook. He married a Shan woman from the Christian Village and fathered seven children. In 1961, Dr. and Mrs. Olmanson, our predecessors, arrived in Namkham and Wong was assigned to do their cooking. Now he was taking over the big job for our family.

After that first day I rarely entered the kitchen except to use it as a passageway to the back door. Wong had things well in hand, and he openly resented any intrusion. Occasionally I made suggestions or helped him make out the list for bazaar, but otherwise he did everything himself. He shopped, planned the meals, cooked, served, and washed the dishes. Sometimes Joe complained that the meals were monotonous, but that was due more to the lack of variety in the bazaar than to Wong's planning. I ate everything and enjoyed it. The nannies trod lightly when they entered the kitchen, for Wong tolerated no nonsense. To his Chinese way of thinking, all women were inferiors and useful only for hard labor and reproduction. Since I paid him his monthly salary, the equivalent of $40, he made some allowances in my case.

At lunch the first day Joe reminded me that we were expected to attend the weekly softball game that afternoon at four. They were a tradition at the Namkham Hospital, and, come hell or high water, the game went on. Monsoon rains, winter chills, or summer heat were no obstacle to the eager players. We had read about these games and were prepared with our own gloves, ball, and bat.

A few minutes before four, Joe, the boys, and I were on our way to the ballpark. In the coming years we made that trip many times and the route became very familiar. From our back door we went down the lane past our wash house and woodshed, past the carpenter's shed where the workmen always seemed to be having a cup of Shan tea, then on to the truck garage and mechanics shop with its odd assortment of vehicles. There were two jeeps, one weapons carrier, and two large trucks left from World War II, and the old DeSoto. Never were all five in working order at one time, for parts were swapped back and forth and used as needed, a practice commonly called cannibalizing. The best vehicle was the Jeep ambulance in which Dr. Seagrave had met us, and it was used for everything from transporting patients to making long trips to Lashio, Mandalay, and Rangoon. Directly across from the truck park was the building which housed the generator. We developed a great respect for that generator, for it had its temperamental moments. When it refused to run we were without electricity for several hours.

After passing the truck park and generator, we took a shortcut past the water reservoir. Water from streams up in the hills poured into this large tank through ditches and hollowed-out bamboo. It was then piped into several houses on the compound —ours included—though it was highly contaminated and used only for washing. During the time when the rice paddies were being flooded, the water flow was occasionally diverted to the paddies and we had to do without washing water for a few days.

The path led on to the road and past the compound church. That church was the pride and joy of the Christians, for they had built it with their own hands from the same river stone with which the hospital had been constructed. The grounds around the church were beautifully kept and there were always flowers in bloom. A fence restrained hungry cows and water buffalo. Down the road we passed several little stands made of bamboo where food was for sale. We came to call this place our "local Howard Johnson." Generally we bought sunflower seeds to chew on during the game, but there was a variety of other edibles such as pickled green fruits with chili powder, fried banana fritters, sugarcane stalks, and an assortment of strange-looking candies. The old Shan ladies who ran the business sat quietly on their stools behind the rough bamboo counter.

At the ballpark the nurses had begun to gather. When they saw us they smiled shyly and conversation stopped. They were dressed in their *longyis*, and I wondered how they would be able to run and keep those things up at the same time.

The black Rambler arrived with Pansy behind the wheel. She was so tiny she had to sit as far forward as the seat would allow, with one cushion behind her and one beneath her. Even with this bolstering she strained to reach the accelerator and had to tilt her head back to see over the steering wheel. Beside her slumped the Old Man and in the back seat were Fanny and Augusta. Pansy maneuvered the car so that it stopped directly behind two wooden benches; this gave us something to lean on while waiting for our turn at bat. Pansy opened the back door of the station wagon and the girls gathered around to take out the ball, bats, and gloves.

Dr. Seagrave was captain of one team and Joe was captain of the other. I was made one of the shortstops on Dr. Seagrave's team, and he was the third baseman. There must have been twenty to thirty people on each team, but it worked out beautifully. There was one pitcher, one catcher, and one player for each base, but there the similarity to softball ended. There were two short shortstops on each side of the pitcher and four long shortstops farther back, and all the rest of the players arranged themselves about the field. The less familiar a girl was with the game, the farther back in the field she stood. When a batter usually hit to left field, all the players deserted right field and congregated where the ball was expected. Sometimes they were fooled and the happy batter made a home run. Many of the rules had been changed to suit the needs of the players. Joe laughingly called the game Namkham ball instead of softball.

Joe's team took the field first and I sat down by Dr. Seagrave on the bench. He had taken his shirt off and sat smoking. He was in an unusually good mood that particular day and kept calling out to the players, teasing some and shouting instructions to others. His command of the languages of the area was astonishing —he called to one girl in Shan, to another in Kachin, and to a third in Burmese, all the while speaking English to Fanny and me.

I asked Dr. Seagrave about the few males who were playing and he drawled, "We do let men play if they behave themselves. That fellow over there is Chit Tin. He came up from Rangoon a few months ago. Right now he is working in the drug room, but he wants to learn laboratory work so I want you to teach him how to do a few of the routine procedures. I guess he's got sense enough to learn. That fellow out in left field is Plai Paw, and he works in the office. I call him Play Boy because he thinks he's such a hot shot with the women. We don't want the men hogging the game because it's primarily for the girls."

My turn came, and I walked over to the batter's box. It had been a long time since I had played softball, and I felt rusty all over. Joe pitched a nice slow ball, just a little low, and I swung with all my might. No one was more surprised than I was when I hit the ball squarely and it went sailing over the heads of the four shortstops and bounced into left field. There were squeals of surprise and delight from my teammates when I arrived safely at first base. Hits by the two batters after me brought me panting back home, where I dropped onto the bench. The Old Man said, "That was wonderful, just great. The girls all love you. They've never seen an American woman play ball like that before. The few American women they've known have just sat on their asses and acted like playing ball with the girls was beneath them."

When it was his turn to bat, he walked slowly to the plate. His gait was more of a glide than a walk, and his head leaned slightly to the right. Pansy handed him a bat and prepared to run for him. He hitched up his pants and assumed the batting stance. Joe pitched two balls which were not to the Old Man's liking, whereupon he bawled out, "Damn it, stop throwing those curves and throw one decent ball in here." When one came in like he wanted, he swung around and the ball bounced out to right field. Pansy held her *longyi* a few inches above her ankles and raced for first base. Dr. Seagrave tossed down the bat and returned to the bench where he had left his burning cigarette. The exertion left him panting. For a few seconds he didn't say a word. His toothless mouth gaped open and his massive chest heaved with each torturous breath. He reached under the bench for a bottle of water, and took a long gurgling drink. At last he rumbled, "It's a damn shame when a man is so old he can't even walk or make enough spit to wet his mouth. Fanny, I want you to tell those dandies back in New York that I'm still as good as any man in spite of it."

The next batter was a short, stocky Karen girl. She had let down her long hair, and it flowed to her waist. "See that girl, Sue?" Dr. Seagrave inquired. "She can't hit the ball worth a damn. Too bad she can't use her rear."

"She looks like a very attractive girl to me."

"You haven't seen a thing. You ought to see her with her clothes off," he replied. Then he yelled to the rotund staff nurse who was the first baseman on the other team, "Say Paw, get your big fat frame off first base. How in the hell do you expect any of our players to touch the base?"

I wondered if he always talked to them that way. Apparently so, for they hardly seemed to notice.

I had developed a special fondness for Pansy. She was quiet

and warmhearted, and it was obvious that she had dedicated her life to caring for Augusta and for Gordon Seagrave. Later, I moved near where she was leaning on the car. "Pansy," I said, "what is that group of buildings beyond the ballfield?"

"That is the Shan Christian Village. Wong Jack's house is the first house you see there."

"Is everyone in the village Christian?"

"Most of them. Shan people do not usually like it when their people become Christians. They must live in all-Christian communities such as this one."

There was a loud outburst from the ball players. Joe, in retrieving a slow bounding ball, had stepped squarely into a large fresh pile of water buffalo dung. The girls shrieked and howled, and he laughed and joked with them about it. That set the mood for the remainder of the game, and the afternoon was a huge success. We had made a good start in our relationship with the nurses.

When we returned home around six p.m. Wong Jack had supper waiting for us. The nannies had cleaned the house until it shone and had washed and ironed the many dirty clothes.

After supper began the ritual of the bath. There was a tub and running water (a luxury in Burmese homes), but there was no hot water. We could well have bathed in the cool water, at least during warm weather, but the nannies decreed otherwise. Around four p.m. they built a fire under the large iron pot in the wash house, then filled the pot with water. After supper, they carried the hot water into the house by the bucketful and filled the bathtub. After they bathed the children, the nannies then filled a large metal container with boiling water and placed it in the bathroom for Joe and me. Thus we had hot "running" water, but the nannies did all the running.

The trip to the filthy bazaar, the ballgame, plus adjusting to an entirely new way of life had made for a very full day. We went to bed early and immediately dropped off to sleep.

Later, the silence of the night was shattered by a sharp sound, an automobile backfire or possibly a gun shot. Joe and I awakened with a start and sat up in bed. "What was that?" I half whispered.

"I don't know." Joe went to the window and I joined him. It was pitch black outside. We walked through the house, peering into the blackness. No one was about and we heard no further noise, so we returned to bed and forgot about the incident.

After breakfast the next morning we went over to the nurses' home, where morning chapel was held. There was no set time for chapel to begin; things got rolling when the Old Man arrived and rang the bell. That morning exactly at 8:30 Pansy drove the Rambler to the door of the nurses' home and she, Fanny, and Dr. Seagrave got out. Near the door an old metal tire rim was suspended by a wire from a crossbar between two poles. Dr. Seagrave walked to the tire rim, picked up a metal bar, and struck the rim sixteen times. That was the call to chapel.

Nurses all over the hospital put down their work, if possible, and began to gather. Approximately half of them were Christians and most attended chapel regularly. The Buddhist girls were welcome but were never coerced into attending. As we entered the room which doubled as chapel and classroom, we stopped to read the inscription on a plain concrete plaque near the door. It commemorated the Seagrave Hospital Unit of World War II and listed the names of the physicians—headed by Gordon Seagrave —and the names of the nurses. I recognized some of the names. There was Naomi, who was fondly called "Grandma," and Esther and Emily. I had heard of others who had married and were no longer serving at the hospital.

Inside we found a large bleak room filled with neat rows of desk chairs. The bare electric light bulbs near the front gave off a bright, eerie glow but only partially lighted the dark corners. Everything about the room was cold, dark, and depressing. At the far end was a low platform in the center of which was a small wooden table covered with a bright, red-checked cloth. Behind this was a large armchair with a cushion. Straight chairs ranged along the platform on either side.

"Joe and Sue, come on up here," Dr. Seagrave called. "This is where the senior staff sits." He indicated the chairs on the platform.

The highest-ranking staff members sat nearest the Old Man. Those of lesser importance sat farther down the line. I was directed to sit on his left, Joe on his right, with one chair between them for Tun Shein.

The room began to fill. The girls came in quietly, took their seats in the crowded rows of desk chairs, and bowed their heads reverently for a few moments. The fourth-year girls sat in the first two or three rows, and behind them were the third, second, and first-year students. In the rear were a few male members of the office staff. The junior staff nurses sat in a corner to the left of the room, beneath the stairs which led up to the students' sleeping quarters.

Dr. Seagrave watched the girls arrive from his seat in the cushioned chair. He sat in that same chair throughout the morning as he taught class after class, so the cushion was necessary for his comfort. Shortly after seating himself, he had begun to adjust the table. "Goddamn this thing, if it isn't in just the right spot it isn't level and it rocks back and forth." He continued to push the table backwards, forwards, then a bit to the left. When it suited him, he pulled at the cloth until it was properly centered. Then he leaned back, loosened his belt and the top button of his trousers, and surveyed the room. "Excuse me," he said, "but this thing," indicating his belt, "is too damn tight for my big belly and I can't sit here and get strangulated."

When everyone was assembled, Dr. Seagrave called out the number of the hymn to be sung. The hymnbooks were printed in English and the tunes were the familiar ones I had sung and loved all my life. At one end of the platform was an old foot-pedal organ, but no one could play it so we sang unaccompanied. After the singing everyone joined in the reading aloud of a scripture passage from a Burmese translation of the Bible. Neither Joe nor I could read Burmese, but we silently read the identical passage using an English translation. After the scripture reading, one of the students gave a short prayer in a voice so quiet that it was almost inaudible, after which the whole group recited the Lord's Prayer in Burmese, and we were dismissed.

As the nurses rose to leave the room, Dr. Seagrave's voice boomed out: "Find out if that girl has laryngitis." He meant the frightened girl who had led in prayer. "If she does, treat her, and if she doesn't, kick her in the ass." After a short pause he added, "There will be no classes today."

As time passed and we attended more chapel services, we learned that the routine was always the same. Dr. Seagrave struck the tire rim sixteen times (whether there was any specific significance to the number sixteen he never said), and while the girls gathered he adjusted the table, its cloth, and his belt. He proceeded straight through the hymnbook, from number one to the end, singing one hymn a day and omitting only the ones with which the girls were unfamiliar or which he didn't like.

Scripture reading also followed a certain pattern. He began with the first chapter of Genesis and read part of a chapter a day until Revelation was finished, skipping only the books which were difficult to read and understand. Always, there was a prayer, and dismissal with the Lord's Prayer.

Dr. Seagrave usually spent a few minutes after chapel cussing and discussing important matters with Tun Shein and other staff members. Those "few minutes" might drag on for an hour or more while the Old Man's students waited patiently to be called into class. On our first day in chapel, however, he had many things to say, so he had dismissed all classes for the morning. Tun Shein, Pansy, Fanny, Joe and I remained.

"Well, Joe," Dr. Seagrave said as he lit a cigarette with a shaky hand, "have you been around the hospital yet?"

"Yes sir, I had a quick tour yesterday morning and I want to take Susie around today."

"Good, and how about escorting Fanny around the place, too. There are lots of things she needs to see and she wants to make a note of all the things we need before she goes back to meet with the board in Philadelphia next month. God knows, those fancy fellows don't have any idea of the real situation out here.

"Now, Joe," he continued in his slow drawl, "you have an open field here. Do whatever you like, make what changes you think are necessary. We've been needing someone out here with a little know-how and knowledge of the latest medical discoveries. I can't keep up with everything and Silgardo doesn't even try. You notice he wasn't here at chapel. He never comes. He's Roman Catholic and he avoids chapel like the plague. Besides, he's the most damned uncooperative fellow I've ever seen. He's a pretty good doctor, though. All he knows about surgery he's learned from me."

I had rarely heard one man speak about another that way. I studied the shaggy-haired old man slouched in the big chair. There was nothing in his expression to indicate that he had meant to degrade Dr. Silgardo; he had simply made a statement, the final part of which indicated that he thought rather highly of himself. I had been around Dr. Seagrave enough in two days to know that he always said exactly what he thought and that he seldom thought well of anyone.

I was aware that he was talking to me.

"Sue, do anything you want in that lab. It needs a lot of changes. When Olmanson was here he had some Kahn antigen sent in and it's never been used. I'd like to set up a way of doing Kahn tests for syphilis on every patient coming into the hospital. I had that idea long before Olmanson did. Esther hasn't had time to do anything with that antigen, and she really doesn't want to mess with it. She's awfully busy in that lab, and she doesn't give a damn about starting any more work. I also wish you'd try to teach those student nurses a few of the basic lab tests. They rotate through the lab and spend a month there and don't learn a thing. Esther doesn't like to teach and she just has them washing glassware and doing all the messy work."

He lit a fresh cigarette from the stub of his last one, which had been smoked down until it was about a half-inch long. His hand shook, and we waited anxiously to see whether or not the two cigarettes would meet. All conversation ceased until the new cigarette sent up a curl of smoke. Then he continued. "Fanny brought along some rough plans drawn by an architect for a maternity and children's building. The A.M.C.B. had a campaign on to raise funds last year during my fortieth year celebration. I'd like to get all of you together soon to go over those plans and get your opinions on what we should have in the building. We'll want it built out of stone like the rest of the hospital."

Fanny commented about the funds which were available and how much more money was needed. Tun Shein said where he thought the building should be situated, considering the space available. Dr. Seagrave listened, smoking, and occasionally took a sip of water from the covered porcelain cup which was always on his table.

As we were about to leave, Dr. Seagrave asked Tun Shein if he had heard the loud noise the evening before. "Yes," Tun Shein replied. "Some of the soldiers from the camp below the compound caught a man they thought was one of the Kachin insurgents, or, at least, cooperating with them. They took him outside town on the road which runs near Joe and Sue's house and shot him, leaving the body beside the road. I hear the lieutenant is raving mad, not because they shot the fellow, but because they were so indiscreet about it. Usually, they take the poor devils out in the jungle somewhere before shooting them."

That was the first I had heard about any insurgency and I wanted to know more, especially if people were going to be shot practically in my own front yard.

"For the most part," Tun Shein told me, "the insurgents are people who have some quarrel with the government, or maybe they just don't like the Burmese. The Kachins would like to set up their own independent state. The majority of the rebels in this area are Kachins and there are a large number of Shans, too. The Kachins operate more to the north of us around the Bhamo area, and the Shans are most active to the south around Lashio. There is never much organization to them and it seems more like simple banditry and murder."

Dr. Seagrave lit another cigarette from the butt of the last one. He inhaled deeply and the smoke came belching forth from his wide nostrils. "Well," he said, "there has been some form of insurgency in this country ever since independence in 1948, and even before. First it was the Karens, and they put up a darn good battle. If their leader had not been such a maniac they might have won. Back during the Karen Rebellion was when I was put in jail for high treason. Now it's the Kachins and half a dozen other groups including the White Flag Communists and the Red Flag Communists. If they'd ever stop fighting among themselves and join forces they'd have the government whipped.

"After independence from Britain in 1948 the leader, General Aung San, and his fellow leaders were mowed down with a machine gun. Then U Nu took over and he ran things pretty well in his own placid way. There were numerous ups and downs and the army took over for a short while. In 1961, the army took over again. That s.o.b. coward, General Ne Win, is the leader now and he has a Revolutionary Council under him, all military officers. They're pursuing what they call 'The Burmese Way to Socialism' but I won't repeat in front of the ladies what *I* call it.

"By the way," he directed this to Joe and me, "be very careful what you put in your letters going out of here. Most of them are censored so don't say anything about the political situation or about the insurgents. Lots of our letters are 'lost.'"

The talk about insurgents, the Revolutionary Council, and censors really stirred me. I wasn't sure whether I was a bit frightened or simply excited. After all, this was a far cry from Main Street, U.S.A.

When our group finally broke up, Joe, Fanny, and I began our tour of the hospital. Our first stop was at the old hospital, or O.H., as the girls affectionately called it.

"This is the same old wooden building Dr. Seagrave found when he arrived here in 1922." Joe told us. "Be careful going up those stairs. I think they must have been the original ones, from the looks of them!"

The old building was built in a U shape, with the female ward on one side and the male ward on the other. In the middle was the nurses' station and a small treatment room. There was no glass at the windows, but the openings could be closed at night with sliding bamboo partitions. The floor was full of holes, many of which had been patched and repatched, but we still had to be careful where we stepped. The beds were made of wood and covered with thin mats. Though O.H. was by far the most primitive of all the hospital buildings, it was the favorite with the patients because it was more like home to them. The holes in the floor gave them a convenient place to spit their betelnut juice. The two wards were crowded, and most of the patients sat up in their beds to stare at us. They were dressed in their regular clothes and there were no sheets on the beds.

A number of patients and their families were gathered at the rear door. Some squatted around a small fire, cooking rice. Others were washing clothes, and a woman was bathing near a spigot. She was wearing her *longyi,* and after bathing she changed to a clean, dry *longyi* without ever completely disrobing in her very public bathhouse. In the distance a few patients were waiting their turn at the latrine.

"See those fellows all huddled together in the corner of the men's ward?" Joe asked. "They're opium addicts, and they're under sedation now. I understand there are fields and fields of opium poppies growing around here."

From O.H. we crossed over to the newest and finest of the hospital buildings, the Private Building. It was a two-story structure with rooms of various sizes. There were anywhere from one to five beds in each room, causing me to wonder why this was called a private building. Possibly because five roommates offered more privacy than thirty. Each floor boasted a bathroom with running water and an Asian-type toilet, a hole in the floor over which the patients squatted. The downstairs floor was of cement which gave the whole place a cold, dreary look, but upstairs the teak floors had been polished to a high gloss with a mixture of melted candle wax and used motor oil. The Private Building was the only building with screens in the windows, but many of them had been kicked out by the patients. Instead of seeing the screens as a means of keeping out mosquitoes and flies, they looked upon them as a hindrance to fresh air.

It was only a short walk to the medical ward, also a two story-building, but here there were no individual rooms, only two very large wards. The men's medical ward was downstairs and the women's upstairs. Children were accommodated everywhere. Most of the female patients had at least one child in bed with them. Sometimes the mother was the patient, sometimes the child was the patient, and often both were. The most advanced tuberculosis patients were grouped together in small sun porches at the end of both wards; but lack of space forced some to remain in the large ward with the other patients.

Shortly after we entered the women's ward it was time for the morning meal. Two meals a day were served, one at about ten a.m. and one at four p.m. Four student nurses came struggling up the stairs; two were carrying a large kettle filled with steaming rice, and the other two had a kettle of some strange-looking liquid with green leaves floating in it. The two kettles were placed on the floor in the center of the ward and the patients crowded around, each holding his bowl. They were given a heaping bowlful of rice, and some of the liquid was poured over it. They returned to their beds and squatted on the floor to eat with their fingers.

Some of the patients preferred to cook their own food in a small cookshed provided outside. Even so, many built fires out in the open and cooked their rice.

In the wards and outside we saw numerous children being carried in slings on their mothers' backs. One little fellow had the eating and sleeping problem well under control, for as his mother carried him on her back he leaned over as far as he could, ducked under her left arm, and was nursing.

Joe pointed to a group in the corner of the room. "That's a whole family, father, mother, and three children—all patients."

"Isn't that interesting!" Fanny exclaimed. "I recall from Gordon's books that it's a common thing for whole families to come in together, sometimes even the better part of a village. They might walk for days to get here."

Next we visited the maternity ward. That small building also had a depressing effect on me, for I had associated mothers and small babies with sparkling white nurseries, the finest of equipment, and an aura of great love and happiness. Perhaps the love and happiness were there, but I did not detect it, and there was certainly a definite lack of the other items. The undelivered mothers wandered about, dressed in their filthy tribal costumes. The hall was lined with makeshift beds, and some of the occupants were in various stages of labor. The two small wards were jammed with postpartal patients nursing their babies. The delivery room was small and no different from any other room in the building except for two crude homemade delivery tables. A delivery was in progress, with one of the student nurses in attendance. Fanny had never seen a baby born, so she and Joe went in to have a look. Actually, I had never seen a delivery myself, but I didn't feel that this was the time, so I waited in the crowded hall. In a few minutes, a nurse hurried out of the delivery room carrying a bloody, screaming little mass of humanity. Fanny, when she appeared, looked considerably shaken.

We were about to leave when we were confronted by two pairs of bright eyes. Two small boys, twins under two years of age, were staring at us with something between fear and amusement in their dark eyes. Suddenly, as if by signal, they turned and ran down the hall as fast as their short legs could carry them, emitting high-pitched, happy shrieks. They opened a screen door at the other end of the hall and disappeared.

"Who are they?" I asked in amazement.

Khin Nyunt, the very fat and jolly nurse-midwife who had accompanied us on our tour of the maternity ward said, "Those are our Shan twins, who live here in this building. Their mother died when they were born. She was unattended, in a small village near here. I went there in the ambulance soon after their birth, too late to help the mother, but the babies were very small and needed care so I brought them back to the hospital. They have been here eighteen months now because the father refused to come for them. All the nurses help in caring for them and they are much loved by all. The girls have decided to name them James and John, but everyone calls them KoKo and NyeeNyee. That means older brother and younger brother in Burmese."

I remembered reading in Dr. Seagrave's book that twins were often rejected by the Shans and others. "But why won't the father claim them? What kind of man would do a thing like that?"

Khin Nyunt smiled as she replied, "The Buddhists do not like twins. It is thought to be bad luck to have them. This man had many other children and no wife to care for them. Maybe he could not keep them or perhaps he did not want them. I cannot say. They would surely have died if they had stayed in the little house where they were born."

We stepped from the maternity building, across a path, and into a flower garden tended by an aged Shan gardener. Roses and many other flowers were in bloom. The contrast between the drab hospital ward and this beautiful garden was startling. I had noticed similar flower gardens near some of the homes on the compound and also in front of the nurses home. Pansy had a beautiful garden surrounding Dr. Seagrave's home.

As we turned from the flower garden to enter the back door of the surgical building, an elderly female patient leaned out from a window on the second floor. Without a moment's hesitation, she opened her mouth and spat a large amount of bright red fluid onto the ground.

"My God," Joe said, more to himself than to Fanny and me. "That woman's having a massive hemorrhage." And he dashed into the building.

A few minutes later he was back, wearing a sheepish grin. "I just learned something. That wasn't blood but betelnut juice. The patient, like most of the others, chews betelnut, which produces copious amounts of red-stained saliva. Also, like most of the others, she isn't a bit fussy about where she spits."

In the women's surgical ward Joe led us to the patient in question, who, by that time, was squatting beside her bed eating a few handfuls of rice. Through sign language he persuaded her to open her mouth. A lifetime of chewing betelnut had left its mark. Her few remaining stumps of teeth were black as tar, but everything else in her mouth was bright red.

"I think I'll write a new song," Joe said. "With betelnut you chew and snack and wish you had the yellow back!" he sang to the tune of a well-known toothpaste ad. Fanny and I laughed, but the patient didn't understand and went on with her eating.

In the men's ward we saw two student nurses working intently around one of the wooden beds which had been stripped of all mats and blankets. Each had a lighted candle and was dropping some of the hot wax into the cracks of the bed. Instantly, scalded bed bugs came scurrying from each crack, whereupon the waiting nurse smashed them with her fingers.

The operating room was the most modern-looking section of the hospital. The lower walls had been tiled within the last few years, and everything was gleaming white. The lights above one of the two operating tables had been fashioned in the compound carpenter shop by placing three large electric bulbs inside a shiny metal shield. It produced quite a bright light, and also generated a large amount of heat in this un-airconditioned room. To the rear of the operating room a fire was roaring in an open grate, the smoke escaping through an open space beneath the rafters. Over the flame sat a large kettle filled with water. Here surgical instruments were being boiled.

"There is a modern sterilizer," Joe commented, "but no one knows how to use it. Boiling is a lousy way to sterilize. Maybe I can get the sterilizer going. The same is true of the gas anesthesia machine over there in the corner. The soda lime crystals needed are missing and no one knows how to make it run besides. There's a fluoroscope machine in the X-ray room that hasn't even been put together. I'll have fun tinkering with these things in my spare moments."

On the way out of the building we passed through the outpatient clinic. The waiting room was packed. One old woman had just been brought in on a chair strapped to poles and carried by two men on their shoulders. They had made a twenty-mile trip over the hills with that contraption. Mothers were nursing babies dressed in several layers of shirts, a cap, and nothing below the waist. Two student nurses were dressing an angry-looking, infected wound on a boy's leg, and a child sat staring out of sightless eyes due to a long-neglected infection.

I wondered what small impression we would be able to make in relieving the misery we saw all about us. There was so much to be done and so little with which to work. Dr. Seagrave and his dedicated nurses had been struggling for over forty years and had only been able to scratch the surface. Joe and I had entertained such grand visions of curing hundreds and helping them to a new and healthful way of life, and now I seriously doubted that we would accomplish anything at all. The people's absolute ignorance of hygiene and preventive medicine was appalling, and only after ignorance and superstition were overcome could there be any significant improvement in the health standard.

Joe began his work in the hospital immediately. He and Dr. Silgardo arranged that each should take alternate days in the outpatient clinic and do whatever surgery was necessary on the other day. Dr. Seagrave was not in good enough health to do surgery, but he taught nursing classes in the morning and held a late afternoon clinic in which he reviewed all the patients admitted since the previous afternoon.

Joe was amazed by the patients, their diseases, and their apparent unconcern about life and death. Medical cases, as opposed to those requiring surgery, were the biggest problem. Malaria, tuberculosis, typhoid, beri beri, bronchitis, pneumonia, malnutrition, and parasite infestation made up the bulk. Most patients ignored their diseases until it was no longer possible to do so; then they consulted a Shan masseur for a rubdown and massage. When that failed, they took several bottles of Chinese herbs and tonics. Generally they were near death before they came to the hospital.

Surgical cases were also prevalent. Namkham was in the Himalaya Goiter Belt, where a scarcity of iodine caused a majority of the hill people to have enlarged thyroid glands, commonly called goiters. They seldom wanted to have the goiters removed unless they had grown so large the patients had difficulty lifting their heads or swallowing. Dr. Seagrave was known all over Burma as the goiter specialist, having developed his own technique for their removal.

Joe soon learned what Dr. Silgardo called the "Namkham Approach" to therapy: what could and what could not be done to help the patients. Cases which might have been cured readily in the United States had to be left untended because of the lack of proper drugs or other necessary materials. There was no blood to give surgical or maternity cases who desperately needed a transfusion. It was almost impossible to get anyone to donate blood, even to a relative who would die without it. Few people had any blood to spare, and almost everyone had had malaria, hepatitis, or some disease which made him ineligible as a donor.

On his first day in the outpatient clinic, Joe treated a child who died a few minutes later from diphtheria, and saw another who died in his mother's arms in the waiting room after having had severe diarrhea for five days. Many more such incidents, seldom seen in a medical practice in America, were Joe's introduction to Namkham.

Esther invited us to attend church with her and her family on our first Sunday morning at Namkham. Joe was working, but Tim and I went. Ordinarily the family walked the short distance to the compound church, but that morning they were riding because they were also going to visit the Shan church in the Christian Village. They owned a jeep which ran occasionally, but not often, and never well. Ja Naw, Esther's husband, was a handsome man with a broad smile, curly hair, and a trim, athletic physique. He was a Kachin and Esther a Karen. As Tim and I climbed into the jeep, their children smiled shyly and moved over to make room. Each was dressed in his or her best Sunday clothes. The oldest was nine-year-old Ja Nan, "number-one-girl" in Kachin. They called her Nanette. Next was seven-year-old Charlie, whose Kachin name was Ja Li, or number-one boy. Then there was Ja Naw, Jr., number-two boy, who was nicknamed Jr., like so many American boys. The youngest was Ja Bawk, or simply Bawky, the number-two girl, four years old. This was a common way of naming children among the people here.

The church was crowded, mostly with women and children. The worshippers were students and staff of the hospital, children from the compound private school, and a few people from the town. The choir sang two special songs in English, but the congregational singing was in Burmese. It made me feel good to listen to the old hymns sung by strange people in a strange language, so I sang lustily, using the English words which were drowned out by the Burmese singers. The pastor, Saya Daniel Tun Baw (Saya is Burmese for teacher), gave the sermon in Burmese and followed it with a resume in English for my benefit. I appreciated the translation, but somehow it wasn't really necessary. I had found that one did not need to understand every word the pastor said in order to enjoy a church service and be uplifted by its message. A worshipful state of mind was the first requirement. I thought of the hundreds of times I had sat in church at home and sung those same songs and heard those same words. I felt more strongly than ever that God's people are the same the world over.

On Sunday evening, Joe, Tim, and I attended the song service at Dr. Seagrave's home. This service was as much a tradition at Namkham as chapel and the weekly softball game. When we walked into the living room, Dr. Seagrave was sitting in his favorite chair in a corner of the room reading and listening to records. Reading was his hobby, and when he was not teaching he was reading. He also enjoyed classical music.

"Come in," he said. "Pansy has some chairs set up for you. Everyone else will sit on straw mats on the floor. Some of these girls never saw a chair until they came to Namkham. They can sit on the floor for hours with their feet tucked under them on one side. In fact, the word for chair in Burmese is *kalahtain,* which literally mean 'foreigner sits.' They didn't have a name for one of those things until foreigners started bringing them into the country."

The front door opened and in came about fifty of the student nurses, carrying the hymnbooks from the chapel. They came quietly, meekly—not daring to look in our direction—and sat on the floor in the way Dr. Seagrave had said they would.

When everyone was seated the service was ready to begin. One of the girls in a far corner of the room quietly called out the number of the hymn she wished to sing. "What number?" the Old Man shouted. The number was called out even more faintly than before. "What?" he thundered for the second time. Embarrassed silence. "Pansy, what in hell does she want to sing?"

"Number sixty-five."

Everyone turned to number sixty-five, Dr. Seagrave began to sing and all joined in. I thought the singing was beautiful. The girls' harmony was near perfect, and their slight Burmese accent as they followed the English hymns was fascinating.

After about thirty minutes of singing, Dr. Seagrave read a passage of scripture from the Bible and led in the group in prayer. Then the girls rose and left as silently as they had come. Joe and I remained to visit, as did Tun Shein, and of course Fanny and Pansy were there.

The Old Man lit a cigarette and settled back in his chair. "How are your boys getting along, Sue?" he asked.

"Fine, sir. Timmy is finding friends and Philip and Paul are about over the diarrhea they've had the past few days."

"Joe, why does she always call me sir?" Not really expecting a reply he went on, "I have so blamed many names here. They nearly choke on a name like Dr. Seagrave, so they call me the Old Man, or, if they don't hate my guts too much they call me Daddy. Customarily missionaries are given terms of respect. For instance, they call the female missionaries mama. Ma means sister, and when doubled up it means big sister. I ought to know enough about missionaries and their names because my ancestors have been missionaries for generations. I'm the twenty-eighth member of my family to serve in this country."

"Yes sir, I read that. Wasn't your great-grandfather one of the first Baptist missionaries?"

"Two lines of my forebears, the Vintons and the Haswells, came to Burma a hundred and thirty years ago, only shortly after

Adoniram Judson himself. I'm the last of the line. Ever hear of Adoniram Judson?"

"Well, I don't know much about him, but I did hear about him in a Baptist Church I attended in St. Louis a few years ago," I answered.

"That's where you'd hear about him, all right. To the Baptists Judson was some kind of gold-plated god. He was the first missionary to set foot on Burmese soil a hundred and fifty years ago and he started the whole Baptist movement here. Judson was a tough old bird in more ways than one because he outlived two wives and was living with the third when he died. I'll tip my hat to any man who can do that. Did you know that he made the Burmese translation of the Bible that we use, and also wrote an English-Burmese dictionary?"

I shook my head no, and he was off again.

"It was seven years before Adoniram had any converts and they were Burmans. Today there are more Christians among the Karens than any other group in Burma.

"My great-grandfather, Justus Hatch Vinton, was born in 1806 in Wellington, Connecticut. As a young man he met Adoniram Judson, who was back in the States for a short rest. When great-grandfather heard Adoniram tell some of his tales about pioneer missionary work in Burma, he vowed that was the work he would do too. In 1834 he and his bride, Callista, left for Burma.

"In 1852 they moved from Moulmein to Rangoon. It was during the second Burmese-English War and they wanted to aid those who had been hit hardest by marauding bands of Burmese soldiers. Great-grandfather made the move without taking time to write a letter to the American Baptist Mission Society to get their permission. It would have taken at least a year for an answer. Besides, he probably thought they had enough gumption to see where the real need was. But the Mission Society considered the move a 'flagrant dereliction' and voted a formal vote of censure. The worst of it was that many of the Christians couldn't understand why Great-grandather fed everyone who was starving, Karen or Burmese, Christian or Buddhist. Great-grandfather must have thought, 'to hell with them,' because he carried on alone without aid or recognition from the Mission and they never got around to forgiving him for twenty years. By that time he was dead and his son, Brainard, was carrying on the work.

"I like this story, not only because it shows Great-grandfather Justus was a determined old cuss with a mind of his own, but because it's so similar to what happened to me after World War II. The Mission thought I was directly on the road to hell, and I thought they were . . . well, anyhow, we came to a parting of the ways. But I'll come to that later."

He spoke slowly and deliberately and omitted no details. We heard more about his family in Burma, including the Haswells, and eventually the story of his father, Albert Ernest Seagrave.

"My ancestors were all teachers and Bible pounders but I decided I wanted to be a medical missionary. My parents thought I was going to be an evangelist to the Karens of Lower Burma like my father, grandfather, great-grandfather, and many uncles and aunts, but I held out, and finally they were convinced that I was going to be a medical missionary or nothing at all."

"How did you happen to get up here to Namkham?" Joe asked.

"The Baptists had this hospital here and one at Kengtung. Dr. Harper, who had been here in Namkham for several years, was almost ready for retirement, so it was decided that this was where I was needed most. We had a small daughter then, and another baby to arrive soon, but my wife, Tiny, and I started up here from Rangoon as soon as the decision was made. You thought you had a tough trip up here from Rangoon! We went by train to Mandalay and then by river steamer three days up the Irrawaddy to Bhamo. From Bhamo we rode native ponies down to Namkham. That's about forty miles, and on the fourth day we crossed the Shweli River, rode through the town of Namkham, and up the hill to this place. The Shan compound was on the right and the Kachin compound on the left side of the road.

"Finally we saw the hospital, and I still feel nauseated when I think of it. The old wooden building we're still using was all there was to it, and there was only one patient. The floor was covered with dirt, blood, pus, and the red saliva of betelnut chewers."

He took a sip of water from his cup. "God, it was awful, but Tiny and I set about to clean up the place, and then to learn the Shan language. My first surgical case was a Kachin with a huge adenomatous goiter. I sterilized the instruments in a pressure cooker on our stove, then Tiny poured the chloroform. I darn near cleaned everything out of that man's neck and it's a wonder his head didn't fall off, but the next day he was out eating pork curry with some of his friends! This must have broken the ice, because surgical cases began to dribble in and pretty soon I had all I could handle."

He went on to tell about how he started the nurses' training school. "Some of those first girls were the dumbest and the dirtiest I have ever seen, but with a lot of scrubbing and drilling some of them turned out to be pretty fair nurses."

Then he told about the need for new buildings and how they were constructed. "The nurses and I hauled stone from the river-bed after the hospital work was done and we held those stones together with mortar to form the walls. Hell, no one at Johns Hopkins taught me how to mix lime and sand mortar, so we had to have a little outside help for that. After the surgical building was completed there was no money left for beds, so we sawed up the lumber which had been used for scaffolding and used that. God, what bedbug hideouts those were!"

He brushed away the long gray curl of an ash which had formed on his cigarette. Then he took another sip of water from his cup. By that time it was getting quite late, but I wouldn't have left for anything. I was fascinated with his account of the outbreak of World War II, the return of his wife and children to the U.S., the Japanese invasion of Burma, and how he and many of his nurses were commissioned as the medical unit of General Joseph Stilwell's army. He told in his colorful drawl about the long march from Burma into Assam, and how they performed major surgery out in the open within a few feet of combat. In India there was not much to do but wait and time passed slowly, as he was anxious to get back into Burma and to his hospital.

"One night I was so damned lonely and bored and miserable that I took one drink, then another, and God knows how many more until I collapsed on the floor. Some of the nurses found me there and tried their best to get me into bed. Finally they made it."

After long weary months the push back into Burma began, and once again he had plenty of surgery to do as the pitch of battle increased. After the battle to retake Myitkyina the march contin- ued down past Bhamo and into the Shweli Valley and back to Namkham, though the war was not yet over and he was not free to take up work at the hospital. However, in March, 1946, he did return to Namkham to reopen the nurses' training school and begin full operation of the hospital.

"For a long time," he said, "I had had the dream of making this the biggest and best hospital in Burma. I wanted to train doctors as well as nurses, and treat Buddhists as well as Christians with- out twisting their arms when they were down, trying to convert them. The Baptists wouldn't hear of it. When I was in the U.S. in 1946, I contacted the president of the American Baptist Foreign Mission Society and explained that I wanted to operate this hos- pital on a nonsectarian, nonpolitical, nonprofit basis. I asked him to lease me the property on which the hospital stood without any connection with the Mission Society. He had heard enough stories about me to wonder about my sanity anyway, but when he real- ized that I wasn't going to fight the American Baptist Foreign Society tooth and nail, but would cooperate with them medically, he agreed to my plans. I was finally strictly a medical missionary, and since then I have left the preaching to others.

"Then I had to find some means of support, so with the help of influential friends the American Medical Center for Burma was formed. I organized a Namkham Hospital Committee here in Namkham to work along with the American committee. Sometimes this bunch here acts like a bunch of jackasses, but they've been helpful for the most part."

He seemed to be tiring—the pauses between incidents were becoming longer and longer—yet he went on.

"Since 1949 there have been dozens of simultaneous insurrections. When the Karens staged their big war, the hospital compound was overrun by insurgents. And when they began having a pitched battle with government troops right here on this hill I was so damned mad I ran halfway down the hill screaming my head off for them to stop shooting in the direction of the hospital. It's a miracle I didn't literally lose my head. Later, several people told some filthy lies about me, and suspicion arose that I was aiding the insurgents. I was arrested and tried a year later on two charges of treason against the government of Burma. I'll die before I'll ever go to jail again. They treated me pretty well, but my amebic dysentery really flared up and I suffered the torments of hell. My sister, Dr. Grace Seagrave, tried to hold this place together for me. The court convicted me and sentenced me to six years of hard labor. The whole staff of the U.S. Embassy in Rangoon went to bat for me, as well as lots of Burmese citizens. My hard labor consisted of house arrest in a place owned by the embassy. Finally, the Burmese court did clear me of the charges, but I was not permitted to return to Namkham for several months, until Burmese public opinion demanded it.

"During my absence, Grace was taken ill and died, but she had kept this hospital open with the help of Grandma, Esther, and others."

At that point in his narrative he began to refer repeatedly to "that Shan s.o.b." It wasn't until much later that I learned that he was referring to Dr. Albert Ai Lun, a young man whom he had partially raised and sent to medical school, and whom he had asked to come to Namkham as medical superintendent after Dr. Grace's death. When Dr. Seagrave was finally permitted to return to Namkham, he and Dr. Ai Lun had serious personality clashes and Dr. Ai Lun was eventually forced to leave, thus ending their professional association and what had once been a close familial relationship. When I questioned various people about the nature of the disagreement I heard different views, but my general impression was that Dr. Ai Lun had tried to make a few changes which the Old Man didn't like. Some told me that Dr. Seagrave treated Ai Lun like a child and expected him to do as he was told. I heard it summed up: "Well, Ai Lun was young and childish, and the Old Man was old and childish. They just couldn't get along."

The Old Man wound up his tale by saying, "Well, that about brings you up to date. In 1961, the A.M.C.B. got the Olmansons to come out here. Now, you two are here, and I can relax a little."

A few nights before Fanny was due to return to the U.S. we asked her to have dinner at our house. I wanted to invite Pansy and Dr. Seagrave but hesitated because I knew it would break the Old Man's routine and he might think it an imposition. I couldn't imagine how long it had been since he had gone to another home for a meal. Finally, I consulted Pansy. She didn't reply right away, and her face reflected serious thought. Then she said, "Yes, I think he would like to come, but he is so sensitive about his teeth. He cannot eat properly with them because they keep popping out, and he cannot eat any solids without them. Also, he must be very careful about what he eats for fear of causing a relapse of his amebic dysentery. But I think he would like to go to your house."

The last thing I wanted to do was cause a relapse of anyone's dysentery, but Wong Jack knew what foods would cause trouble. As for the teeth, I had seen plenty of people having trouble with their dentures, and I couldn't imagine the Old Man being bashful about anything. When I asked him if he would come to dinner, he seemed pleased to be remembered.

Wong Jack worked for two days buying and preparing the food for his special Chinese dinner. I watched him when I had time, and asked a few questions, but he did all the work.

When the three guests had arrived the night of the dinner and we were all seated at the table, Wong served each dish silently as he padded about the table in his bare feet. The first course was a noodle soup. Then there was sweet and sour pork, fried noodles with diced pork, green beans, cabbage, pork skin, bean sprouts, and green onions all fried together, fried beef strips seasoned with soy sauce, and eggrolls. Wong told us to heap a generous serving of rice in the center of our plates and put some of each of the other foods around it.

Dr. Seagrave wore his teeth throughout the meal, without mishap. Actually, he did more talking than eating, which didn't surprise me. One of his topics of conversation was Wong Jack. "You know he used to cook for me, don't you, Sue?"

"Yes sir, I read that in your book. We feel very lucky to have him cooking for us. It was nice of you to let us borrow him."

"My god, you're welcome to him. I kicked him out. He treated Pansy like dirt. Besides, he's a pretty lousy cook and my stomach said it was time for a change."

Wong Jack was serving around the table and listening to every word. He made no comment, and there was no change in his deadpan expression. However, I suspected that he had a few opinions of his own.

After dinner we moved into the living room. As he passed the fireplace, Dr. Seagrave pointed to a spot where an attempt had been made to patch a large crack in the concrete between the stones. "That's about the only mark left that shows the damage done to this house by U.S. bombers."

"Were you here then?" I asked.

"No, I was operating in some swamp hole between Myitkyana and Assam. The Japanese general in charge of this whole area was living in this house. Our pilots knew it and they were out to get him. You can still see a few bullet holes in the tin roof, too. I built this house just before the war for my family. After the war my wife and children returned to Namkham from the U.S. where they'd been during the war. But they didn't stay long. Insurgent uprising, need for schooling, and other things sent them back to the U.S. I stayed on and lived here until two years ago when I had the smaller house built where Pansy, Augusta, and I are now.

"There were Japanese troops quartered on the compound during the war. They even put bamboo strips down on the hospital floors to sleep on because they didn't like our teak. The general who lived in this house must have been completely ignorant of Western-style plumbing. He had the bathtub ripped out and we found it downtown set up for the use of prostitutes. As for the toilet, he had been climbing up on it and squatting instead of sitting. What a mess that was!"

Suddenly from somewhere in the distance we heard the soft, sweet sound of children's voices singing "Rock of Ages." "Do you know where that's coming from?" I asked Pansy, who was sitting next to me.

"Yes," she said. "Esther's family. They have a little song service and prayer every night before bed."

"What a fine tradition!" I thought. "Few families have their own services anymore."

The Old Man growled, "Why the hell don't they sing on key?"

After a few moments he continued his story about the house. "We heard that the Jap general had had an air raid shelter dug beneath that big banyan tree out by the back door. In case any bombs fell the limbs would scatter the blast. When the Japs were being driven out several of them were trapped in that hole and refused to come out and surrender. Some Americans simply drove a bulldozer up the hill and closed up the opening to the hole."

I wasn't sure whether that story was true or not. However, from that time on, whenever I went out the back door and passed that tree I wondered what might be beneath it.

We soon discovered other interesting things about our house. One morning shortly before day-break I got out of bed and went to the bathroom. The generator wasn't on yet so there was no electricity, and I felt my way in the darkness. Suddenly, something dashed from underneath the bathtub and brushed past my ankle. I ran out of the bathroom, slammed the door shut, and went into the bedroom to get the flashlight. Then I gathered up my courage and went back into the bathroom. I shone the light into the corners, under the tub, and behind the toilet. Nothing, but then I heard sounds coming from the dirty-clothes basket. Two beady bright eyes reflected the flashlight and there sat an enormous rat happily snacking on soiled spots on the boys' pants. He hopped out of the basket, and there followed a mad scramble as I swung wildly at my uninvited guest with a long-handled back brush. Finally, the rat jumped to the bathroom window and hid behind the curtains. Although I couldn't see him I knew where he was and I attacked the curtains with vigor, landing blow after blow with the back of the brush. When I finally stopped, one very battered dead rat fell to the floor.

A similar chase in Tim's room one night resulted in a catch for Huckleberry. Sometimes it sounded as though whole herds of horses were racing back and forth in the attic overhead as the rats ran around. We put out some poison, but because we were afraid of harming the children all poisons were used sparingly. We did manage to thin out the rat population, and by keeping the attic door closed we kept most of the rest upstairs.

Bats also inhabited our attic. Their high-pitched screeches were heard each morning and evening. Many times I watched them take off at dusk from beneath the eaves of the house; they returned by the drove with the first light of dawn. Occasionally one lost his direction and came plunging down the attic stairs into the dining room. When this happened the boys swung everything from brooms to baseball bats at the frightened creature before it was finally captured.

Fanny stayed at Namkham three weeks. I shall never forget my feeling of near-panic the morning she left for home. Our short acquaintance with Fanny had been most pleasant and I was sad to see her go. Her going severed the last connection with home and friends, leaving us isolated in a strange place. We said our good-byes the night before her departure, and early the next morning as the roosters began to crow I awoke to hear the ambulance start up in the distance and drive away. I wanted to run after it shouting, "Wait for me!"

CHAPTER FOUR

NECESSITY AND INVENTION

One morning early in November, 1963, the entire valley was shrouded in fog. It was difficult to see the few feet from our back door to Esther's house, and impossible to see the hospital a hundred yards away. The mornings and evenings had been much cooler for two weeks, but according to the Old Man, the fog heralded the real beginning of winter.

As November faded into December, the fog was even more dense in the mornings and it lingered until around ten o'clock, when the sun made its first appearance in the valley. The temperature often fell to the low forties at night, but rose to at least sixty by afternoon. The ambulatory patients wrapped themselves in blankets and squatted outdoors in the sun for warmth. The girls in the lab made charcoal fires in small portable burners. It was impossible to warm the whole room, but they always kindly set a burner on the floor near me so that my feet and one side roasted while the other side was freezing. Two large burners were placed in the classroom to raise the temperature a few degrees before Dr. Seagrave came for chapel. Because the doors and windows were kept closed the fumes from the burners became stifling. Dr. Seagrave complained bitterly. "Get that damn thing farther away from me and open a window a bit. I can't breathe in here."

The winters were especially hard on him. He wore several shirts and a sweater or two, and topped it all with a heavy overcoat. When he sat in his chair during chapel service he looked like an overstuffed walrus with his gray mustache and gray mop of hair. He kept a small electric heater on the floor near his feet. When he turned it on the lights in the room dimmed noticeably. Huckleberry often visited chapel, and he soon learned that the most comfortable place was on Dr. Seagrave's feet near the heater. Huck was indeed a privileged character, for no other dog was allowed in the same room with the Old Man, much less on his feet.

Chapel was not the only place where Huck took liberties. He followed Joe as he made his rounds in the hospital and acted as though he were a consultant. Sometimes there were bits of food near the patients' beds to which Huck helped himself. The extent of his brashness revealed itself one day in the operating room. A nurse had opened the door to carry in a tray of instruments and Huck casually strolled in. Joe was operating. No one challenged Huck, so he found an old wicker chair in the corner of the room, hopped into it, and settled down for a nap until the operation was over. Once he had been in the inner sanctum, there was no keeping him out. Joe finally gave up and accepted his presence there. After all, Huck was cleaner than most of the patients and had fewer worms.

Early that first winter Tun Shein made a trip to Rangoon. It was time for us to apply for an extension of our three-month visa so that we could finish our first year. Tun Shein filled out all the necessary papers and presented them personally at the Department of Immigration in Rangoon. When he returned, he brought with him Dr. Violet Po Nyo and her husband, U Thet Wah. Dr. Violet was a charming, quiet girl, a Christian Karen, who had worked at the Namkham Hospital in 1961–1962 and had gone to Rangoon for a year's internship at Rangoon General Hospital. Her husband—we called him Chuck—was a big handsome Karen with many talents and a varied background. He had recently returned to Burma from Thailand when General Ne Win, the chairman of the Revolutionary Council of Burma, had granted an amnesty to members of various insurgent groups. We never knew his full story, for when we questioned him he simply smiled and gave some evasive answer. Chuck became Tun Shein's right-hand man, and his official title was Assistant Administrator of the Namkham Hospital.

After Dr. Violet's return, the workload became somewhat lighter for Joe and Dr. Silgardo. Dr. Violet had had no surgical experience, but she was a competent and conscientious clinician, and with Joe's guidance she gradually acquired surgical skills. In addition to her hospital duties, she became the regular organist for the chapel services.

As we adjusted to life in Namkham, it was inevitable that time should pass rapidly, almost unnoticed. Each day was exactly like the day before; breakfast, chapel, hospital work, lessons for five-year-old Tim, supper, bedtime. There were no other American families to visit, no places to go, no television, no real diversion of any kind. Even the weekly softball game became so routine as to be boring. An occasional movie, shown in the nurses' dining room, relieved the monotony. I had not fully appreciated Johnny Weissmuller's Tarzan movies when I had seen them twenty-five years before.

My first birthday in Burma did provide a break in the routine. Joe had arranged for a surprise party, though it was impossible for me not to be suspicious when I noticed lavish preparations underway in the kitchen. Wong Jack spent a good part of the day baking a huge cake and making ice cream in the old hand-crank freezer. His cake was a thing of beauty, though not nearly as tasty as it was pretty. There were three layers, two chocolate separated by a white one, and all covered with white icing decorated with blue trimming. Unfortunately both the chocolate and the white layers tasted the same, like the peanut oil Wong Jack had used in their preparation.

In the evening guests arrived, singing "Happy Birthday" as they came in. Dr. Seagrave, Pansy and Augusta, Esther and her family, Tun Shein and Lulu, Dr. and Mrs. Silgardo, all the staff nurses, and a few of the student nurses came to help me celebrate. They brought a wide variety of gifts, including a Burmese outfit consisting of a beautiful silk *longyi* and lace *engyi*, a Burmese parasol, *hpynats* (Burmese slippers), several lengths of cotton material, flowers, a chicken, and some sticky rice cakes called *kawpoke*. My family gave me a beautiful Shan hand-knit sweater.

After I had opened the gifts Wong Jack served the ice cream, cake, and coffee. It was the first time some of the guests had tasted ice cream, and only a few had ever eaten cake. The nurses seemed ill at ease. Most of them sat on the floor and quietly ate the strange food, probably wishing they had rice and curry instead.

Dr. Seagrave made me feel very happy when he said, "We all hope that you have many more birthdays and that you spend them all in Burma." Right then I felt content enough to want just that.

On one of my earliest visits to the lab I had noticed a cabinet filled with glassware which had never been removed from the packing boxes. When I asked Esther about it, she replied, "Pansy and I brought that glass back with us from the U.S. in 1948. Much of it I do not know how to use, and the rest I do not have time for."

After hearing this I couldn't rest until I had examined every bit of that equipment. There were dozens of petri dishes and several jars of prepared media for bacteriological work, flasks of all sizes and description, pipettes, and even an ancient, rusty microtome for cutting tissue sections. Any lab staff would have been tickled to have such a supply. This equipment had lain untouched for fifteen years! The biggest find was two beautiful Zeiss microscopes, still in their cases, with eyepieces, objectives, and other accessories still wrapped in tissue paper. I asked Esther, "Why under the sun aren't you using these microscopes instead of that old monocular?"

She gave some explanation, but what she meant was that she had used that old, dirty microscope for years, was used to its idiosyncrasies, and saw no reason for changing. Besides, there was no electricity in the afternoons, therefore no microscope lamp, and it was almost impossible to use the larger microscopes without artificial light. She just turned her old monocular to the window and usually got plenty of light for it.

My first big project was to set up a method for doing routine Kahn tests for syphilis on each patient admitted to the hospital. As Dr. Seagrave had said, there was an ample supply of Kahn antigen in the cabinet, so I got it out, along with the pipettes and test-tubes necessary for the procedure. Then I studied the laboratory manual which described the technique, for it had been over fifteen years since I had done any Kahn tests. There were not nearly enough test-tube racks to set up the tests. I summoned the carpenter, and after much talking, drawing, and describing, he shuffled off to the shop. He returned later with something approximating what we needed, and I was in business.

After a patient had seen the doctor and been admitted to the hospital, he was given a slip to take to the lab indicating what tests were to be done. At that time blood was also drawn for the Kahn. The student nurses on duty in the lab drew most of the blood and put it in the tiny refrigerator to clot so that serum might be ready for the next day's batch of Kahns. Esther and I tried to teach the students the proper technique for drawing blood, but without much success. They simply had to learn by practice. Perhaps I had a morbid sense of humor, but it was amusing to see an old Shan man seated on a stool, his arm bared and his expression terrified as one of the girls moved toward him with a 10-cc syringe and a long needle with a visible barb.

I set up the tests in the morning, and after I had done this enough times to be sure of the technique, I showed the girls how to do it. Before long some of them became proficient enough so that I had only to supervise and read the results. Then their month of lab duty would end and I had to start all over with another group.

At one point during the procedure the patient's serum and the Kahn antigen had to be shaken vigorously for three minutes. There is a regular shaking machine devised for this purpose, but of course we did not have one of these. When shaking time came I simply handed each of the girls a rack of tubes and we shook them together for three minutes.

When Tun Shein observed this procedure he said, "I could make a machine for you that would do the shaking. All we need is a small motor and some pulleys. I'll get to work on it and have the carpenters make it."

Two days later Tun Shein and one of the carpenters came to the lab straining under the heavy load of his invention. I had never seen the likes of it. They had constructed a crude but sturdy table, and strapped to one end was a motor which looked adequate enough to run a small car, let alone shake a few tubes. A pulley belt was attached to a wheel on which sat a wooden tray. After we had located a suitable electrical outlet, Tun Shein took two test-tube racks and strapped them to the wooden tray with strips of rubber cut from innertubes. "Now stand back," he said, and he plugged the cord into the outlet.

What happened then was enough to stampede a herd of water buffalo. The wooden tray with its burden of racks began to shake back and forth violently while going around at the same time. The noise was deafening. The tubes did not fit securely in the homemade rack and two of them flew into the air and crashed on the cement floor.

When Tun Shein finally turned the machine off I was almost convulsed with laughter. Feeling that some comment was necessary, I managed to remark, "I'll have to admit it *really* shakes those racks."

"Sure, and look here," he said, "With these other little trays we've made you can attach white-cell pipettes and you won't have to shake them by hand either. Here, let me show you." He picked up a pipette in which blood had been diluted with the counting fluid, strapped it into the small tray with rubber strips, put it on the larger tray on the machine, and plugged it in once again. The noise began and the pipette whirled. Three minutes later Tun Shein unplugged the machine and removed the pipette. Not one drop of solution was left in the bulb. The shaking had been so violent, and from end to end rather than from side to side, and everything had been shaken out.

Tun Shein shook his head. "We'll have to work on that a bit. If it shakes too fast, just take this small block of wood and hold it against the pulley belt. That will slow it down."

Our machine became famous throughout the compound, and people dropped in to see it in operation. We did use it to shake Kahns occasionally, but it never did work well for white-cell pipettes.

After the Kahns were under control, I began to work on blood sugar determinations. There were always several diabetics in the hospital and it was invaluable to know the level of sugar in a patient's blood before and during treatment. By searching through the cupboards again I found the necessary reagents and equipment. The biggest hurdle came when I started to make standard solutions with known amounts of sugar against which the unknown amount in the patient's blood would be matched. The procedure required a very delicate balance, in order to weigh minute amounts of sugar before they were dissolved in a known amount of water. I had no such balance, only a very crude instrument which was not nearly accurate enough, but I weighed out the sugar anyway, hoping that my solutions were not too far off. After all the reagents were ready I tried a test on myself and on several others whom I assumed to have normal amounts of sugar in their blood. In each case, the results were within the limits of normal.

In my laboratory training I had had the minimum basic instruction in bacteriology and it had been my weakest course, but there was so much need for this work at Namkham that I decided to make an attempt. I removed some of the jars of dried prepared media from the cabinet, along with a few petri dishes. Esther and the students watched as I dissolved media in water, then washed and dried some of the dishes. We carried everything to the autoclave in the surgical building to be sterilized, and then I poured the hot solution into the dishes, taking great care to avoid contamination. As the solution cooled it hardened, and then it was ready to be inoculated. By preparing different kinds of media I could do throat cultures, stool cultures, and many others.

Before long I had an opportunity to try out my media. Joe came to the lab and told me, "I just saw a small child with a severe eye infection. I suspect that his mother has gonorrhea and has transferred some of her 'bugs' to the child's eyes. Of course, it could be some other organism, so why don't you make a culture?"

We both examined the child. He was about two years old. I had never seen eyes so inflamed and puffy. The infection had been allowed to continue for weeks before the mother had brought him to the hospital, even though the family lived close by. I took a sterile swab from a tube, rubbed it gently inside the eye lid, picking up some of the discharge, and then placed the swab back in the tube. In the lab, I rubbed the swab about on the surface of one of the dishes of media. Then I placed the dish in the incubator, which had been set for 98.6 degrees Fahrenheit, body temperature, and also the temperature at which bacteria grow best. I fully realized that at eleven p.m. the electricity would go off and the temperature would drop, but that was the best I could do.

The next morning I hurried to the lab, opened the incubator door, and carefully removed the dish. Scores of tiny white colonies of bacterial growth were spread over the surface of the media. I removed a tiny portion of one of the colonies with a sterile wire loop, stained it, and examined it under the microscope. I felt a tremendous surge of excitement and pride as I beheld millions of tiny, red, round organisms, appearing in pairs. They fitted exactly the description of *Neisseria gonorrhea,* the organism which causes gonorrhea, and, in this particular case, a serious eye infection.

Fortunately, *Neisseria gonorrhea* is sensitive to certain antibiotics. The boy's eyes cleared up rapidly and he went home.

I did not do any more cultures that day or the next, and my prepared media sat untouched in the plates. On the third day I took a look and discovered that each plate was growing a beautiful blue mold. They were supposed to be sterile. There was only one explanation: the autoclave was not doing a thorough job of sterilization.

I showed the plates with the mold to Tun Shein. He merely said, "I'll check into it. Most likely whoever is running the sterilizer is not doing it properly. Let's hope there's not anything wrong with the sterilizer itself, because I don't know where we would find another."

The Old Man was not so placid. He was furious. "What in hell is wrong around here? Can't these girls run an autoclave without someone hanging over them? Damn it all," he said to Tun Shein, "kick a few of them out if necessary, but get that thing working right. No wonder we have so many infections after surgery."

Tun Shein checked every possible angle, but the fault was

never found or corrected. My bacteriological media continued to grow mold after two or three days, so I made fresh media every time I needed any. The percentage of postoperative infections was staggering, but most cleared up after massive doses of out-dated penicillin. Optimistically, we concluded that poor sterilization was better than none at all.

One morning I walked into the lab to see black smoke curling up from the incubator. Rushing over, I found the door very hot and the inoculated plates inside charred. I hurried into the office for help and found Fred Taw, office manager and general handyman. "Fred, come quickly and see what has happened to this incubator."

Fred ambled after me, wearing his usual big grin. He touched the hot handle and quickly withdrew his burned finger, shaking it about as he laughed. "Maybe the thermostat control has gone out," he said.

"Well, what do we do about that?" I was very much annoyed.

"Not much we can do. There are no spare parts here. Maybe you should write to Fanny and see if she can have a new thermostat sent."

"But that would take months! Isn't there anything else we can do?"

Fred smiled all the while, and looked as though he was enjoying my predicament. The Burmese were never upset by such trivialities and the impatience of us Westerners amused them. "I'll ask PoZo to look at it. Maybe he can help. Ha ha ha."

"Ha ha ha yourself," I muttered as he headed toward the door.

Within a few minutes PoZo walked in. He was a Karen of some sixty-five years, and a man of many talents. His official title at the hospital was Chief Engineer, but the thing he did best was chase cows off the compound with his slingshot. He was a dead-eye with that slingshot and an extremely fast runner for a man his age. Few cows escaped him. He also had musical talents, for he directed the church choir and played several instruments. But it was soon obvious that he knew nothing about incubators.

It looked as though my bacteriology days were over. But, I wasn't entirely licked yet, for I had a sudden brainstorm. Several patients had just been admitted with an apparent diagnosis of typhoid fever, and I had wanted to try some stool cultures to see if I could isolate the typhoid organism. We saw dozens of such cases, and there was some question in Joe's mind whether this was really typhoid or something closely related. I prepared the media, inoculated several plates with stool specimens from the patients suspected of having typhoid, and took them home with me.

When we left the States we had foolishly brought along an electric blanket. I say foolishly because the electrical current at Namkham was not suitable, and anyway, the generator was turned off at eleven p.m., just when we would have wanted to turn on the blanket for the night. Now I thought I would try connecting the blanket to the transformer ordinarily reserved for the iron. I could turn the blanket on very low, just enough to warm the plates. Of course, once the electricity went off there would be no heat, but perhaps there would be enough warmth for the organisms to grow. I made the necessary connections and carefully wrapped the plates in the blanket. When I checked a few minutes later the blanket was much too hot, so I lowered the control knob. After ten minutes there was no heat at all. Again I adjusted the control. After several attempts, I thought it felt right. Throughout the evening I couldn't keep my hands off that blanket, and kept wrapping and unwrapping the plates as though I expected some growth to appear by magic.

The next morning I hurried to my "incubator." Although the electricity had been off for hours and the blanket was cold, there were hundreds of tiny colonies of bacterial growth on the surface of the media. After breakfast I dressed quickly in my *longyi* (by now I was wearing them, too) and went to the lab. More cultures of suspicious colonies had to be made. By evening further studies were ready and my "incubator" was again in service.

When all the cultures were completed I showed the results to Joe, and he came to the same conclusion I had reached. "It looks as though the pathogen is not the typhoid bacillus, but one of the paratyphoid group which can cause a similiar disease," he remarked.

There had been too many variables and changes in technique, to be sure, but it seemed that his observation was correct. Had any cultures ever been incubated in a blanket before, and with such variations in temperature? The value of my work was purely academic, but I'm sure Madame Curie was no prouder of her great discoveries than I was of my electric-blanket paratyphoid bacilli.

Distilled water used for glucose and saline intravenous solutions was made in the lab in a small electric still which sat on a shelf against one wall of the lab. It was a simple enough contraption, but without it the hospital could not have run. Rain water was collected in a large drum near the stairs leading up to the lab. The nurses carried that water in buckets to the lab, where one nurse stood on a high stool and ladled water into the still. The finished product, a clear, pure water, trickled out the bottom of the still into jugs. Esther weighed out the correct amount of salt or glucose for each jug, put the jugs in the autoclave for sterilization, and then sent them to surgery.

One day, in a rare moment of frivolity, a first-year student nurse bumped the glass tip on the still and broke it. This put the still out of commission temporarily, and Esther was furious. She reported it to Tun Shein, and he told the Old Man, who blew a fuse. Luckily, we were able to make the necessary repairs, but the humiliated student was not allowed to wear her cap for a month.

Dr. Seagrave was anxious that Joe and I should begin teaching classes to the students. Within a few months some of the trainees would be taking their government midwife examination, so with Pansy helping as interpreter, Joe started a course of lectures in obstetrics. Pansy also interpreted for me in training laboratory technicians. Both Joe and I started off rather ambitiously, using outlines and formal lectures. After the first quiz we relaxed a bit, and after the second we gave up trying to give tests because few of our students were absorbing anything.

I had five students in my class; two junior staff nurses, two senior students, and one boy, Chit Tin. Of the five, Chit Tin was the only one who showed interest, and he seemed to have the least talent. However, as time went on, Chit Tin emerged as the real scholar in the class. At the end of six months he was the only one who had completed the entire course. He was then assigned to help Esther in the lab part-time, in addition to his duties in the storeroom.

One of our biggest headaches was the lack of blood for transfusions. It was almost impossible to persuade anyone to donate, and we lost several patients who might otherwise have been saved. Joe often operated on a patient with so few grams of hemoglobin that he would not have touched the case in the United States without several transfusions before surgery.

Shortly before noon one day he came hurrying into the lab. "A Chinese girl was just brought into the maternity building. Her baby is due, but she's been bleeding for twenty-four hours. The baby is dead, I'm sure, and the mother is in severe shock. If she doesn't have some blood right away she'll die. Her husband is willing to donate if he's the right type."

I grabbed the anti-A and anti-B typing serum, both about a year out of date. I had learned not to bother with the Rh typing serum, which was so old that it no longer reacted properly. The patient was still alive and her husband was terrified. He was the first man I had seen in Burma who showed real concern over whether his wife lived or died. I took two drops of blood from each of them and mixed the drops with the typing sera. But the patient was type O and her husband type A, making it impossible to use him as a donor.

Joe rolled up his sleeve and said, "I'm type O; let's go over to the lab and draw off a pint of my blood. Let's hurry. I don't mind giving the blood, but I don't want the patient to expire just before she gets it."

We didn't even take time to do a crossmatch, a usual precaution to ensure blood compatibility of donor and recipient, but immediately withdrew a pint of blood from Joe. We had no modern disposable plastic bags with tubing, and the old rubber tubing and glass bottle had been used and reused. When the bottle was full Joe rushed it over to the patient and began dripping blood intravenously as fast as he dared.

Fortunately, the patient was young and strong, and she recovered. Her only ill effect was a sharp rise in temperature shortly after receiving the blood, probably from contaminated equipment. She and her husband were most grateful, and the day she was discharged from the hospital they brought us some beautiful silk brocade material and a Chinese tea set.

Joe gave blood on two similar occasions, but of course he did not have enough blood to give to all who needed it. He had to develop the callous attitude adopted by Dr. Silgardo: If the patient needs blood, give him several injections of iron and some synthetic plasma. If that's not enough—and it seldom was—don't worry about it.

I had an idea, so I went to have a talk with Tun Shein. "We've got to do something to have blood available when it's needed. We don't have the facilities for storing blood. That would take 24-hour refrigeration, and we don't have a refrigerator or electricity all day to run one. What we need is a list of donors we can call when there is a need for blood. We could have all prospective donors typed and keep the list on hand for emergencies. We might pay fifty kyats (about ten dollars) for every bottle they donate."

Tun Shein smoothed back his hair and tightened up his *longyi* before replying. "OK, I'll send out a notice to all the male workers on the compound, and distribute a few downtown. We'll ask for volunteers to donate blood and offer to pay them for each donation."

"Fine," I fairly beamed. "We won't take blood from anyone more often than once every three months. Please put on the notice that anyone interested should report to the lab. We'll have to type them and do a hemoglobin determination to be sure they can spare a little blood. I'll even do a Kahn to be sure they don't have syphilis. How's that sound for efficiency?"

The next morning I got all the typing sera in order and waited for my first customer. Noon came and no one had volunteered. "I'm too anxious, tomorrow they will come," I thought.

Tomorrow came and went, and the next day, and the next. After a week I told Tun Shein, "I haven't had a single blood donor volunteer."

"I'm not surprised. I'll send out another notice and make the language a little stronger this time."

Another notice went out, and days passed. Still no volunteers. Finally, two boys from the weaving school in town presented themselves. The first had eight grams of hemoglobin, not nearly enough to donate blood, and the other had even less.

Needless to say, I never was able to set up an available blood donor system. Patients continued to die in shock for lack of blood. Occasionally a patient who needed blood was known to some of the student nurses, and they would donate. As a rule, Kachins gave to Kachins, Karens to Karens, Chinese to Chinese, and Shans to Shans.

The majority of my working days in the laboratory in the U.S. had been spent in hematology—the study of blood—and there were enough blood diseases at Namkham to keep me occupied. Nearly everyone had a moderate degree of anemia. I had assisted at hundreds of sternal bone marrow aspirations (the bone marrow is where most blood cells are made) but had done only two aspirations myself. At Namkham I was the hematology specialist. When a bone marrow study was indicated to properly diagnose the type of anemia or some other type of blood disorder, I stuck a large needle into the breastbone, drew out a little of the marrow, made the preparations for study, and made the diagnosis. The first few times I did an aspiration my hands shook violently and my heart felt as though it was in my mouth. Soon, however, I found myself bravely aspirating marrow from the top of the flat hipbone just for the sake of variety. By doing those marrow studies I was able to uncover four cases of leukemia and one case of aplastic anemia—a rare disease in which the bone marrow ceases to function—and to study other cases of strange anemias.

The patient with aplastic anemia was a fourteen-year-old Shan boy. When I first saw him he lay on his crude wooden bed, huddled under a blanket, in the darkest corner of the men's ward. Joe pulled back the cover, and I could see two very frightened eyes.

"This boy has a little of everything wrong with him," Joe said. "Just name it, he's got it. His stool is positive for hookworm ova and blood; his Kahn test is two-plus positive; his hemoglobin was too low to be read on the hemoglobinometer. Esther estimated it to be around two-and-a half to three grams. And he's obviously malnourished. Hookworm and malnutrition will give anemia, but not usually as low as this. Oh yeah, and he has these small red spots on his extremities, which makes me think he might be bleeding because of a lack of platelets."

The boy reminded me of pictures of inmates liberated from Nazi prison camps. He was just skin and bones, and his wizened face was like that of a very old man while his size was more like that of an eight-year-old. I felt compassion beyond words as his eyes, which seemed much larger than normal in his shrunken face, turned to me.

"Has he any relatives here who will give blood?" I asked. "He needs lots of things, but it looks as though he must have some blood first, and quick."

"No, some relative brought him in yesterday from near Mongyu and left right away. You type him, and if he's type O I'll give him a pint of blood. Maybe it will tide him over for a while. Do a bone marrow, too, to see if there is anything there to indicate why he has such a severe anemia."

On the way out of the ward I stopped at the nurses' station and asked the nurse in charge to set up a prep tray for me; then I walked the few steps to the lab and got out clean slides, pipettes, a sterile bone marrow needle, and typing serum.

Back in the ward, I made a finger stick and took two drops of blood for typing. He was type O, so Joe would be able to give him some blood after all. Next, I proceeded to do the bone marrow aspiration. The procedure was not very painful, but it was frightening to a patient and I was anxious not to upset the frail boy. He was unusually responsive and kept smiling at me as though he knew how much I wanted to help him. I cleaned off a small place over the breastbone with iodine and alcohol, then injected a few cc of a local anesthetic and waited for the deadening effect to take place. Next, I pushed the large bone marrow needle into the skin with a quick, hard shove, and it went through the upper layer of the breastbone. "Now the tip of the needle should be right in the marrow cavity," I explained to the student nurses who had gathered to watch. I carefully placed a large syringe on the needle and drew back on the plunger. The boy gave a small groan but did not move as a few drops of bloody material came up into the syringe. Speed was essential at that point to get as many preparations made as possible before the blood containing the small marrow clumps clotted. I placed a drop of the material from the syringe on each of several slides, and then made an even film by smearing out the drop with the tip of another slide. The student nurse from the ward put a small bandage on the patient's chest and I hurried back to the lab with my slides.

After the slides were stained and dry, I examined them under the microscope. Normally the marrow of the breastbone contains countless numbers of early forms of white and red blood cells in the process of development. When the development is complete, the cells enter the bloodstream to perform various functions. When their lifespan is over (three to four months for red cells, a few days for white cells and platelets), they are removed from the circulation by the spleen and other "filtering" tissues of the body. Normally there is a proper balance between new cells being formed and old cells being removed, and the individual has adequate numbers of red and white blood cells as well as platelets.

What I saw on that boy's slides was most unusual. There was a complete absence of the blood cell precursors and there was no evidence of platelet formation. Platelets are tiny cell fragments necessary for blood clotting; their absence would account for the numerous bruises and tiny red spots called petechiae on the boy's body. After examining all the slides, which all showed the same changes, I knew that the boy was suffering from aplastic anemia, a disease in which the bone marrow ceases to function. Rarely is the cause of the condition known, and only rarely will the marrow respond to treatment and begin to form blood cells once again. The boy's body was destroying his old cells and not making new ones, thereby rapidly depleting his blood supply.

That night I told Joe of my findings. "First thing in the morning," he said, "I'll get Esther to draw a pint of my blood and we'll give it to him. Then I'll start him on various medications to try and stimulate his marrow back into business."

With Joe's good rich blood the boy brightened a bit, but his hemoglobin was still too low to be determined accurately. Through the following days we watched him closely, checking his hemoglobin regularly, but it continued to fall. A week later I repeated the bone marrow examination, and it looked just as it had on the previous occasion.

"I'll give him a pint of blood, too. We've just got to keep him going," I said to Joe.

"Absolutely not. I can't let you do that," was his answer. "We'll do all we can for him, but you keep your blood."

Each day I visited the boy, and each day I found him weaker. He was too weak to sit up anymore and could barely move his head on the hard pillow. Then he stopped smiling at me and I knew his time was running out. He died during the following night and was taken to the damp morgue. The next morning the carpenters made a box, placed the body inside, carried it to the marshy place below the hill on which our house sat, and buried it in a shallow grave beside scores of other unclaimed bodies.

Other cases of anemia ended less tragically, and one was particularly interesting. A first-year student nurse, Shwe Kgi, constantly complained of weakness and was extremely pale. She was a dainty and graceful Shan girl from one of the two Christian families in Namkham. The Old Man had treated Shwe Kgi with iron, vitamin B12, liver, folic acid, and every other available blood-forming medicine, but she had failed to respond. He asked me to check her blood to see if I could suggest anything. She had only seven grams of hemoglobin, roughly half the normal amount, and the stained film indicated that her red cells, instead of being uniform biconcave discs, varied greatly in size and shape.

A few weeks after this test Shwe Kgi's father was admitted to the hospital for some abdominal complaint, and when I studied his blood it tested exactly as his daughter's had. Arming myself with syringes, needles, tubes, and all the other necessary paraphernalia, I had a driver take me to Shwe Kgi's home. There were several other children, and I took blood from all of them, as well as from the mother. The mother's blood was essentially normal, but the children showed the same low hemoglobin with odd sizes and shapes of red blood cells. It was clearly a familial type of anemia which had been passed on by the father. I yearned to do further studies to learn more about it, but this was beyond the realm of possibility in a valley in North Burma.

Joe, too, was constantly frustrated by his inability to study and treat patients as thoroughly as he would have wished. "But the hardest thing is the absolute lack of control the doctor has over whether the patient stays in the hospital or goes home," he told me. "When the patient comes into the outpatient clinic, a nurse takes his history and he tells her whether or not he will stay in the hospital, and whether he will agree to surgery. By the time I see him everything is decided. If he has fulminating tuberculosis and doesn't want to stay, he goes right out and infects a few more people. If he just wants a bed for the night so he can go to bazaar the next day and doesn't have anything wrong with him, he stays. Yesterday I saw a patient with the most horrible-looking cancer of the lower lip, but he didn't want to stay in the hospital and wouldn't agree to surgery."

"What did you do, let him go?"

"One of the students called Grandma Naomi. She understands most of the languages spoken around here. The man was a Shan, and she laid it on the line to him. He finally consented, but said he couldn't stay more than two weeks. In two weeks I have to cut off that cancerous lip and make him a new one. What I know about plastic surgery would fill a thimble. I've got to do some reading between now and tomorrow morning."

"What did Grandma say to persuade him?"

"Well, maybe it wasn't so much what Grandma said when you come right down to it. The deciding factor was that he couldn't eat rice anymore. So much of his lip is gone that food keeps falling out of his mouth before he can swallow."

The next morning Grandma put the patient to sleep. Drip chloroform had been the anesthetic of choice since the days when Dr. Seagrave did most of the surgery. He kept a nurse standing by with a lit cigarette so he could turn for a puff occasionally.

Being highly combustible, ether was out, but chloroform did very nicely.

When the patient was asleep Joe performed the surgery on his lip. First, he removed the cancerous portion, and then, by taking flaps of skin from the patient's cheeks, he was able to fashion a new lip of sorts. When the bandages were removed a few days later the old fellow was not a raving beauty, but soon he was eating rice and holding it in his mouth. Before two weeks were up he had gone home.

Apparently the operation was a success, for we never saw this man again. Sometimes we felt we had done the impossible, and helped a patient despite himself. And so our work continued, a frustrating but rewarding blend of compromise and improvisation.

CHAPTER FIVE

PATIENTS

Shortly after our arrival at Namkham, I was awakened from a sound sleep one night by an eerie glow of light and strange sounds just outside our bedroom window. "Joe, wake up," I whispered hoarsely.

"Huh, what, what? Is something wrong?" he mumbled.

"Wake up! There's something or somebody outside."

As he roused we heard a voice calling, "Doc-tor, doc-tor." Joe got out of bed, walked to the window, and parted the curtains. There stood two student nurses holding a kerosene lantern. "Yes, what do you want?" Joe asked.

"Doc-tor, please come. Patient shot, much bleeding."

That was our Namkham telephone system, and it was very effective, for the nurses always brought the news. Actually, Joe was glad to be spared the harassment of the telephone, and we soon become accustomed to these visitations in the night.

So I was surprised a few months later to see several of the main-

tenance men hanging some kind of wire among the trees outside
the lab. I noticed that one end of the wire was attached to the lab
building; the other end seemed to be going to our house. Curious,
I went into the office, where I found Tun Shein.

"Tun Shein, what is this wire the men are putting up in the
trees?"

"That's a telephone wire. We're going to have all the buildings
on the compound connected by phones."

"You're kidding. Phones at Namkham? I can't believe it."

"That's right. All the major buildings on the compound will be
connected. This whole outfit came over with the last shipment of
goods from New York."

We were to have phones, indeed, but it was some time before
they were actually connected and working. Just before the final
work was completed, one small but important part was found to
be missing. Tun Shein dispatched a letter to Fanny, who sent the
missing part from New York, but the whole operation was delayed about three months.

A year or so before, Dr. Seagrave had hit upon the idea of having phones at Namkham and had applied for the necessary funds
through the United States Public Law 480 grant which helped to
finance the hospital. The officials at the U.S. Embassy in Rangoon
had a good laugh when they read Dr. Seagrave's reason for wanting such a communications system. "We need telephones so the
girls won't get raped when they have to run around at night carrying messages and calling the doctors," the application said.
With the need so great, the money was granted!

Finally all lost and forgotten parts were replaced and the
phones were connected. Joe grumbled bitterly at the prospect of
being at the beck and call of the jangling black monsters once
again.

The first time our phone rang, I hurried to answer. The woman
at the other end of the line began to speak rapidly in Burmese,
and when I tried to interrupt there was a timid giggle, then a soft

click. Obviously a wrong number.

Later the phone rang again. This time Joe answered, and the situation was repeated. After several wrong numbers we left the phone off the hook. We never got anything but wrong numbers, and the few times I tried to call Pansy or Mrs. Silgardo there was usually some trouble along the line. The nurses used the phone to call each other between wards, but they continued to come for Joe in person. None of the nurses were ever raped while on duty, but I don't know whether or not the phones were responsible for that good fortune.

One morning shortly before dawn the nurses came for Joe. He dressed and hurried to the hospital through the dense fog. It was noon before I saw him again and heard about this particular emergency.

"When I got to the hospital the only light we had was the lantern the girls were carrying. That wasn't much, but I could see that there were three stretchers on the floor of the admitting room. The patient on the first stretcher was an old woman whose head had been completely cut off. The same thing had happened to the young man on the second stretcher. On the third one was a younger Chinese woman so covered with blood it was hard to tell how many wounds she had. But there was a faint pulse so we took her up to the operating room. That's where I've been for the last six hours."

Joe's description left me feeling cold and sick. "Who were these people? What happened to them?"

"They were a Chinese family—man, wife, and the man's mother. They had a little store in the village up past the junction of the Burma and Lido Roads. About ten o'clock last night some bandits attacked. Nobody knows how many there were. They had those long knives they call *dahs*. It seems to be general practice to kill robbery victims, but somehow they didn't complete the job on the poor wife. I've never seen so many deep cuts. One cut on her head went clear through the bone and left a section of brain exposed. A blow on the back of her neck left all the muscles severed between the vertebrae. She must have held up her arm as protection—most of the muscles on her lower right arm were sliced back to the elbow. I don't even remember all the cuts she had.

"The bandits probably thought she was dead; they took what they wanted and left. She must have lain there for hours before she was discovered, and her loss of blood was terrific. Why she wasn't dead I'll never know. If I had operated on her back in Bradenton I'd have given her at least three or four pints of blood, but as usual there wasn't a drop to give her and no one to donate. So far, she's still alive."

We both went to the surgical ward to see what we could do for this woman who refused to die. She was still under anesthetic and lying perfectly motionless on her hard mat. There were bandages from the top of her head to her waist. Only her eyes and a portion of one cheek were visible. "See this bandage here?" Joe asked, as he indicated her right shoulder. "One cut went through the muscle and broke the shoulder blade."

We had little hope for this patient, but one and then two days passed and she continued to live. On the third day, when I visited her, I expected to find her still in shock. But as I approached the bed there was a quick movement and the woman jerked the sheet up over her head. A staff nurse standing nearby laughed. "Patient very shy. She no want you to see her shaved head."

Gently I reached over and pulled back the sheet. I was totally unprepared for the sight which greeted me. The girl was surprisingly young, not more than eighteen at the most. All of her larger bandages had been removed. In their place were numerous smaller bandages, over her head, arms, and shoulders. As soon as the girl saw me she buried her face in the pillow and tried to cover her head with her hands. I learned from the nurse that she had been out of bed, walking about the ward, and was already asking to be sent home.

The only thing that seemed to bother her was her humiliation at being seen with her head shaved. If she felt the least bit of grief over the loss of her husband and mother-in-law it certainly wasn't apparent. Two days later she left the hospital, her trim figure dressed in a gay *longyi* and her head with its short black bristles carefully wrapped in a gray bathtowel.

We encountered many other patients who were equally amazing. There was a Lisu couple who had walked for two or three days from their village to bring their baby to the hospital. Joe was immediately impressed by these young people because we had met very few parents who would make such an effort to get medical help for their children. When he questioned them through an interpreter, he learned that the baby had been crying almost constantly. The father held the baby so it could be examined, and Joe noticed that the father's fingernail beds were absolutely white instead of a healthy pink. A look at his eye grounds showed the same. Setting aside the baby, Joe continued to examine the father, who showed all the classical signs of severe anemia.

"Send the mother in here," Joe ordered the nurse.

The examination of the mother produced exactly the same findings, and both parents were sent to the lab for a blood count. Both of them had hemoglobin levels far too low to be read accurately with our hemoglobinometer. I estimated them to be in the range of two grams instead of the normal twelve to fourteen.

The baby's trouble was very simple. He was being breast fed, and his mother was so anemic that the breast milk was about as nourishing as water. The poor little fellow was simply starving to death.

The parents consented to stay at the hospital for a few weeks for treatment, and Joe placed them on large doses of iron. After a week they were already feeling stronger. As the mother improved, the baby began to thrive and stopped fretting. Both parents had lived with subnormal hemoglobin levels so long that they had adapted to their miserable existence and did not know what it was like to really feel well. When their hemoglobin rose to seven grams, about half the normal level, they didn't believe it possible to feel any better, so with their baby they left the hospital and walked the long distance back to their village.

In the rear of the dingy little building known as the surgical annex was a small room with a dirt floor. The only opening from the outside was a window a few feet above ground level which doubled as both window and door. The furnishings inside consisted of a bed of wooden slats covered with a thin mat, and a small table. Those accommodations were used to isolate patients with contagious diseases. Occasionally, a suspected case of smallpox was kept there, but usually the occupant suffered from Hansen's disease, better known as leprosy.

We had two such cases who visited us periodically, one a man and the other a woman. Both had rather advanced cases of the disease in nodular form. I particularly remember the man, who was a pitiful sight. His face, arms, and upper trunk were covered with large, unsightly nodules ranging from the size of marbles up to some as large as hen's eggs. Because of fear and superstition, he was not allowed to live in a village, but managed a meager, animal-like existence in the jungle. Occasionally he came to the hospital for treatment, but mostly for food. Each time he stayed for a month or two until there was some small improvement in his disease, and then vanished again. There were numerous leprosariums in Burma, but he refused to go to one.

Another patient who made regular visits to the hospital was a Kachin girl with a mosquito-borne disease known as filariasis or elephantiasis. Her right leg was four or five times larger than the left one due to a blockage of the lymph channels by microfilariae. The tremendous enlargement was irreversible, so there was little that could be done to help the girl. She was terribly self-conscious about her deformity, and wore her *longyi* down to the ground to cover her legs. Otherwise, she was far healthier than most of our patients. That was the only case of filariasis we saw at Namkham, though it was quite common in the south of Burma.

The patients for whom I felt the greatest compassion were the children, who were usually brought to the hospital so near death that we couldn't help them. They were filthy, malnourished, loaded with parasites both inside and out, and often had pneumonia, severe diarrhea, or a horrifying skin disease. Many a time I helped treat such a child in the hospital, then hurried to check on my own three children at home. The sight of their smiling faces and healthy bodies gave me courage to return to the children at the hospital.

Every Friday morning after chapel, Esther, Grandma, Emily, and Pansy made rounds of the entire hospital. As the highest-ranking nurses, it was their duty to keep a watchful eye on all phases of the hospital work. Actually, they had little authority since Dr. Seagrave gave all the orders, and the rounds were more of a tradition than anything else. The Namkham Hospital was bound together with tradition. I often accompanied the nurses, not because I had anything to contribute, but because I never failed to be impressed with the great needs of the patients. I was alternately depressed with the hopelessness and misery and then inspired to work harder to relieve the suffering in some small way.

One morning while on rounds we entered the women's side of the Old Hospital. There on the first mat sat a pitiful little Lisu girl dressed in rags. As we walked toward her bed, she turned her head in our direction and the sight made me stop in my tracks, for both of her eyes were swollen shut and oozing copious amounts of purulent pus. Grandma explained to me that the girl had contracted a gonorrheal infection in her eyes which had been left unattended until she had lost the sight of both eyes. "Someone from her village brought her in here and left her. She has no parents and no one to care for her," Grandma added with a sad shake of her head.

"What will happen to her?" I mumbled.

"The doctors will try to arrest the infection. After that, I do not know. Perhaps someone from her village will take her."

Also on the women's surgical ward was a baby no more than three weeks old. She was swathed in vaseline bandages, for her entire right side had been severely burned when her mother dropped her into an open fire. The right arm was completely charred, and the infant was more dead than alive. Her mother squatted nearby, seemingly unconcerned as she chewed her betelnut.

A few days later I learned that she had taken the baby from the hospital, telling the nurse that she intended to throw it in the river. Perhaps she wanted to rid herself of a burden, or she may have thought she was performing a merciful act. I preferred to believe it was the latter.

That mother was the exception, for most loved their children dearly. The seeming neglect of their children was because of ignorance, not deliberate. The women dutifully carried their infants on their backs for hours, pacified them with flabby breasts when they cried, then fed them a pure rice diet and gave them a drink from the nearest contaminated stream. They never bathed the small children because they might catch cold, or because they believed bathing was bad for the skin.

A Chinese lady who lived across the Shweli River brought in her three-year-old child, who was gasping for breath. Joe examined him and found a large white membrane in his throat indicative of diphtheria. Without taking time to carry the child to the operating room, Joe reached for a scalpel and performed a tracheotomy in an effort to clear an air passage for the oxygen-starved body. Then he began treatment with diphtheria antitoxin. Sadly, his emergency efforts were in vain, for the child was dead within a few hours.

The poor mother was overcome with grief. She had lost two other children within a year from different diseases, and this tragedy was more than she could bear. Most of the people with whom we came in contact rarely showed emotion, but simply accepted whatever came their way. That Chinese mother must have passed beyond the point of blind acceptance. I shall never forget her cries and moans as she sat in the damp morgue with the small body while the carpenters constructed a crude wooden box. When the body was placed inside, the carpenters nailed the lid on the box and carried it to the marshy cemetery for burial. The mother followed a few feet behind, still emitting those loud, mournful cries.

One of the most tragic occurrences at Namkham during our stay concerned a four-year-old Shan boy who was not a patient. His father was on the medical ward being treated for an advanced case of tuberculosis, and the rest of the family had returned to their village to harvest rice. The little fellow had been left behind with his father, possibly so he could help him and run errands, or, most likely, because he was too small to help with the harvest. At any rate, he stayed close to his father and slept on the floor beside his bed, undoubtedly breathing in large numbers of tuberculosis organisms in the process. I often saw him wandering alone about the compound in the evenings, amusing himself by kicking stones down the hill with his bare feet. If the boys and I were taking a walk, I would ask him in sign language if he wanted to go with us. He always shyly turned away but followed at a distance.

Christmas Eve came and Joe and I were walking with the boys to the nurses' home for the Christmas party. We met Tun Shein as we passed the door of the medical building. He raised his hand in greeting and said, "I have just been talking to the TB patient who has the little boy staying with him. He says the child went out this afternoon around five o'clock and has not returned. He's probably wandered off somewhere and gotten lost. I'll get a couple of men and look for him."

Later Tun Shein joined us, and sat down beside Joe. "We've searched the compound, but can't find the boy. No one remembers seeing him. We'll have to wait until morning to look more thoroughly."

In the excitement of the party and Christmas morning at home, I forgot my missing friend. After all the presents had been opened, Santa Claus and some of his helpers came to our house to bring nuts for the children and sing carols. The boys and I then followed the group, going from house to house singing carols. As we proceeded about the compound, I saw Tun Shein and several other men huddled around the septic tank which was about twenty feet behind the office building. "Strange," I thought, and paused to watch. The men had removed the lid from the tank and were probing around inside with a long pole. Tim started to run over, but Tun Shein called out sharply, "Get away from here!" Unaccustomed to such a rebuke from Tun Shein, Tim quickly returned to my side and we continued to follow the carolers.

When Joe came home for lunch he said, "Well, they found the little lost boy. I hate to tell you where."

The scene around the septic tank flashed before my mind. "Oh no, not there," I moaned. "Not in that septic tank!"

"How did you know?"

"I saw Tun Shein and some men there this morning. How did it happen?"

"No one knows exactly. The tank has that large cement slab over the top of it, but there's a small opening near one end. The only thing over the opening was an old piece of rusty tin. The boy probably jumped on that tin and it gave way. Tun Shein noticed that the cover was missing this morning, so he looked in and saw the boy's cap floating. No one saw him fall in and the water was deep enough for a little fellow like that to drown."

Not all of our patients had such tragic stories. Indeed, many had a happy outcome, and some even provided moments of amusement.

I remember a ten-year-old Indian boy whom I first saw on a cold foggy winter morning when his father carried him into the lab. The boy's skin was very dark, and he had black eyes and tremendous ears which stuck out at right angles from his head. He was dressed in baggy blue trousers and a ragged shirt which had been white at one time. Actually, it was the father who immediately attracted my attention. He was over six feet tall, extremely thin, and his skin was almost black. He had a large bushy black mustache. His shoulder-length hair, very thick and kinky, stood out in all directions, and it shone from the habitual application of some kind of oil.

Joe had just seen the boy in the admitting room and had sent him to me for routine blood studies. When I approached the boy with a syringe and needle, he began to weep and wail. Tears fell like rain, and a constant stream of fluid came from his nostrils. The father was so filled with pity for his son that he, too, began to weep, with the same copious tears and nasal fluid. The crying distracted me, and my venipuncture was highly unsuccessful. In fact, I got no blood at all. In spite of the chill of the morning, I began to perspire freely as I made another attempt and the moaning became louder. Finally, the blood began to fill the syringe as I pulled back on the plunger, and I heaved a sigh of relief. When the procedure was completed, I placed a small piece of cotton over the wound, patted the boy on the head, and indicated that they might leave. Both father and son ceased wailing, but I could hear loud sniffing as they retreated down the steps and headed toward the surgical building.

After this experience I was anxious to know more about that strange father and son, so I went in search of Joe. He had just finished seeing another patient and was sitting alone in the small examining room filling in a chart.

"What's the matter with that Indian boy you just sent over to the lab?" I asked.

"Why, did you have any trouble with him?"

"No, no, nothing like that." Then I recounted my experience with the boy.

"He seems a bit retarded, Susie, but his father is completely devoted to him. The reason the boy was brought to the hospital is that he has a congenital malformation of the penis and his father wants me to make him a new one!"

"You're kidding! Now I've heard everything. Can you do it?"

Joe began to thumb through the pages of a large book. "Well, urology is a little out of my line, but I've been reading in this book, which describes a similiar operation. It will take at least two operations and maybe three."

He showed me some drawings in the book. "See, this boy has the opening to his urethra—the tube through which urine flows to the outside—at the base of his penis. Usually, of course, the urethra passes through the penis. Now, what I have to do is free the boy's present penis, which is adhered to the soft tissues of the perineum. That's operation Number 1. Then I'll close up the present opening of the urethra and try to make a passage for it through the penis. That's operation Number 2 and maybe Number 3, depending on how things go. I'm going to do the first one tomorrow."

The next morning when I arrived on the second floor of the surgical building I saw that preparations had already begun and that Grandma was giving the anesthetic. Huckleberry was comfortably curled up in his favorite chair. Say Paw was moving slowly about, supplying instruments and sterile gowns. She was normally a large heavyset girl, but was even more so now, as her seventh pregnancy was due to be terminated any day; yet she plodded patiently on. Four or five student nurses were scurrying about the room. One of them brought a cap and mask to me, while another began to wash the patient thoroughly from his waist to his knees. Then she applied a bright red antiseptic to the genital area and covered the patient with sterile drapes.

I was very proud of Joe, who worked steadily and surely, cutting, tying, sponging. A casual observer would never have suspected that he had never performed such an operation, and that only yesterday he had read how to do it. He freed the small, malformed penis from the tissues to which it had been adhered, and finally inserted a catheter, a tiny rubber tube, from the opening of the urethra to the bladder. The outer end of the catheter was inserted into a bottle to collect the urine.

When the last stitch was made, Joe straightened up and removed his gloves. "Well, that's that. Now, we'll see what happens."

It didn't take long for us to see what would happen first. That afternoon I walked past the boy's bed to see how he was progressing. He was partially awake from his anesthetic but still a bit dazed. His father kept vigil at his bedside, and as I approached, the father jumped to his feet, placed his hands together in a prayerlike position and bowed from the waist to me. Over and over he continued to bow, happily smiling all the while. I smiled and bowed back, and the two of us bowed to each other for several seconds before I decided this could go on indefinitely if I didn't stop. I turned to the patient, and just at that moment the boy reached down, took hold of the catheter, and yanked it out. I was too stunned to move. When I finally regained my composure I ran for the nurse, who ran for Joe.

A return trip to the operating room was necessary, and Joe left orders for a nurse to be with the patient at all times. A few days passed and all went well.

It was essential that several weeks go by before the final operation, so the boy and his father went home with instructions to return in about six weeks. The boy was pleasant and gentle, but, as Joe had suspected, not very bright. In fact, Joe privately worried about the wisdom of constructing an organ with which the young man might propagate offspring of equal mentality.

Exactly six weeks later father and son were back. I did not know of their return until I met the father in the hall of the surgical building. He immediately began bowing to me. He had great respect for his son's doctor, and as the doctor's wife I was entitled to a share.

The second, and final, operation was a success, and the father's joy knew no bounds. Each time he saw Joe he bowed, and sometimes he grabbed Joe's hand and held it tightly for a few seconds, his eyes brimming with tears.

The day they were to leave the hospital for the last time I went by to see them. They had been around for so long that the place wouldn't seem the same without them. When the father saw me he rushed forward, bowed several times, and motioned for me to come to his son's bed. The boy was standing beside the bed, and his father hurried over to him, pulled down his pants, and proudly indicated the finished product of Joe's labors. I was a bit startled, but both of them were so happy that I was caught up in the spirit of the occasion, and managed to express my congratulations.

CHAPTER SIX

HOUSEHOLD
HELPERS

I was fortunate to have an abundance of good household help most of the time. Besides Wong Jack, there were two nannies to care for the children, do the housecleaning, and wash and iron.

Karen women are noted for their gentleness and other qualities which made for good nannies. I was told they had lived for centuries in a state of servitude to the Burmese and to the British and the many other foreigners who inhabited Rangoon. Tun Shein secured the services of two Karen girls for us, and we took them from Rangoon to Namkham when we first arrived in Burma.

Shirley, who was twenty-four years old, had worked for years as a nanny and had even helped the Olmansons, who preceded us at Namkham. She understood and spoke English well, worked fast, handled the children beautifully, and there was a sparkle to her personality.

Nella, on the other hand, was young, inexperienced, painfully shy, and understood no English. She followed Shirley about and did as she was told. After three weeks at Namkham, Nella boarded the bus one morning and went back to Rangoon, much to my surprise. Since I could not communicate with her, I had had no idea of her intentions. Esther said that Nella told her that she was very homesick and unhappy at Namkham.

To help Shirley, Tun Shein enlisted the help of one of the many relatives who inhabited his house. Mu Nah was much older, had never done housework, but she worked out very well. The children loved her and we all began calling her Auntie Mu Nah. Alas, Auntie Mu Nah stayed with us only a few months. She became violently ill with a stomach disorder and was forced to spend several days in the hospital, after which she decided to retire to the relative peace and quiet of Tun Shein's house.

I was busy with hospital work in the morning and teaching Timmy in the afternoon, which left Shirley with more work than she could manage alone. For a time, some of the student nurses came over two at a time to watch the children so Shirley could be free for household chores. That worked nicely but was not a permanent solution.

Finally, Wong Jack made a suggestion. His wife, E Poi, had time to spare now that all her children were able to shift for themselves. Why not hire her? It sounded like a good idea to me. She was available, and she was not likely to get homesick and suddenly leave. Pansy and Tun Shein were skeptical, and the Old Man didn't think much of the idea. What did a Shan know about house work? "I've known her all her life and she has always been stupid," was his comment.

E Poi (no. 2 girl in Shan) was hired and she proved the skeptics wrong. She worked slowly but steadily, learned the routine quickly, and immediately won the affection of the children. There was only one thing wrong with E Poi. Although she arrived at work fresh and clean, she soon began to perspire. I never had any trouble locating her in the house. All I had to do was follow my nose. In fact, I could walk into a room and tell if she had been there within the last fifteen minutes. Joe stood it as long as he could. "Susie, you've got to do something. Talk to Wong Jack about it and have him talk to her."

How could I tell someone she smelled terrible? I remembered how easy the TV ads at home had made it sound, but I didn't believe them. The situation was made even more difficult because E Poi couldn't speak English, and I spoke no Shan and very little Burmese. Days passed as I procrastinated, planning my attack first one way, then changing, then deciding the situation was utterly impossible.

Finally, I armed myself with a bar of soap and a bottle of deodorant and cornered E Poi as she was in the wash shed preparing to make a fire to heat water for evening baths. There was a short embarrassing silence, then I went into my act. And act it was, because my Burmese vocabulary didn't allow for much speechmaking. Holding the bar of soap in my right hand, I raised my left arm and rubbed the soap vigorously over my armpit while repeating the Burmese word for bathe, *yaycho*. Then I opened the bottle and demonstrated how to apply the deodorant. All the while E Poi stood nodding her head. She was much more at ease than I. When I had finished my demonstration, I thrust the soap and the deodorant into her hand, and hurried back into the house.

The next day there was a remarkable improvement. Joe was impressed. "Wong Jack will probably give you a medal," he said.

However, after a few days the old familiar odor hung about the house. Apparently, E Poi thought the deodorant was a kind of soap and had used large amounts of it as she bathed, so the bottle was soon used up. I had brought an ample supply from the U.S. so I gave her another full bottle, and periodically saw that she was supplied with the precious solution.

Before long we had another problem. With a Chinese cook and a Karen and a Shan for nannies, we were sitting on a racial powderkeg. Wong Jack ruled the roost, and his wife, E Poi, dutifully sided with him in all things, which left Shirley treading on thin ice. After about a month of this arrangement, Shirley told me she had received a telegram stating that her father was very ill in Rangoon and she should come quickly. She burst into tears telling me about the emergency. This was a real blow to me, for I depended on Shirley a great deal. Reluctantly, I gave her money for bus fare. She promised to keep me informed of her father's condition and to return to Namkham as soon as the situation permitted. The next morning she was on the bus and on her way to Rangoon, but not alone. The young Karen girl who worked for Dr. Seagrave and Pansy had decided to go with her, which brought forth untold rumblings and grumblings from the Old Man.

Days and weeks passed with no word from Shirley. After about a month one of the Karen student nurses returned from vacation in Rangoon with the news that she had seen Shirley, who was now happily married. Her father had not been ill at all, and the telegram had been from her boyfriend, urging her to hurry to Rangoon to meet him. I was furious that I had fallen for such trickery and disappointed in Shirley.

E Poi managed the work very well alone, and she did not mind working longer hours to get everything done, so I didn't bother to look for another nanny right away. However, three months later, while in Rangoon on vacation, we met a seventeen-year-old Karen girl who wanted to work in Namkham so that she could be near a sister who was in the second year of nurses' training. May was hired, and she went back to Namkham with us.

At first she was more like another child whom I had to care for than a helper, but gradually she learned what to do and worked like a demon. She tried so very hard to please that sometimes I had to ask her to slow down a bit and take it easy. Her eagerness soon got her into hot water with E Poi. Though E Poi was slow, she was steady and dependable, and she resented May taking over as though she were the only one capable of doing the work.

In my presence they were quiet and never spoke to each other, but Tim told me of spats they had while I was at the hospital. The old Chinese-Shan-Karen triangle was back in action, but we all managed to live through it to the very end.

May was a sweet Christian girl, and she was blindly devoted to our family. She had quit school after about the eighth grade, partly because she needed to work and, I suspected, partly because she wasn't a good student. She had aspirations of returning to school and going on into nurses' training. After she had been with us almost a year, I arranged for her to attend school on the compound and work for us after school hours and on weekends. That setup pleased her, and pleased E Poi as well, since their working hours rarely coincided anymore.

CHAPTER SEVEN

GATHERING
CLOUDS

Irene Silgardo was a large woman who dressed in the traditional Indian *sari* and seemed always to be smiling. I discovered one day while visiting in her home that the smile belied her true state of mind, for she was really very unhappy at Namkham.

She and Dr. Olwen B. Silgardo ("Dr. O.B.S.") had married seven years before, while he was in India on a short vacation from the hospital, and she had returned with him to Namkham. Before her marriage she had never been very far from her family, but at Namkham she was completely cut off from them. The first two years she was bitter and miserable; then she gave birth to two daughters, and then a son. The children kept Mrs. Silgardo's thoughts from dwelling too much on family and friends in India. Eventually she learned to speak some Burmese and made friends with the staff and student nurses. The nurses thought she was grand, and since many of them were far from home and lonely also, they sought her company.

Tun Shein, Administrator of the Namkham Hospi-
Lettering on the Jeep reads in full: A Gift to
nkham Hospital for the people of Burma from the
ple of the United States through C.A.R.E.

Wong Jack, personal cook t
the Newhall family.

The Nurses' Home.

Grandma Naomi, matron at Namkham Hospital.

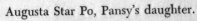

Esther Po, in charge of the laboratory a X-ray.

Pansy Po, dean of the nursing school, secretary and personal driver to Dr. Seagrave.

Augusta Star Po, Pansy's daughter.

HOMER PAGE

Dr. Seagrave addresses a class.

The Friday afternoon softball game was a tradition at Namkham. Dr. Seagrave, in his undershirt, stands at third base.

The Newhall family and staff nurses.

Patients bathing, sunning, and eating behind the Old Hospital.

Nurses in native costume.

Kachin women sell vegetables at the town bazaar.

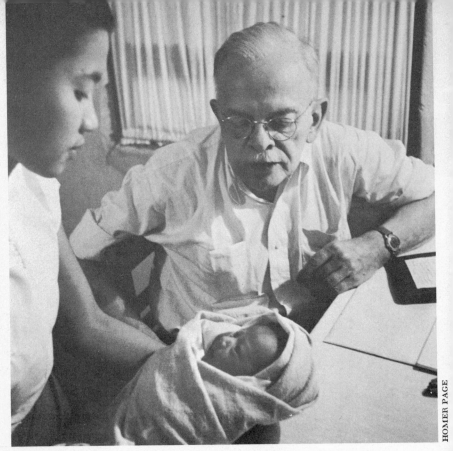

A nurse holds a newborn baby for Dr. Seagrave's inspection.

"Dr. Joe" and Dr. Olwen Silgardo (right) with a group of nurses.

Dr. Violet.

HOMER PAGE

March 31, 1965. Nurses and townspeople carry floral pieces at Dr. Seagrave's funeral.
The sign below reads "Namkham Townspeople."

Sue Newhall models Burmese clothes, a birthday gift.

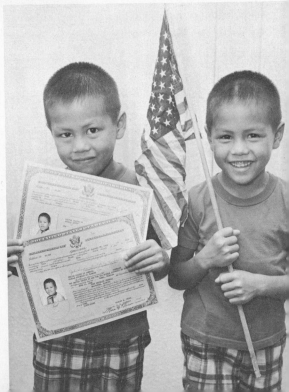

ohn and James, the orphan Shan wins adopted by the Newhalls, be- ome naturalized U.S. citizens in ne, 1968.

"Are you happy here?" she asked me, but before I could answer she went on, "Mrs. Olmanson did not like Namkham at all, and I do not like it either, but I cannot convince my husband to go back to India. His mother and my mother keep writing letters begging us to come home. The situation in this country is getting very bad. The government does not like foreigners and there is no future for us here."

"Why do you say that?" I asked.

"Well, ever since this Revolutionary Council has been running the country they have been changing so many things. They make it very hard for all foreigners because they say foreigners are here only to exploit the people. Some Indian friends of ours in Rangoon had their business taken from them and had to leave the country without any of their possessions. I feel that this is going to happen to us, and we cannot afford to start all over again without any money. We have saved some during these years and it is possible that we may not be able to take any of it out of Burma."

"But surely the government would not treat Dr. Silgardo that way. He hasn't been exploiting anybody, and he's been helping a lot of people who really need him."

"That does not seem to matter. Dr. O.B.S. has spent most of his life in Burma. He was educated at the University of Rangoon and even served in the army during World War II in this country, and still he is considered a foreigner who is exploiting the people.

"Also, the government is rapidly nationalizing everything, and it is only a matter of time until they get around to this hospital. When they do, we will all have to get out. I do not understand what they are trying to do, and it has me very worried."

"Yes, I can see why it might worry you," I admitted. "But if the government is so much against all foreigners, why do you suppose they let us come into the country?"

Irene smiled. "I do not understand that either. The Burmese Government has practically stopped issuing visas. Maybe it was because I prayed so long and hard that you would be allowed to come. I wanted Dr. Joe to come very much, because now that he is here and Dr. Violet has come back, maybe I can convince my husband to go back to India. Always before he has told me that he could not leave the Old Man without someone else to help do the work."

"Dr. Silgardo seems to have a deep feeling for this work," I said. "He must feel that he is accomplishing something to have stayed on so long. How many years has he been at Namkham?"

"Twelve years. He first met the Old Man at the close of the war when they worked together for a time. Dr. Seagrave offered him an opportunity to go to the United States and serve an internship if he would come back and help out here at Namkham. So Dr. O.B.S. went to Louisville, Kentucky, for two years in the late forties. Since then he has spent most of his time here. He feels deeply indebted to Dr. Seagrave for this training and has said that he will stay here as long as the Old Man lives."

We were sitting in her living room and our conversation was constantly interrupted by her three children and my three, who kept racing around the room. The Silgardo children owned a three-wheel vehicle which all six children wanted to be on at the same time.

"Children are the same the world over," I remarked. "If there were a dozen toys here they would all want the same one."

"Yes," she said. "Marietta, now you let Timmy ride the wheel for a while!"

Then, turning to me again, she said, "My children are another reason why I am so anxious to return to India. I am Roman Catholic and we cannot bring up the children properly in our faith here. We only have mass occasionally when one of the priests from Kutkai or Bhamo passes through Namkham. My oldest daughter wants to know why she cannot go to the Baptist Church on the compound with some of her friends, and I just cannot let her go. Then there is the matter of schooling. Marietta has started to school this year and she is becoming fluent in Burmese, but these things will not fit her for what she will need to know back in India."

"Well, you surely do have lots of reasons for wanting to leave this place," I admitted, "but I hope you don't go soon for I'll surely miss you. You've done a lot for me, and these afternoon visits have kept me from being lonely. Surely Dr. Seagrave doesn't want to see you go either."

"I wasn't going to say anything about that, but he is the main reason I want to get away from this place. He is like a tyrant in his own little kingdom, and he does not treat Dr. O.B.S. fairly at all. He never treats him as a professional equal. He never asks his opinion on any subject, he constantly says very bad things about him before the staff and students. He does not appreciate the fine, unselfish work my husband has done here, and I do not understand why Dr. O.B.S. continues to put up with such humiliation."

I could see that this was a sore point with her and I was surprised at her frankness. "But Dr. Seagrave has been very kind to us, surely. . . ."

"That will change. When Dr. Olmanson came, the Old Man received him with open arms, and within a few months he was criticizing everything Dr. Olmanson did and making life very difficult for him. It has always been the same way with doctors who come here. Only Dr. O.B.S. remains while others come and go. You wait and see. Soon the Old Man will begin to find fault with the way Dr. Joe does his surgery, the diagnoses he makes, and even petty things like the way he writes on charts. He is completely unreasonable.

"Please forgive me, I did not intend to say nearly so much. So many things are building up inside of me lately and my husband is tired of hearing me complain and there is no one else to whom I dare talk."

Suddenly her mood brightened and she said, "I have been meaning to tell you, Father Divine from the mission up near

Bhamo will be in Namkham this weekend. He usually stays overnight with us and says mass either in our home or somewhere
downtown. There are very few Catholics in Namkham. You have
been wanting to find a fourth person for a bridge game and Father Divine is an excellent bridge player. Maybe you, Dr. Joe, Dr.
O.B.S., and Father Divine can play while he is here."

"Oh, I hope so! Please be sure to let us know when he arrives so
we can work out something."

Joe was home when the children and I arrived. I began to discuss with him some of the things Irene had told me. "She really is
bitter about the situation in Burma and about things right here in
Namkham. I was surprised because I've talked with her many
times and she always seemed happy."

"There's no doubt that the present Burmese Government is
making some radical changes and discouraging foreigners as
much as possible," Joe said. "There is also no doubt that the Old
Man is hard to get along with. I've heard some of these stories,
and I'm beginning to find out a few things myself. Yesterday I
saw a boy with a typical case of chickenpox and admitted him to
the medical ward. In the afternoon when the Old Man held his so-
called clinic he saw the boy and wrote in his big red letters across
the chart: 'Any damn fool would know this is smallpox!' Then he
had the boy put in strict isolation. That's the way a staff doctor
might talk to a medical student, but not one physician to another.
I'm still certain the boy has chickenpox.

"A few days ago I was talking with the Old Man and Tun
Shein about this matter of the Burmese Government charging ex-
horbitant duty on drugs and equipment the A.M.C.B. is waiting
to send us. The Old Man asked me what I thought about it, and I
told him I'd rather do without the things than pay that duty.
They've never charged duty in the past and there's no reason why
they should now. That was obviously not what the Old Man had
in mind, because I wasn't asked anything else. Since then he
hasn't spoken to me.

"I guess when a man has lived in such isolation and loneliness for so long he has a right to be temperamental and autocratic. He's done a wonderful work here under very difficult circumstances, and we'll have to overlook some of his idiosyncrasies, but it's getting mighty tough."

"I know it's hard," I said, "but please don't be too independent, and do try to get along with him. I hate unpleasantness so much."

"I'll do my best, but if he asks my opinion I'll tell him, even if it's not what he wants to hear."

Before long we began to see the truth in what Irene Silgardo had said about the Burmese Government. Under "The Burmese Way to Socialism," General Ne Win and his Revolutionary Council were the supreme authority, and outside Rangoon each commanding officer in the army camps was the little dictator in his district. Behind our compound was a small camp which housed twenty or thirty soldiers with a lieutenant in charge. Not only was the lieutenant in command of his straggly band of soldiers, but all the township officers bowed to his every whim. He was automatically a member of the Hospital Committee, which met every three months. The committee was meant to perform the duties of a Board of Trustees and to act as a local counterpart of the A.M.C.B. At least, that was its purpose, but circumstances had caused it to deteriorate considerably, and there was constant contention between Dr. Seagrave and the committeemen. The lieutenant liked to throw his weight around, and the local people were too afraid of him and the power of the government to object.

One morning we arrived at chapel to find the Old Man more agitated than usual. He bellowed at the girls to "Speak up, damn it," and when they held a quarter note for a half-note count, he stopped the music and gave a five-minute tirade on correct timing. Finally the service was over, and he began to unburden himself to us.

"That sneaking egotist of an officer at the camp is trying to ruin us," he said. "We had a committee meeting yesterday and it was a farce. Two of the town people came in drunk, and they all sat around, afraid to open their stupid mouths in front of the lieutenant. There are three girls in the first-year nursing class who haven't passed a test since they got here, and they're too dense to absorb anything. All they have their minds on is something in pants. One of them is Tun Shein's relative, so he knows what I'm talking about. I refuse to let these girls have their caps and I'm going to kick them out. This stinking s.o.b. of a lieutenant got up and shouted about how I was discriminating against these girls and he was going to see that they stayed. These damn Shans in town have yelled for years about how I was prejudiced against the Shans and favored the Karens, and how I was unfair to the followers of the Lord Buddha, so they just sat there and nodded their heads. Besides, they didn't dare contradict him. They're scared to death of that rat.

"Ne Win would like nothing better than to see me back in jail, or, better yet, kicked out of the country. He's really got it in for me ever since my lawyer made him look like a fool at my trial. I'll die before I'll go back to jail, and I refuse to go back to the U.S. and sit around and rot like a senile old ass."

The more he talked, the more agitated he became. He hated having his authority challenged, and he was not accustomed to having his orders questioned. Yet he had a great fear of running afoul of the government and being put in jail. Even more, he dreaded the thought that he might be sent back to the U.S. and have to leave his little kingdom. He smoked cigarette after cigarette and his hand shook as he took sips of water from his cracked cup.

"And you, Tun Shein, you didn't help matters yesterday. When the officer sent for you to come see him you didn't go. That threw him into a rage. We've got to pacify him at all costs."

Tun Shein was accustomed to such scenes. He spoke calmly

and politely. "When the officer sent for me I was sick in bed. This whole situation has worried me so much that I had a terrible headache, so my wife, Lulu, told the messenger I couldn't go. When he came back the second time I got out of bed and went downtown to meet the officer. He had been interviewing the girls you want to expel."

The situation rocked on for several days and I stayed away from Dr. Seagrave as much as possible. Our relationship had been good, and I didn't want anything to disturb it during this critical period. Finally, one of the girls was sent home for medical reasons, and the other two stayed on a while longer. Neither received her cap with her class, and eventually both gave up and left.

Trouble with the lieutenant and the Namkham Hospital Committee was not all that was bothering the Old Man. For some time he had been dissatisfied with the way hospital affairs were being handled by the directors of the American Medical Center for Burma. I had no way of knowing whether or not he had genuine grounds for complaint, but he would go on for hours about how he was being "robbed blind," among other grievances. Often his diatribes included attacks on the personal behavior of some of the directors. Right or wrong, he could not rest until changes were made, so at the first board meeting after Fanny's return from Burma a new chairman was appointed and new policies instituted.

A few days after his selection, the new chairman sent a lengthy cablegram to Dr. Seagrave. Joe and I were present when he began to read. His massive face clouded, his hands began to shake, and he took a sip of water between puffs on his cigarette. When he finished reading, he did not say a word, but handed it over to Joe. In the cablegram, the chairman had discussed a few items of business, said how proud he was to serve in this new capacity, then went on for two full pages to reminisce about his and Dr. Seagrave's days together during the war. I did not know what it

cost to send a cablegram half way around the world, but it occurred to me that this one must have cost plenty. That was pre-
cisely what troubled the Old Man. "How much do you think it
cost to send that damned thing? He could have written all those
things in a letter and saved a lot. Don't those jackasses on the
board know how to save a buck? They live so high and mighty
and forget that we need a lot of things over here more than we
need four-page cables."

"Never satisfied," I thought. "He forgets that all of the people
who serve on the board do so on their own time and don't get one
cent for it. All he does is criticize them. Some gratitude."

CHAPTER EIGHT

KUTKAI

Luna Luther was an English teacher at the Shweli Valley School, the school located on the compound. She was a Karen whose home was near Rangoon, but she was living at Tun Shein's house along with some seventeen others who worked in some capacity at the hospital or were teachers or students at the school. I had asked her to help me learn Burmese.

"I am free every afternoon after four o'clock, and also on Saturdays. When would you like to have your lessons?" she asked.

"Well," I replied, "I teach Timmy his first-grade class every afternoon from one to four, but after that I don't have anything to keep me busy. How about five to six every day?"

"O.K." she said, "I will be at your house tomorrow at five o'clock."

And thus I found myself taking lessons in Burmese. Luna was a perfect teacher. She spoke excellent English and insisted that I give the proper inflection to the Burmese words. That is much more difficult than it sounds, for, as I learned, the same word can have three entirely different meanings, depending upon whether it is spoken quickly and sharply, whether the tone of the final syllable is dropped, and whether all the syllables are spoken evenly. For instance, one day I gave Luna the Burmese translation for the sentence "The children have gone to school," whereupon she burst out laughing and said, "You have just said that the children have gone to the cat!"

I had other problems, too. I had never been a good language student, mostly because I felt too shy to converse outside of the class. I had the same difficulty with Burmese. Occasionally I would muster up enough courage to say, "Nay gaund deh la?" meaning "How are you?" And I could hear the person giggling after I had passed. That didn't do much for my morale.

The text we used was "Lessons in Spoken Burmese," which had been prepared especially for missionaries newly arrived in Burma. In the course of a conversation with Dr. Seagrave after a Sunday evening song service, he asked how I was progressing with my lessons.

"Pretty well, I guess, but it is difficult for me. Luna taught me the numbers yesterday. Would you like to hear me practice counting?"

"Sure, go ahead."

"*Tit, hnit, thon,*" I began, and continued through number seven but could not remember the word for eight.

"I'll tell you how to remember the Burmese word for eight. It's pronounced exactly like the good old English word s-h-i-t. It's one of my favorite Burmese words. I find it very expressive sometimes."

I never again forgot number eight. Occasionally when Dr. Seagrave was in my presence and wished to tone down his "Anglo Saxon" a bit he merely said, "Oh Burmese number eight!"

My lessons continued every day for a few weeks. Then I found that I did not have enough time to study between classes, and

Luna was busy with a Christmas program at the school, so we started a three-day schedule. That was quite successful for a time, until Luna went to Rangoon for the Christmas holidays. When she returned to Namkham two weeks later, the original momentum had been lost and we never picked up where we had left off. In March, which was the end of Luna's school year, she resigned from the Shweli Valley School to study at the University of Rangoon. I had learned very little, but I was able to follow conversations and understand some of the more common words. The nurses did not know how much I had learned and how much I could understand, and stopped speaking about me in my presence. Little did they know they would have been perfectly safe 99 per cent of the time! I developed their habit of smiling knowingly whenever anyone was speaking. I looked intelligent, at least.

Joe never did learn much Burmese. The majority of the patients could not speak Burmese either, and it was always necessary to have an interpreter, sometimes two or three before the English got back to Joe. Of course, this wasn't the most accurate way of getting the patient's history, but it had to do. "It's kinda like veterinary medicine," Joe often complained. "If the patient is Chinese, he tells about his aches and pains to a Chinese nurse, who translates into Burmese for another nurse, who tells it to me in English. By that time I can only guess what the trouble is."

He really didn't have to worry too much about making a diagnosis. According to custom, if a patient had a fever he had typhoid, unless the fever rose and fell at regular intervals; then it was malaria. Similarly, if a patient was anemic—and all were—he could safely be treated for malnutrition and hookworm. If he had a longstanding cough, he had tuberculosis. Acute abdominal pain usually indicated a ruptured amebic abscess.

In spite of all the patients and the hospital work, we eventually began to feel the lack of something to do during our free hours. Downtown Namkham featured a moviehouse which along with two pool halls provided the only entertainment in town. Joe and I never visited the pool halls, but we did go to a few movies. Each evening about dusk, we could hear loud music coming from the loudspeaker in front of the theater, a sign that the show would soon begin. The theater was a large, grotesque barn whose façade had been patterned after a theater in Rangoon. All along one side was a large area with a dirt floor which was fenced in and covered with a tin roof. Here the patrons bought refreshments during intermission.

One evening during our first few months in Namkham, we received an invitation to attend an American movie at the theater. The invitation came from Sayama Koy. (Sayama is a Burmese term of respect which, literally translated, means teacher. All nurses were given the title. Koy is a Shan word for "the last one.") Koy and her husband were coowners of the theater. We had met her previously and knew that she had been one of Dr. Seagrave's wartime nurses and had also spent a short time doing postgraduate nursing in the U.S. after the war. Joe and I got into the Jeep, stopped to pick up the Silgardos, and drove to town.

As soon as we stopped in front of the building a group of spectators gathered. By that time I was accustomed to stares and smiles, and stared and smiled right back. Koy came out to meet us and in her gracious way showed us to our seats. The inside of the building was far nicer and more modern than I would have imagined. Large ceiling fans overhead turned slowly to keep the warm air moving. The four rows of seats in the extreme rear were the most comfortable and the most expensive, costing three *kyats*, about sixty cents. Our hostess directed us to those seats, which were the kind whose uncushioned bottoms flipped up when not in use. The few rows immediately in front of us, composed of folding wooden chairs, cost two *kyats;* while the rows nearest the screen, wooden benches with no backs, cost one *kyat.* The Silgardos, Joe, and I were the only people sitting in the highest-priced seats, and we were of far more interest to the townspeople

than the film. They didn't understand the English dialogue anyway.

Midway through the film there was an intermission. We four
remained in our seats, but everyone else went out to the fenced
area for refreshments and returned with an assortment of
goodies. The one which interested me most was made of small
pieces of sugarcane stuck on the tops of long bamboo sticks. It
looked like a giant cluster of lollipops. Other people had sunflower seeds and peanuts, and it wasn't long before the floor was
littered with debris. The chewing and spitting continued during
the entire second half of the film.

It was a rare occasion when an American film was shown because the Burmese Government was making it more and more
difficult for them to be brought in, supposedly because of adverse
Western propaganda. Most of the films shown were Burmese and
Chinese. When the old picture about the Ringling Brothers Cir-
cus, *The Greatest Show on Earth,* found its way up to Namkham,
Sayama Koy invited the entire senior staff of the hospital to see
the film as her guests. We all turned out, even Dr. Seagrave. It
was the only time he left the hospital compound while we were
there. Everything was set up for his comfort and convenience at
the theater. He had an aisle seat and a small table, placed within
his reach, held a cup of cool water and a flask of hot coffee with a
pitcher of sweetened condensed milk to be used with the coffee. I
didn't think it was very gracious of him to grumble throughout
the movie about that "damned Koy."

I discovered another diversion which was infinitely more rewarding. One afternoon while I was passing through the maternity building I spied the Shan twins, Nyee Nyee and Ko Ko, peering at me through the screen door to their little room. When I
started toward them, they screamed with laughter and hid beneath their cribs. I told the staff nurse on duty that I wanted to
take the twins over to our house to play with my boys, but since
the twins refused to go with me, two of the student nurses went

along too. When the boys got to our house they clung to their nurse friends and cried most of the time. Philip and Paul eyed them suspiciously and each time one of the twins tried to touch a toy there was a loud protest. Finally, we solved the problem rather nicely by taking them all out in the yard to swing. Fortunately there were enough swings to go around. When the twins went back to the hospital they weren't quite so shy and our boys weren't quite so belligerent.

That was the first of several afternoons when the twins came to play. We became very attached to the bright-eyed little fellows, though they were still somewhat cautious about being too friendly with us.

In spite of the children, and my work at home and in the hospital, I had time to be lonely, and I was getting depressed. I had never required a gay social life, but this isolation was getting the best of me. There were long periods in the late afternoons and evenings when I had to search for ways to keep myself occupied. I wrote letters, read, and took long walks with the children until we had explored every inch of ground within walking distance of the compound. Many evenings I sat at the top of the hospital hill and watched the sunset. I became troubled about many things.

What probably bothered me most was Timmy's lack of playmates. There were plenty of boys near his age living on the compound, but he couldn't find his way into their inner circle. One barrier was the language difficulty. The other boys understood very little English, and Tim knew almost no Burmese and no Shan or Kachin. Tim's efforts to speak Burmese consisted of adopting the broken English the other boys spoke. Another difficulty was that Tim was often overbearing and bossy with them. When the boys came to our house to play with the toys we had, Tim got along fine, but otherwise he didn't fare so well. Sometimes they let him play marbles or shoot slingshots with them, and sometimes they just ran off and hid. When Tim finished his lessons at 3:45 every afternoon he raced out to wait along the path the other boys took on their way home from school. When the boys caught on to that habit, they took more devious routes in order to avoid him. As a result, Tim was unhappy and I was miserable. Joe kept telling me I was worrying too much, but I noticed that he was spending more and more time with Tim. Philip and Paul were too young to be bothered about the lack of outside company.

Finally, my troubles, both real and imaginary, began to get the best of me. I felt if I could just get away for a while my outlook would be brightened. But all local travel was hazardous and uncomfortable, and, besides, there were so many travel restrictions. The road to the north of us, which led to Bhamo and Myitkyana, had been closed by insurgents, and there were no Rangoon or Mandalay Hiltons where one might rest and play for a few days.

Finally we decided to take a few days off and travel to Kutkai, which was about eighty miles away. On our way from Rangoon to Namkham the previous August we had spent a night there.

The ambulance was packed to the hilt the morning we left for Kutkai. As we drove down the hill from the hospital, Joe kept mumbling, "Left is right, left is right."

"What are you talking about?" I asked.

"This is the first time I've ever driven on the left side of the road in a car with the steering wheel on the right side. Thank goodness there won't be much traffic. Help me remember to stay on the left side of the road."

The road was narrow and rough and we were slowed down by the many small villages, but I was enjoying the ride. I suddenly felt lighthearted and free. It was cool weather for early December and the rice paddies were brown and bare. We rode for miles beside the Shweli River, now just a trickling stream, but swollen to many times its present size during the rainy season. We passed the marker indicating the Burma-China border. We went through Muse, bustling with people on bazaar day, and were stopped on the outskirts of town by a soldier beside a barrier. When he recognized the hospital car he raised the barricade and waved us on.

"What was that all about?" I asked Joe.

"They have checkpoints up and down the road. They search all cars and buses for smuggled things, mostly guns and ammunition, I guess. As long as we're in the ambulance they won't bother us. The army, and the insurgents, too, for that matter, respect the hospital. They never know when they might need it."

The small village of Mongyu was a familiar sight. We had stopped there for customs check on our way to Namkham the first time. "Hope he doesn't ask us to have tea with him," I thought.

We were detained only a few minutes. There was a new customs officer on duty, who had been Joe's patient only a few weeks before. He made no search and asked no questions. "How do you do, doctor? It is nice to see you again. Please be careful as you drive across the hills between here and Kutkai. Don't stop for anyone. Two nights ago while I was sleeping our village was attacked and my house was set afire. I managed to jump up and run out the back door and hide in the jungle until morning." Then he glanced in my direction as he added, "It was mighty cold without my pants!"

A few miles farther, we had our first "bush" stop and noticed that the left rear tire was dangerously near to being flat. Joe rummaged about in the back of the ambulance and found a spare tire but no jack. As we were lamenting our bad fortune, a truck drove up behind us and half a dozen men got out and walked toward us. "Friend or foe?" I whispered to Joe.

Joe began to explain the situation, but no one understood him. The driver kept answering, "Yes, yes," and then spoke in Kachin to the others. While we stood by in amazement, five of the men held up the rear end of the ambulance while the sixth replaced the tire. Then they let the car back down, climbed aboard their truck, and drove off.

The rest of the trip was without incident, except when the nanny became terribly nauseated from motion sickness. She stuck her head out of the front window of the jeep and with one mighty heave sent her misery flying down the mountainside.

Four hours after starting our trip we had covered the eighty miles to Kutkai. As we drove onto the Baptist Mission Compound I was struck with its beauty. The church was situated on a hill overlooking the rest of the compound. It was constructed of stones cut from a nearby quarry and had stained-glass windows. The mission residence was of the same stone; smaller wood and bamboo houses were for the students of the Kachin Bible School. On one side of the compound was a long low sprawling building where classes of the secondary school were held. In the distance I could see the farm where students were taught the basic elements of farming, with emphasis on poultry and eggs. Numerous pine trees added beauty to the grounds.

The next three days were a physical and emotional lift to our whole family. Due to the increased altitude it was much colder in Kutkai than in Namkham, and we spent the evening hours hovering about the bright fire in the grate while visiting with missionary friends. During those talks I learned a lot about what missionary life was really like, and it was a far cry from my original impressions. I had pictured a missionary as a person who went to some foreign country because he couldn't do anything well at home. On the mission field he preached constantly and still didn't do anything well. But I learned that the dedicated missionary was a leader at home and abroad whose greatest service and witness was simply living among the people, helping when needed, counseling, and trying to present a Christlike example. I found out that there were many rewards to missionary life and many sacrifices to be made.

On our first afternoon in Kutkai, Joe, Tim, and I went for a walk while the two smaller boys were napping. We decided to visit the Buddhist pagoda we saw in the distance atop a nearby mountain. A quarter-mile walk through knee-high grass led to the base of the mountain, where we were instructed by a small sign to remove our shoes before beginning to climb. I wasn't wild over the idea of going barefoot, but the three of us took off our shoes and left them beside the path. From that point onward rough steps had been hewn out of the clay to aid worshippers in their ascent. I could imagine what that clay must have been like during the rainy season. Tim ran on ahead and was at the top long before Joe and me. We had to stop every few feet to rest, but it was well worth the effort just to admire the scenery. Never had I seen more beautiful rolling green hills. The town of Kutkai, with its three dozen or so small buildings, was nestled at the foot of the hills, and the Burma Road wound into town from the south and disappeared into the hills to the north from which we had come the previous day. On the eastern edge of the town I saw several buildings with what looked like a church nearby. "Do you know what that group of buildings over there are, Joe?"

"That must be the Catholic mission. I've heard there was one here. Maybe we can get over there and look around sometime."

At the top of the hill two large white stone *chinthits,* or winged lions, symbols of the Buddhist faith, guarded the entrance to the whitewashed pagoda. It was only a small pagoda, perhaps ten feet square at the base, with a spire which was twenty to thirty feet high. A few wilted flower petals and lumps of candle wax lay about, the remains of offerings and prayers to the Lord Buddha. No one else was around, and all was still. A gentle breeze moved the small prayer bells near the top of the pagoda, from which came a soft, musical tinkle.

The next afternoon, Joe, the boys, and I drove to the Catholic compound. We had heard that two Italian missionary priests were in charge of the place, with some Burmese nuns to help with the school. As we drove onto the compound I noticed that the church was so new that a few workmen were still putting the finishing touches in place. The concrete block church was of moderate size and had the traditional cross atop a steeple. It could have been the parish church anywhere in America.

Nearby was a long, low building also of concrete block. Through the door a short, heavy-set, nearly bald man came rushing toward us with arms outstretched. He had a long, straggly black beard, and he wore a long black robe, coarse black trousers, and heavy muddy boots, but the most striking thing about him was his broad smile. He had noticed the hospital Jeep and immediately surmised who we were. "Ah, you must be the new doctor at Namkham," he bubbled in his perfect English with only a trace of accent. "How good to see you, my friends! I am Father Adrien Cadei."

"Joe Newhall, Father, and this is Sue. Our three sons are in the back of the Jeep."

"Welcome, welcome, how nice to meet you! My, what a pleasant surprise to have you come to see us! Please come in, Mrs. Newhall, and bring the boys."

By that time another priest had appeared in the doorway. He wore the same clothing, but he had more hair on his head than Father Cadei and a shorter, neater beard, both of which were tinged with gray. "Father Aquaviva," Father Cadei shouted, "this is the new American doctor at Namkham, Dr. Newhall, and his charming family."

"Doctor who?" asked the father, cupping one hand to his left ear.

"Newhall, Father," Joe answered as he extended his hand.

We followed the priests inside the rather dreary, cold building, and they insisted on taking us on a tour of their home. Each of the priests had his own small, bare room, and there was a spare room for overnight visitors which reminded me more of a cell than a guestroom. There was a small first aid room for the schoolchildren, a primitive kitchen, and a living room where guests were entertained.

"Please sit down," Father Cadei said, indicating the hard chairs lining the wall. "I have just returned from three weeks in the jungle. I rode ponies from one village to another giving the Christmas Mass. Father Aquaviva will leave tomorrow to serve others. We must travel because where there is no priest there is no church. Before Christmas I hope to spend two days in Namkham. Dr. and Mrs. Silgardo are Catholic, and a few others, too, so I must have Mass for them."

Father Cadei sat on the edge of his chair and spoke excitedly, waving his arms and slapping his knees for emphasis. I liked him immediately. In spite of his long black robe, beard, and bald head, I could tell that he was a young man, probably not more than in his mid-thirties. Father Aquaviva was ten or fifteen years older.

I was amused at Joe. He has never been noted for his ability to remember names, and he kept calling Father Aquaviva, Father Aquavelva, probably because of his familiarity with the shaving lotion with that same name.

Father Cadei suddenly jumped to his feet, waved his arms, and said, "Please, my friends, come. I must show you our beautiful church."

Once we were inside, Father Cadei went to the altar and knelt in prayer for a few seconds, then proudly showed us about. "I am so happy," he beamed. "During my seven years in Burma I have continually worked toward this church. Much of the money for its construction came from donations made by generous Americans."

After our tour of the church we drove back to the Baptist compound. I knew that if I had as much enthusiasm for my work as wife, mother, and erstwhile medical missionary as Father Cadei had for his work I would be an unquestionable success. We never saw Father Aquaviva again, but Father Cadei visited us in Namkham on several occasions while on his way to or from the villages in the hills.

The following morning Joe and I attended the graduating exercises of the Kachin Bible School in the Baptist Church. Because it was such an important occasion, the faculty and graduating class were dressed in the traditional Kachin outfit. The women wore bright red, handwoven wool wraparound skirts with yellow and black designs woven into the material, and leggings of the same material that reached from the ankles to mid-calf. Their jackets were of black velveteen, to which were stitched myriad silver ornaments that jingled loudly when the wearer walked. About their hips they wore a dozen or more thin bamboo hoops painted with black lacquer. The married women wore black turbans; the single women were bareheaded. The men were much less colorful in their ill-fitting brown trousers and jackets. On their heads they wore cotton turbans of red and black plaid, *gaungpauns* in Burmese, literally meaning *head wraps*.

The organist began pumping on the old organ, and the fifteen graduates and handful of faculty members marched in and took their places. The principal of the Bible School, Lahpai Zau Yaw, said a few words in Kachin, and then to my utter surprise and horror, he said in perfect English, "We are happy to have Dr. and Mrs. Newhall from Namkham visiting us today. Will they please come forward and say a few words to us? I understand Mrs. Newhall can speak a little Burmese and we would like her to say something in Burmese for us."

Every eye in the church was turned on us. Finally, Joe got up and walked to the pulpit and "said a few words," none of which was understood by the average person in the audience. Then it was my turn. I tripped on the steps on my way to the pulpit, said a couple of sentences in English, then finished with what few words I knew in Burmese. "We are happy to be with you today. Thank you very much." It was not a great gem of oratory, but I saw a few smiles of comprehension.

Then there were speeches, solos, awards, and the main address by an aged Kachin pastor who had helped make the first translation of the Bible into Kachin many years before. The program lasted more than two hours. The Kachins were better adapted to hard benches than I was.

The next morning Joe chopped down two of the lovely longleaf pines which grew in abundance on the Baptist Compound. Christmas was two weeks away and these would be fine Christmas trees, one for our home and one for the nurses' dining room. After tying them to the top of the ambulance, we all climbed aboard and headed back to Namkham.

That was our first trip to Kutkai, but certainly not our last, and I fear that we must eventually have worn out our welcome. Occasionally we stopped there on our way to or from Lashio for a meal or for overnight.

One trip to Kutkai in the spring of 1964 was especially memorable. Again, I was getting a little fed up with Namkham and decided to get away for a few days. Joe didn't feel he could leave the hospital at that time, so Tim and I drove to Kutkai one morning in the ambulance with Tun Shein. Tun Shein was on his way to Mandalay and expected to pick me up on his return trip Saturday. However, on Friday afternoon I was wakened from a nap and told that Tun Shein had returned a day early and wanted to leave immediately for Namkham. Hastily I gathered my things and met him in the living room of the mission house. "What's the matter, Tun Shein?"

He was sprawled in a chair, more lying than sitting. "I don't know, maybe nothing. I got this telegram from the Old Man yesterday." He handed me a folded piece of paper.

The message contained five words: "Suggest you return soonest Seagrave."

Within a few minutes we were on our way. We fairly flew around the curves and up and down the hills. I frequently closed my eyes and hoped that no one was coming from the opposite direction. Few words were passed between us for Tun Shein was busy with his driving and I with my thoughts. The government had been clamping down on the hospital. What if they had decided that now was the time to take over completely? Then I thought about my family. Maybe one of them had taken seriously ill. There my mind stopped wandering and remained fixed with anxiety.

Finally we bounced up the hill to the hospital compound. As we approached our house I could see the children playing in the yard with the nannies keeping watch. Well, everything looked all right there. What about Joe? I jumped out of the Jeep and grabbed Philip and Paul in my arms. They squealed with delight and hugged my neck. E Poi said, "Paul walk now. See?" and she took him and put him on the ground. He obligingly took several faltering steps in my direction and I picked him up again. "Paul, that's wonderful. Mommy's been waiting so long for you to walk, and she goes away for two days and misses the first steps!"

Wong Jack was in the kitchen preparing supper. "Wong, is everything all right? Is Dr. Joe here?"

"Dr. Joe playing ball now."

Yes, it was Friday afternoon and time for the softball game. So far I saw no reason for our hasty return.

I was sitting on the livingroom floor playing with the children when Joe walked in. "Susie! We didn't expect you until tomorrow. Why are you home so early?"

He looked well and hearty, and the last trace of my fear vanished. I gave him a quick hug. "That's what I'd like to know. Tun Shein got a telegram from the Old Man telling him to return right away. What's wrong?"

Joe threw up his hands. "He did that? Why, that old s.o.b., to use his own expression. Nothing's wrong, but he's so panicky he can't stand to let Tun Shein out of his sight. The day you left, a letter came from the Revolutionary Council saying that private organizations were required to register, giving the names of all members or employees. Tun Shein knew this was coming, and he had already prepared the report. Besides, it doesn't have to be returned for another two weeks. I knew the letter had come, but I didn't know the Old Man had gone into a complete tizzy and wired Tun Shein. This makes me mad. You'd been wanting to get away and then you had to come back early for nothing."

I was pretty upset myself. The Old Man could have stated the nature of what he considered an emergency, but this was all part of the pattern which Joe and I were learning to accept. We found it wise to avoid contact with the Old Man as much as possible because that was the only way to maintain harmony. One could not discuss anything with him, one could only listen. Any opinions contrary to his were taboo, and his word was final regardless of the consequences to anyone involved. He thought he was a king in his own world, and nothing else mattered so long as that kingdom remained undisturbed. The trouble was that many things were happening to upset it, and while he had successfully kept his power through many years of various conflicts, his entire world was being threatened by a socialist government. His disposition did not improve with increasing pressures. This was understandable but hard to live with. Whereas he had welcomed us with open arms and had given us a free hand to make any changes we thought necessary, now he constantly blocked Joe's attempts to improve techniques as being "not the way we have done it for over forty years." "My way works best out here" closed many a discussion. He read constantly, but never any medical journals.

Dr. Silgardo was the only doctor who had been able to survive very long at Namkham. He did his work at the hospital in the best way he knew, and spent the rest of his time at home. He took no part in the softball games, chapel, or any other activity on the compound and almost never met Dr. Seagrave face to face. To be sure, he read the insulting remarks the Old Man wrote on his patients' charts, and heard from others the names he had been called, but none of this seemed to bother him. Joe, deciding to take the same approach, stopped associating with the Old Man except at the Friday afternoon softball game, and those games were often fraught with contention.

So far as I was concerned, the Old Man was quite pleasant and we had a very amiable relationship, though I was on pins and needles at every encounter. He complimented me on changes I had made in the lab and actually asked my advice on matters pertaining to recent advancements in hematology. He even told Joe that I was the only American woman he had ever known who was "worth a damn." "Any other gal who has ever come out here was trying to run things the minute she arrived, and trying to get the hell out of here soon afterward." I was angry with myself for being flattered.

Soon after my trip to Kutkai a pregnant woman was brought into the hospital bleeding profusely. She had been bleeding for several hours and was in shock. Joe operated on her immediately, but the baby was dead and the bleeding difficult to control. The patient needed blood desperately, but the relatives who brought her in refused to act as donors. Joe had been forced to begin the surgery without a transfusion, but it went well until Joe put in the first sutures. Then the patient began to take very shallow breaths and her heartbeat became faint. It continued to get weaker and weaker and then the heart stopped. All attempts to make it start again were fruitless. The patient had bled to death.

Dr. Seagrave read the hospital report every morning while drinking his coffee. On the morning he read that a patient had died on the operating table he must have jumped to the conclusion that the surgeon had been negligent. There was no other explanation for his strange behavior. By the time he reached chapel he had worked himself into a frenzy. Before chapel began I heard him questioning the operating-room nurses and Tun Shein. I tried not to listen and, at the same time, strained to hear every word. The Old Man made it clear that he suspected Joe had been careless and had killed the patient. He had not discussed—and never did discuss—the case with Joe, who was not at chapel.

When the service began I sang the hymn and read the scripture, but my mind was elsewhere. Why did he have to behave that way? As soon as chapel was over I hurried from the room to avoid hearing any more, but at the lab I couldn't work for thinking about the whole mess. I finally decided that I had to talk to Tun Shein. Not finding him in his office, I went to his home. He was in his living room sitting close to his old radio and listening to a short-wave broadcast, and he didn't look any happier than I felt. When he saw me at the door he turned off the radio and asked me to have a seat near him.

"Tun Shein, I'm worried and miserable and sick of everything. What does the Old Man want of us anyway?"

"I don't know what to tell you. We all get discouraged, but most of us have learned to appreciate the Old Man's good points and overlook the bad ones."

"But things like this are driving me crazy. Indirectly he is accusing Joe of a terrible thing and he airs his views before everyone but Joe. Would he be happier if we left here? Does he want us to go home?"

"That's probably the last thing he wants. At one time or another everyone at this hospital has felt the way you do."

"Well, Tun Shein, why do you stay here then? I mean, you don't have to take all this. You can work someplace else, so can we. Nothing Joe does seems to be right, and now this thing this morning."

Tun Shein settled himself into a more comfortable position, tucking his bare feet under him in the chair. "Let me tell you a little story," he began. "During the war when the hospital unit was in India there was a lot of drinking and immorality going on in the group. Some of the nurses were shocked and didn't want any part of it. The situation became so bad and the restlessness so great that part of the group wanted to be transferred. Oh, there was much more to it than that, and no one was completely without guilt, but that was the general setup. They came to me for help, and I did what I could to find them other posts. The Old Man was so angry with me that I didn't dare go near him. He called it a strike against him.

"Months after the war, I came up here on business and he ordered me out of the hospital. Then four years ago he wrote asking me to take this job as hospital administrator. At first I didn't want to come, but after thinking it over I agreed. I want to help people, and what better place than here? The Old Man wasn't angry with me anymore, he needed me instead. He isn't easy to get along with, and never was, but now he is old and sick and discouraged. What he says and does shows that. What he has done here is far greater than the wrong we sometimes think he does, and I have to honor him for that. As you Americans say, his bark is much worse than his bite. Sure, he says some things about Joe, but I think he respects him, too. Try not to be discouraged."

I went away both puzzled and somewhat relieved. Tun Shein, I thought, was either the most dedicated man I had ever known or the most stupid.

I had decided to stop going to chapel, but the next morning I found myself back at the same old place. Much to my surprise, Dr. Seagrave was smiling and greeted me pleasantly. He asked how the boys were getting along and I mumbled some reply. Again after chapel he talked to me, in the most pleasant way. I hadn't heard him talk that way since the first day we arrived at Namkham. Furthermore, his good humor in my presence continued for several days, and I felt sure that Tun Shein had discussed my visit with him. Still, his relationship with Joe did not improve.

But over the months Joe and Dr. Silgardo were coming closer together. Dr. Silgardo was not a warm, friendly man, and at first he had acted almost hostile. He liked to do his work alone and openly resented intrusion by another doctor. Joe had been accustomed to practicing with doctors who discussed their problems with each other and consulted with men in other specialties. If Joe asked Dr. Silgardo's advice about a patient, Dr. Silgardo refused to help unless the patient was turned over to him for all future care, and he never asked Joe's help with any of his patients. Later, when they became better acquainted, he explained to Joe that no doctor in Burma asked advice of another for fear of losing face. It was strictly unethical for one surgeon to walk into an operating room where another was operating lest his colleague think he came to spy or to give unwanted advice. Any physician who had gained a reputation in his profession had done so by hard work and he was reluctant to teach anyone else what he knew. Let others find out the hard way, too. That line of thinking made it difficult for medical students and residents to learn medicine if specialists and teachers were not willing to teach what they knew. Dr. Silgardo and Joe finally were able to discuss their patients' problems and each offered advice to the other when asked.

CHAPTER NINE

FIRST
DEPORTATION
ORDERS

As a child I had anxiously awaited the annual visit of Santa
Claus, but no more eagerly than I looked forward to the daily
visit of the mailman at Namkham. He wore black baggy pants, a
faded shirt of dubious color, a black cap with a crushed bill, and
when he wore shoes they were *hpynats,* or thongs. He carried the
mail in a traditional Shan bag, a handwoven cotton bag with a
long black strap over his shoulder. The mail was generally for the
hospital personnel, since few others received letters.

Nothing ever happened according to schedule at Namkham,
and that was true as well of the mailman's arrival. He might come
trudging up the steps to the office of the hospital anytime from 10
a.m. to noon, or even later, if he found someone who invited him
to stop for Shan tea or some rice and curry.

Occasionally, if I wasn't busy in the lab, I sat on the office steps
to wait, so that I might catch an early glimpse of the mailman.
And several times I walked to the top of the hill in front of the

hospital, from which I could see the road to town. From that van-
tage point I could see him in the distance as he plodded slowly
up the hill.

Airmail arrived two days a week, usually Mondays and Thurs-
days, and my excitement reached even greater heights on those
days. Sometimes I waited in vain, but usually there was some letter or papers from home. On the really wonderful days when
there were three or more letters I wasn't much help to Esther in
the lab for the rest of the morning. Many of our Bradenton
friends were good correspondents, but none was so faithful as
Jackie Holton, a former neighbor. Jackie wrote every two or three
weeks whether she heard from us or not, and thus earned my undying gratitude.

Dr. J. D. Moran and his wife Bev gave us a subscription to our
local newspaper, *The Bradenton Herald*. Of course, the papers
came by ship and we got them irregularly, two to three months
late. We received them about twice a month, in batches of fifteen
to twenty, and for the next two or three days our living room
would be ankle deep in scattered newspapers. We read about the
Christmas dances, teas, and charity balls, and reveled in photo-
graphs of familiar people dressed in their best formal attire. Then
we felt a nostalgic pang as we threw the papers in the fireplace to
perk up the blaze and went back to the cold hospital wards.

One day shortly before Christmas, 1963, our mail included an
unimportant-looking letter in a brown envelope. It was addressed
in English to Dr. Joseph Newhall, Namkham Hospital, Namkham
N.S.S., but the return address was written in Burmese, and the
form letter inside was also in Burmese. On the letter, the name,
Dr. Joseph Newhall, was typed in, but that was all I could read. I
had more interesting mail to read, so I put that letter aside until I
could get someone to help me with it.

Sometime later, Joe and Dr. Violet came into the lab to check
on a report. As I looked up from the microscope I handed the letter to Dr. Violet. "This Burmese is all Greek to me. Will you

please translate?"

She opened the letter, scanned its contents, and paled. "We'd better take this over to the Old Man."

Joe looked up from the letter he was reading. "Can't you read it?"

"Well, yes." She hesitated. "It is from the Immigration Department, but I'd rather let the Old Man discuss it with you."

So the three of us went over to Dr. Seagrave's classroom. When Dr. Violet handed him the letter she said politely, "Daddy, this letter arrived in the mail today for Dr. Joe."

He took the envelope in his massive hands with their club-shaped fingers which shook slightly as he removed the letter. Then he began to read as we all waited silently. Suddenly his expression changed, and he seemed at a loss for words. The pause was only momentary, however, for in a few seconds he spat forth a lengthy string of "Anglo Saxon" which would have made any drill sergeant proud. When he cooled down a bit he told the girls who had assembled for class to "get the hell out of here, there won't be any class today."

Needless to say, the suspense was killing me. Finally the Old Man spoke. "Those stinking rats in Rangoon have denied your application for visa extension and have given you until January 13th, that's just three weeks away, to be out of Burma. Those God-damned s.o.b.'s."

He reached for his cracked porcelain cup and took a sip of water, then opened his can of Burmese cigarettes and lit one. "They're doing this just to spite me. That coward Ne Win. What is this country coming to, anyway? Next thing you know they'll be putting me back in jail or sending me out of the country. Next March they probably won't renew my visa either. That's what Ne Win would really like to do, deport me."

"Where in the hell is Tun Shein?" he demanded.

Joe answered that Tun Shein and Pansy had gone to Mandalay. "They left two days ago in the ambulance to buy Christmas presents for the nurses. I think they should be back tomorrow."

"Oh, hell, I knew that. When he gets back he'll have to turn right around and head back to Rangoon. We'll write up a petition asking that you be allowed to stay and we'll get the signatures of the local army officer and the Shan State officials in Taungyi and hand it to the immigration officials in Rangoon. God only knows what will happen then."

It was a dejected group that dispersed and went back to the daily chores. A dozen questions kept whirling around in my brain. Leave Namkham? After only four months? Why would the Burmese Government want us to leave their country? I couldn't believe it was just to spite the Old Man, as he seemed to think. I was happy, and we had just begun to work; why couldn't we stay? Still, I thought how nice it would be to be back home again! No, by gosh, I didn't want to leave! Our coming to Namkham had not been a fly-by-night decision. There was a real purpose behind it and a definite task to be done. I felt that God intended us to do this work, both for our own betterment and for the betterment of others. Most of all, I resented being told that we had to leave for no reason at all.

"Well, Joe, what do we do now?"

"For the present I have a cesarean section to do, two tonsillectomies, and a gunshot wound of the leg to work on. After that I'll have time to worry about the Burmese Immigration Department. Don't worry about it. I'm sure everything will be okay."

I was pretty busy myself. Esther and her family were on a short vacation, so I had my hands full. Luckily, a few of my students were competent enough to help out with the routine tests and I relied heavily on them.

Not until the children were in bed that night and Joe and I were comfortably seated before the fireplace did we have time to discuss the matter again. "This business has really got the Old Man going," Joe said. "He's mad as hops, and scared, too, and without Tun Shein or Pansy here—the two people he depends on most to keep him on an even keel—he doesn't know which way to turn.

"As for us, I think we'd better wait until Tun Shein gets back and talk to him before we decide what to do. I'm afraid I've lost my incentive to work very hard. After all, I've never been kicked out of a country before."

"Me either, and it burns me up. It makes me want to say Burmese number eight a few times. What do you suppose it's all about?"

"It's all a part of this strong nationalistic or socialistic trend. They just don't want any foreigners in the country."

Shortly after noon the next day, Tun Shein and Pansy drove up in the old Jeep. They were tired, but pleased with the purchases they had made, and the Jeep was loaded with gifts and baskets of delicious citrus fruit. Their joy was cut short when they heard the story of our letter. "It's unbelievable," said Tun Shein, and Pansy's eyes brimmed with tears.

That evening, Joe and I, Tun Shein, and Chuck met at Dr. Seagrave's home. A long letter of petition was drafted, and Dr. Seagrave wrote a personal letter to U.S. Ambassador Byroade. Tun Shein was to deliver the letters in person.

Before the meeting broke up, Joe asked Tun Shein, "Have you any idea how long you'll be gone?"

"No. First, I'll go to Lashio, then I'll stop in Taungyi to get signatures from the Shan State officials. If they're all available that won't take more than one day. After that, I'll go to Rangoon and try to see the Controller of Immigration. As soon as I get some kind of an answer I'll be back. In the meantime, I'll send telegrams and letters. Keep calm and pray. I'm sure everything will be all right."

The next day, December 21, 1963, Tun Shein and a driver were on their way before five a.m. The thoughts and prayers of all the people on the compound went with him. Though none of them said anything to us, there was obvious concern in their faces.

In spite of the atmosphere of gloom, everyone entered whole-heartedly into the Christmas celebration. It was the gayest time of the year at Namkham. There were enough Christians to spark the excitement, and the Buddhists were ready to play and cele-brate anytime, no matter what the occasion. The nurses worked hard to decorate the wards. The drab old rooms took on a festive air as red and green crepe paper streamers were draped from the bare light bulb in the center of the room to the four corners, and around the walls. Some of the girls had fashioned stars and tiny trees from tin foil, and MERRY CHRISTMAS appeared in large letters over the doors to the wards.

The tree we had brought back from Kutkai was placed in a bucket in our living room, and ornaments of all sorts—both store-bought and homemade—were hung from the branches. One eve-ning Joe's class in midwifery and mine in laboratory technique came to help decorate the tree.

On the night of December 24th a party was held in the nurses' dining room. The large tree was decorated and hundreds of gifts were beneath it. The room was packed with the whole hospital staff, the student nurses, and several invited guests from the town and the army camp. It was always a mystery to me how so many people could get together and be so quiet and look so gloomy. If that many Americans had been in the same room there would have been a hubbub of talking and laughing. Not so with those people. Hardly anyone spoke to his neighbor, and there was no shouting across the room.

After a dinner of Indian curried rice, chicken, and Shan tea, a skit depicting the Christmas story was presented by several of the nurses with the help of a few men. They spoke in Burmese, but I was familiar enough with the story to follow what they were doing. Actually, I was surprised with how many words I under-stood. One of the Buddhist girls played the part of the Virgin Mary!

The highlight of the program was a cantata, "Night of Miracles," presented by a chorus of about thirty voices. The singers wore choir jackets of white trimmed in red, and it seemed that their long hours of practice under U PoZo's leadership had produced a fine chorus in spite of their untrained voices.

Then Joe appeared dressed as Santa, but everyone knew who he was. The first time he lost his beard, Timmy said in a voice loud enough for all to hear, "Look Mom, it's Dad!" Santa proceeded to distribute the gifts beneath the tree, and everyone went home.

Joe and I had been concerned about how much Santa was going to be able to find for our boys. We warned them that Namkham was a long way from the North Pole and that Santa Claus might not be able to carry many gifts all that distance. We need not have worried, for there was more than enough to make them very happy.

On Christmas afternoon, I sat down before the fireplace, and Paul, who was then less than fifteen months old, climbed into my lap. As I held him and looked into the dancing fire, it occurred to me that this had been one of the most pleasant Christmases I could remember. There had been no mad dash to the stores to spend a lot of money for unnecessary gifts, no frantic addressing of cards to people who would never remember whether they got one from us or not, and no staying up too late at boring parties. We had made cookies and candy for the children on the compound, and had done our best with what we had to make those dear to us as happy as possible. It seemed to me that Christmas as we had known it in the past had become far too commercial, and that the Christ Child had been lost in the process. The most important thing about this Christmas was that our family was all together and all well.

My thoughts turned to the many about us who were less fortunate, and I thought about the Shan twins who lived in the maternity building. My mind had dwelled on those boys quite a lot in the past few weeks. I stopped by to see them often and still brought them home to play with our boys. Before Christmas I had made each of them a little pair of overalls from some remnants of material, and they were thrilled to have new clothes. As the nurse dressed them in the suits they said, "Hla, hla," meaning *pretty, pretty* in Burmese. The boys were so darling, almost two years old. Though they seemed happy my heart ached for them, knowing that they had no one really to care for them, and pitifully few clothes to wear, and a doubtful future at best.

"What do you suppose KoKo and NyeeNyee are doing on Christmas Day?" I asked Joe, who was pacing back and forth, stopping occasionally to gaze out the widow.

"Probably the same thing they do every day, running up and down the hall in the maternity building. Though I did see them out this morning. They were in the crowd following Santa as he gave fruit and nuts to the patients. There were a couple of guitar players in the group, and everyone was singing carols and having a gay old time. By now the twins must be back in their room."

Without stopping to consider the weight of my words, I blurted out, "What would you think about adopting the twins?" As soon as the words were out, I was surprised at my own boldness and expected a loud protest from Joe. Instead, he hesitated only a moment and then said quietly, "That's funny, I've been thinking the same thing. Do you really mean it?"

"Well, now wait a minute. I said it half in jest, and I don't know if I really meant it or not. At least, I expected more of an argument from you. Let's talk about this. How can we know what's best to do?"

"We can't."

"Do you think even though we want to do what's best for those boys, we might harm them instead?" I laughed. "You'd never know that I was the one who brought up this subject, but as usual, I don't know what to do. I just don't know. By taking them into an entirely different world with another race of people, would we be making life harder for them?"

"Maybe so, Susie, but I doubt it. I think the kind of home we can give them would offset the difficulties they might have."

"Well, then, there's the money angle. There'd be two more educations to pay for, and lots more, too. Can we swing that?"

"You're more of a financier than I am and much more of a money saver. I think we can manage. We'll never be millionaires, but we'll have all we really need. Besides, money is not that important. I really believe that what we can give them in the way of love, guidance, and educational opportunity will so far exceed anything they might get here that it's well worth the risk."

"True. How about racial prejudice? They'd be bound to run into some of it in school and the community, and maybe in our own families. My family already thinks we do strange things. But maybe they'd really understand. I'd want them to."

"Even blonde, blue-eyed, apple-pie Americans have some problems along those lines," Joe said. "America is changing."

"Sweetie," I persisted. "We mustn't forget about our present problem, about having to leave Burma, maybe soon. We might run into all kinds of trouble trying to get those boys out with us if we have to go. The U.S. Government would have something to say about it and who knows what the Burmese Government would say or do."

"I'm sure there'll be a new and different problem every day. We'd just have to take care of them as they come up. The people at the U.S. Embassy in Rangoon would help us all they can from their standpoint."

"Joe, I don't know. I guess I said that before. The more I think about it, the more problems I can see, but the better I like the idea. It all boils down to whether we want the boys or not. I think I do."

"I do, too, Susie. We came to Namkham because we wanted to help people, and what better way could we help two little boys than by taking them into our home and making them a part of our family? I really believe it will work and I think that all of us, not just the twins, will benefit. Few families are lucky enough to have a chance like this."

That very afternoon we made preparations to have the twins moved from their small room to our house. Dr. Seagrave gave his approval, and on a piece of rough brown paper he signed over his responsibility for their welfare to us in his shaky scrawl.

TO WHOM IT MAY CONCERN

This is to certify that the two twins "John Seagrave" and "James Tunshein" were abandoned in this hospital because of the death in childbirth of their mother. This made me their guardian. I now turn over my guardianship to Dr. and Mrs. Joseph F. P. Newhall, Junior.

The nurses called the boys KoKo and NyeeNyee, meaning older brother and younger brother. Actually, no one knew which of the boys was older, since there had been no nurse in attendance at their birth, but it was assumed that the slightly larger one was born first. They were also called James and John occasionally. Joe and I decided to keep these names and added the middle names Tunshein and Seagrave.

There was no such thing as a legal adoption in Burma. Nevertheless, we thought it expedient to get a formal release from the twins' natural father, who was still living. He lived in Monwing, about twenty miles north of Namkham. Chuck prepared a paper for the father's signature and set out for Monwing.

About eight miles outside of Namkham was a suspension bridge over the Shweli River, built by U.S. Army Engineers during World War II when the original British structure was bombed out. Some of the twisted wreckage of the old bridge could still be seen protruding above the swirling water. Whenever insurgent activity flared up, the bridge was a prime target. Two days before Chuck's intended trip to Monwing to visit the father of the twins, an attempt had been made to blow up the bridge, and sporadic pitched battles had broken out in the immediate vicinity between the Kachin Independence Army (known as KIA) and the Burmese Army. As a result the bridge was closed to traffic, and Chuck was forced to return with the twins' release paper unsigned. So Chuck signed the father's name to the paper himself!

On the afternoon after Christmas the twins arrived at our house accompanied by two of the student nurses. They were dressed in the little suits I had made for them, and their eyes were wide with apprehension and fear. They seemed to sense that somehow this day was different from the others when they had just come to play. When I started toward them, they began to cry and clung to the legs of the nurses. It took a long time for the nurses to persuade them to come inside the house, and I finally gave up trying to approach them. The two nannies took charge and the twins accepted them readily.

That first evening and the next morning, the twins cried almost incessantly. They didn't want to eat and they were miserable in every way. According to their routine, they were placed on their potties right after breakfast. It was soon apparent that they had completed their business on the potty, but refused to get up. Fifteen minutes went by, and twenty, and still they would not budge. Those potties were the first familiar things they had encountered and they were not going to give them up. Finally, amid kicks and screams, we lifted them from their thrones and dressed them.

In a few days they became more familiar with their surroundings and were more cooperative. About that time I noticed that NyeeNyee had small red bumps on the back of his neck and up into his hair. The next day there were more bumps, farther down on his back. I wondered about them, but not for long, and went on to other things. Later one of the staff nurses casually mentioned that those were bedbug bites. Bedbugs! In my house? I was horrified.

The explanation was simple. When the boys moved to our house, their crude wooden cribs were brought along with them, and a few bedbugs were transported in the process. Shirley was an old hand at getting rid of bedbugs. She put the bed outside, poured kerosene in the cracks, and nabbed half a dozen bugs as they scurried for drier ground. Our problem was solved for a few days, until some hidden eggs hatched and she had to repeat the treatment.

During those hectic days of adjusting to the twins and helping them adjust to their new life, I didn't forget about our impending deportation; it was only pushed farther back into my mind. But our problem was ever-present, and as each day passed, our dead-line, January 13th, drew nearer. Tun Shein had left Namkham on December 21st, and we anxiously awaited some word from him. Day followed day, and there was no telegram, no letter. On December 26th, Joe decided that we had to start packing. If we received word that we must leave, we would have to be gone from Namkham by January 4th in order to reach Rangoon in time to complete all the necessary arrangements to leave Burma by January 13th.

Dr. Seagrave was in a state of near panic. He felt that all the trouble was designed to spite him personally. He insisted that we be ready to go at a moment's notice so as not to place him in an unfavorable light with the authorities. He had a great fear of being put in jail or being sent out of the country, and that was all he could think or talk about.

On December 31st we received a telegram sent by Tun Shein from Taungyi. The officers he wished to see were out of town and he had been waiting for their return. Finally he had obtained their signatures on our petition, but they refused to let him take the letter on to Rangoon, promising to send it by mail to the Office of Controller of Immigration. Tun Shein was discouraged but had driven on to Rangoon, hoping the letter would soon be there. He advised us to sit tight and not to begin the trip to Rangoon unless he sent word that it was absolutely necessary.

On January 7th we received a letter from Tun Shein dated January 4th.

"We arrived Rangoon in the early afternoon on New Years Day. I contacted Saw Htin him Mya, Deputy Controller of Immigration, the same evening and he advised me to put in an application to the Controller for permission for you to stay in the country while the appeal was pending, because what we were doing was without the knowledge of the Controller. I did that, saying that our appeal had been approved by the Shan State SAC and was with the Central SAC now. Usually, they give permission for stay while the appeal is pending but Htin him Mya was not too sure what the Controller, an armed service man, would say and he tried to contact him till late last night and again this morning without success. The Controller does not attend office regularly. However, Htin him Mya wanted me to inform you, in case the Immigration officials in Lashio or Namkham trouble you, that you have applied for permission to stay during the appeal.

"On January 3rd I went to the U.S. Embassy and was told that Ambassador Byroade was in his office and that he would see me. Dr. Seagrave's letter had been delivered to him before then. We went in at the appointed time and he was very cordial. He said that he had been thinking how he could help. He was really concerned and he asked me what I wanted him to do. I told him that at the present moment we were making an official appeal and so far things were going well. However, during the next few days, if he came across some of the influential officers who were also interested, here I mentioned a few names, he might casually mention the matter. He might get that opportunity tonight at General Ne Win's Independence dinner. We left it at that and I was to keep him informed of the progress.

"I have made repeated trips to the office of the Controller of Immigration, but he is never in and no one knows where or how he can be reached. Nothing can be settled until I can have some word from him.

"Suddenly it struck me that I had been expecting help from a human source rather than from the Divine source. I had to ask forgiveness for this, and I had to stop for a moment's prayer. Of course, I have all along kept up a train of prayers and I feel that our help can and will come from Him.

"I know that this is a very trying time for all of you at Namkham. Please have faith and pray that all will be for the best. God knows that those sick people need you there and He will see that they are taken care of.

"May the New Year bring us new hope. Let us rededicate ourselves for the work that He has for us."

These words from Tun Shein eased our minds somewhat, but we continued to wait each day for a telegram saying definitely, "yes, you go," or "no, you stay." That was not the way the Burmese officials operated, however. Under the military socialist regime, everyone was afraid to take a position for fear it would not meet with favor, so no one did anything at all. Tun Shein continued to make daily calls at the Immigration Department, but the Controller was never available.

Fortunately, in addition to our work there were many things to divert our thoughts. On January 4th, Burmese Independence Day, a giant celebration was held at the government school in town. Aided by some of the nurses, Dr. Violet conducted a baby show in which the healthiest baby was picked from over one hundred entries. There were foot races, many of them won by our nurses and other hospital personnel, and bouts in which a contestant clung to a greased bamboo pole and tried to dislodge his opponent from a similar pole with blows from a pillow. Two teams of three men each raced to see which team could retrieve a flag from atop a greased bamboo pole first. Some type of activity was going on all day.

Sunday, January 5th, was Tim's sixth birthday. Wong Jack whipped up a cake and a freezer of chocolate ice cream, and we invited children from the compound to a party. There were Esther's children, Charlie, Jr., Nanette, and Bawky; Hsu Aung's sons, Ne Win and Ne Tun; Tun Shein's two sons, Sunlight and Moonlight, with their little sister, Ma Dagone; and Lorraine and Marie Silgardo. Philip, Paul, and the twins completed the group. That kind of birthday celebration was a new experience for some of the children and they entered into the games wholeheartedly and gobbled up the ice cream and cake. Birthdays were celebrated in a much more serious way by Burmese Christians. At Namkham, Christian friends were invited to come to the home, where a regular church service was held, including a lengthy sermon by Pastor Tun Baw. After the service, the guests sat quietly on the floor and a meal was served, usually rice and curry. Both children and adults were invited. Such parties held no appeal for Timmy and Philip, and after the first one or two they refused to go.

On January 25th Tun Shein returned to Namkham. He had been told that the decision on our appeal might take a long time and there was no need for him to wait in Rangoon. He never did see the Controller of Immigration, and he had no more definite information about our appeal than he had when he had gone to Rangoon, over a month before. Our letter of petition and the request that we be allowed to stay rested at the Immigration Office while the matter was pending.

It was good to see Tun Shein again. He brought some packages which had been waiting for delivery from Rangoon, and we celebrated Christmas all over again. Grandma and Grandpa Newhall had sent a wonderful collection of toys and clothes for the boys, as had other relatives and friends in Bradenton. There was a large box of goods which I had ordered from the commissary of the Embassy. We had not had dry cereals, coffee (other than Wong's home-roasted brew), cocoa, cake mixes, canned soft drinks, and many other "essentials" for months, and I took great pride in surveying my well-stocked pantry. And there were twelve cartons of Camels to bring smiles to the Old Man's face.

Gradually our trunks and boxes were unpacked for the second

time, and gradually we shed our anxiety over the matter of deportation. No news was good news. We lived quietly from day to day, neither receiving nor expecting news from the Immigration Department. We had no stay permit the entire time we were in Burma, but no one bothered us because we lacked one.

CHAPTER TEN

BROAD
NATIONALIZATIONS

On Friday, March 20, 1964, *The Guardian,* the largest Rangoon newspaper printed in English, bore the following headlines:

BIG STORES, CO-OPS, WHOLESALE BUSINESS,
BROKERAGES DEALING IN ESSENTIAL CONSUMER
COMMODITIES, GENERAL MERCHANDISE
IN RANGOON NATIONALIZED
Business Not To Be Interrupted,
Employees Not To Be Affected
Fair Compensation To Be Given

The article beneath went on to say:

The Government yesterday nationalized with immediate effect all whole-sale shops, brokerages, big stores and shops, and co-operatives dealing in food-stuffs, textiles, and general merchandise, and the warehouses stored with such essential consumer commodities, within the Rangoon area.

The nationalized establishments were given the sale receipts and their bank balances standing at the time of the take-over, after closing the accounts. All the business were carried on uninterrupted with the present employees in their places as usual.

The Government declared that fair compensation would be given for the nationalized enterprises.

Under the General Merchandise are included the following goods: Machineries and their spare parts; spare parts for all kinds of vehicles; all kinds of hardware; watches, clocks and their parts; spectacles and parts; fountain pens and parts; paper all sorts and stationery; electrical appliances; imported raw medicines, Chinese medicines, and foreign proprietary and household medicines; sports goods; photo and cinematographic goods; China ware; glassware; and mirrors and glasses.

The establishments nationalized were taken over yesterday. All their assets, such as buildings and the lands and stocks, stores, and equipment and furniture and fittings were to be handed over to the Government.

The liabilities of these establishments were, however, their own responsibility.

Exempted were small retail shops, hotels, restaurants, tea shops, and other establishments catering food, their stocks and stores sufficient for one month's running of their business.

Also exempted were green groceries, their stocks and stores; fruit shops, their stocks and stores; shops selling tobacco leaves, cheroot leaves, and their stocks and stores; and shops selling meat, fish, and eggs and their stocks and stores.

Exempted too were the big shops and stores and brokerages and whole-sale shops dealing in leather goods and their stocks and stores; and tailoring and garment making shops, but in their case their stocks of textiles must be declared.

Exempted too were also shops dealing in umbrellas, footwear, and hats, and their stocks and stores.

In a statement issued by the Ministry of Information yesterday, it was stated that the nationalization of the big business concerns dealing in essential consumer commodities was designed, in accordance with the policy of the Revolutionary Government, to bring down the cost of living for all the peoples of the Union.

It was also stated that the Government had been constrained to take the step as the foreign and national capitalists and their henchmen had been obstructing the Government in every manner in its endeavour to relieve the consumer public of the burden of high prices. They had been, it was revealed, hoarding, black-marketing, and speculating in essential consumer commodities, and exploiting the poor to queue up for such commodities and buying them up later from the poor people and re-selling at huge profit at their stores and shops.

Tun Shein folded the newspaper and placed it on his desk. I was sitting in the office reading some mail, but I had been watching him to catch his reaction to this startling news. He stared out of the window, then said calmly, "The long-expected has finally happened, and this is only the beginning. With one sweep they have taken all large businesses in Rangoon, and now all small businessmen throughout Burma can only wait and wonder when their business will be taken from them also. It won't be long."

"Are they likely to nationalize this hospital, too?" I asked.

"Yes, if there is no end to it soon. The Revolutionary Council intends to control everything, and the Minister of Health has said that the health of the people is the business of the Government. There are only five nongovernmental hospitals in Burma, so nationalizing them wouldn't be a great undertaking. All doctors are taken into government service as soon as they graduate from medical school and placed wherever the Government feels they are needed."

Tun Shein usually did not discuss conditions in Burma or prospects for the future. Now, apparently, he had said all he was going to say. He tightened his *longyi*, smoothed his graying hair, and went out to inspect the progress of a new ward being constructed in the small space between the medical and private buildings.

Due to the upsurge in socialistic trends which had begun about the time of our arrival in Burma and the subsequent difficulty in finding building materials—plus the fact that the Burmese Government would not grant visas to American doctors—the original idea of building a large maternity and children's hospital had been abandoned. Instead, two small wards were being built to take care of the patients who previously had been housed in the Old Hospital. That ancient structure was finally torn down. The betelnut-stained boards were laid out in the sun for a few months and then reused in a small building for patients' families.

Joe had been extremely critical of even this limited amount of expansion and had angered Dr. Seagrave because of his views. To Tun Shein Joe said, "The government is probably just waiting until the wards are finished before they take over. It's only a matter of time before they step in, so why do you and the Old Man insist on spending A.M.C.B. money to put up buildings for the Burmese Government?"

Tun Shein was harassed from all sides and his difficult administrative duties weighed heavily on his mind. Yet he was always patient. "The Old Man has been working in this hospital for over forty years. His whole life is tied up in it and he has given up everything else for it. Sure, he sees all the changes going on and he knows this hospital won't last much longer, but he hopes against hope that some miracle will come along to save it. Maybe he even refuses to believe he will lose it. At least, he hopes he will be able to live out the rest of his life here and be buried in the little staff cemetery. In the meantime, we must carry on as best we can. We can't just sit and do nothing because one day the government may decide to nationalize the hospital. It may come tomorrow, a year from now, or not at all."

"But Tun Shein, you don't get into a leaky boat and go out into the ocean with the hope that you *might* get where you're going before you sink. That's not a very good example, but you know what I mean. People in America have given money to the A.M.C.B. for Gordon Seagrave's hospital, a private institution, because they believe in his work. They did not give money for a Burmese Government hospital. Our U.S. foreign aid programs do enough of that. Why can't we just sit tight for a while and see what happens in the next few months before spending money on something that might be taken away from us?"

"Joe, whether it's right or wrong I don't know. Try to look at it this way; the sole aim of this hospital is to help sick people get well, and we can do a better job by having a little extra space. If the Government takes over soon, they, too, can help more people by having more wards. A.M.C.B. money won't stop helping people even if *we* aren't still here."

"I wish I could see it that way, but I get so doggone disgusted when I see some of the things the government is doing, and they have the gall to say that all foreigners are here to exploit the people. It really gets me."

Once the first big wave of nationalization had struck, everyone knew there was more to come. But when, and what would be affected? So far, only the large businesses in the Rangoon area had been taken over, and the obvious next step would involve stores and shops throughout the country. Businessmen, even the smallest shop owners, began to get their accounts in order. Most tried to make a fast kyat while there was still time.

We did not have long to wait. The April 10th issue of *The Guardian* carried the following headlines:

BIG ENTERPRISES NATIONALIZED
IN WHOLE OF UNION
All Shops, Stores, Wholesales, Co-ops,
Brokerages, dealing in Consumer
Items, General Merchandise
Taken Over From Yesterday

According to the paper, the extension of nationalization to all shops throughout the Union was due to:

. . . obstructionism and subversion of the former owners of such enterprises in Rangoon which had been earlier nationalized. The step was taken in the interests of the working people, peasants, the working intelligentsia, and intellectuals. Falsification of accounts, hiding and destroying stocks, preventing flow of goods, smuggling were means resorted to by the old owners.

April 10th, nationalization day, was also bazaar day at Namkham. I had not heard the big news until I arrived at the lab for work. Esther was furious. "Ja Naw and I went to bazaar this morning and there was no buying or selling anywhere. Only much confusion. In shops were soldiers and they were taking over the store from its owner. I heard one of the officers tell a shop owner, 'This shop now belongs to all the people. All assets belong to the government, any liabilities are your own business.'"

Palai Paw was about to go into town, so I climbed aboard the jeep and joined him. We made a detour for my camera, and then proceeded down the hill.

In town, the situation was just as Esther had said. Pandemonium reigned. Long lines of people waited for goods at the shops, but there was little business being conducted. No cooking oil was to be had in all of Namkham, and no kerosene for lamps. Officers and store owners were huddled over records, while soldiers with American-made rifles stood guard at the doors. I stepped down from the Jeep and warily approached one of the soldiers, smiled, and indicated my camera. He was most obliging, for he, too, smiled as he stood at attention and posed for his picture.

Over lunch I told Joe of my experience. He had heard the news, of course, but had been busy in surgery most of the morning. "Sweetie, you can't imagine what it was like," I said. "I felt as though I was dreaming. Those poor shop owners were losing everything. They're supposed to be repaid, but I wonder."

"They'll never be paid. The government hasn't anything to pay them with. The thing that surprises me is how quietly these people are taking it. Some of them are griping a little, but there isn't much real resistance. Can you imagine what would happen if *our* government tried to pull a thing like this? Riots, demonstrations, you name it. But these people are more likely to smile at the officer, then stab him in the back tonight."

The next big move in nationalization came two days later, when exports and imports were taken over. All exporters were required to surrender their licences. The State would have complete control over everything that came into or left the country. Not as immediately dramatic as the previous moves, this takeover took longer to show its full effects. Burma is not an industrialized country, and with foreign goods virtually excluded, shortages were bound to develop. For example, within a few months the only vehicles seen on Rangoon's streets were ancient buses, a few jeeps, three-wheeled taxis, and bicycles. The few modern foreign automobiles belong to foreign diplomats.

Government control over imports hampered us too. All medicines and supplies for the Namkham Hospital had come into Burma duty-free, but that policy changed. The A.M.C.B. had accumulated over $75,000 in drugs donated by American pharmaceutical firms, but now we would have had to pay an exorbitant duty to get them into Burma. The Minister of Health told Tun Shein that if the A.M.C.B. made a gift of the drugs to the Burmese Government the medicines would be divided among all Burmese hospitals, and the Namkham Hospital might get its share. He could make no guarantees. His proposal was turned down. From then on we had to operate with whatever drugs we had on hand and what could be purchased from the Burma Pharmaceutical Company. The supplies in our medical store room dwindled rapidly. When the drug of choice for a specific disease was depleted, we substituted whatever else we had on hand.

It was inevitable that the discontent and unrest created by nationalization would step up insurgent activity. Sounds of mortar fire came to us more and more often from the distant hills of the Kachin State. Within a few hours several wounded soldiers would arrive at the hospital to be patched up; there were never any wounded insurgents, for they were not taken alive. Occasionally a man was brought in with both hands or part of his face blown off. His story was that he was preparing a small explosive to dam up a stream for his rice paddy or to trap fish. More likely he had been making homemade bombs for the insurgents. Once a very old Kachin lady came in with pieces of metal embedded in her buttocks and the back sides of both legs. She had been picking vegetables when she squatted on a booby trap the army had set out for rebels. Then, too, in the men's medical ward we had our share of soldiers with vague complaints which could never be traced to anything except fear of going out on patrol.

Late one afternoon a jeep carrying two officers from Muse was crowded off the road by a bus. The officers were brought to the hospital with numerous bruises and possible leg fractures. The nurses in the admitting room nervously flitted about trying to be helpful. One went to get Dr. Silgardo, who was on emergency call for the day. When she arrived at his home, she was told that the Doctor was asleep and would come later. Instead of making the nature of the emergency known, she smiled meekly and returned to the hospital.

In the meantime, the officers lay on the hard stretchers in the hall and received no attention for several hours. Dr. Silgardo finally arrived at the hospital and immediately set about tending the wounds.

When Dr. Seagrave heard about this unintentional neglect, he was livid. After chapel the next morning he delivered a fifteen-minute lecture in Burmese on proper first aid. Then he stormed and swore and unfairly accused Dr. Silgardo of intimidating the nurses so that they were afraid to have him awakened when there was an emergency. (Actually, most of the nurses were very fond of Dr. Silgardo.) At that point in his tirade, the Old Man raised his voice to a high pitch and pretended to knock timidly on Dr. Silgardo's door.

Dr. Seagrave wanted to teach the nurses to give good medical care to everyone, but he was especially anxious to appease the army and stay on their good side. And he had a point.

From that time on, the two officers were given the VIP treatment. They shared a comfortable, airy room, and the nurses went out of their way to provide for their comfort and convenience.

The officers were happy and seemed to enjoy their hospital stay.

I went to their room to collect blood samples, and when I reached for one man's hand beneath the sheet, I touched something hard and cold. Surprised and afraid, I pushed back the sheet and there lay a loaded revolver. I hastily pricked the man's finger, filled the pipettes, and went on to the other officer. He too had a loaded gun beneath the sheet, but this time I was prepared. They were making sure that no insurgent walked into the room and gunned them down.

A few weeks later, Esther said to me in a confidential tone, "I have heard the insurgents are going to attack Namkham tonight."

"Where did you hear that?"

"The rumor is all over the Christian Village. A crowd of boys from the village left to join the insurgents last month. Even some of the boys Fred had in his Boy Scout troop have run away to the jungle. Their parents are nearly crazy. Yesterday the teacher in the Shan school had a message from his son that an attack would come tonight and all the villagers should stay inside."

"Oh Esther, I don't believe it. What is there in Namkham worth having a battle over?" There was a hint of derision in my voice. I was sick of hearing these tales of impending disaster when nothing ever happened, and I almost longed for a full-scale attack to relieve the boredom. I suspected Esther of imagining things and stretching the truth, but she stuck to her story and insisted she had heard it from the teacher himself.

I wasn't going to tell Joe, but decided he might be amused by the latest rumor. "Say," I began, "want to hear the latest? Esther tells me there is to be a big insurgent attack tonight."

He was as unimpressed as I had been. "Well, I'll believe it when I see it. You're not worried, are you?"

I assured him that I had never been more calm, and soon afterward I got into bed. Joe stayed up alone to finish the book he had been reading.

About 11 p.m. he awakened me. "Susie, I believe your insurgent attack is about to take place. Listen."

I listened intently. Suddenly, the stillness of the night was shattered by a single rifle volley from the direction of town. Then there was another, and another, and soon there was continuous firing. It sounded like the Fourth of July, but those were guns and not firecrackers!

"The electricity is off," Joe said. "Go into the living room and stay away from the windows. I'll get the boys up."

He carried the sleeping boys one by one and put them on the floor in the living room. Only Timmy awoke. He was thrilled with the excitement and suspense.

The firing continued from the direction of Namkham for several minutes. Then we were shaken by several very loud shots, close by but from the opposite direction. Immediately afterward we heard excited voices and the sound of running footsteps in the alley behind our house. We flattened ourselves to the floor, and for the first time I felt a sharp twinge of fear.

The shooting spread and the noise reached us from all directions; from downtown, from the army camp, from the road leading to the south, from the hills to the north.

"This is really it," I thought. "By morning the whole valley will be in the hands of the insurgents. What will happen to us?" The insurgents had never bothered us, and sometimes I thought we would be safer in their camp than with the army. Still, no one was safe with so many stray bullets flying around.

For an hour and a half we lay listening to the shooting. Finally it slackened, and then ceased. We waited a few minutes more, and carried the boys back to their beds.

"The nurses will be calling for me soon," Joe said. "As soon as the casualties are brought into the hospital we will be *some* busy."

No sooner had he spoken than there was a knock on the bedroom window and the familiar call, "Doc-tor, doc-tor, please come!"

Two very frightened student nurses were standing at the window in the darkness. Not wishing to attract attention, they had come without their lantern. Joe opened the back door and called to them. "Stay here with Susie and the boys. If anything happens, come running for me." With that he left for the hospital.

The nurses were frightened and shy and it would have been impossible for me to make conversation with them even under the best of circumstances. I invited them to sit or lie down on the couch and make themselves as comfortable as possible, and I went back to bed.

When I awoke it was daybreak. The girls were still sitting in the living room. I thanked them for staying with me and told them to go back to the nurses' home for breakfast.

Soon after, Wong Jack came to build the fires and start our breakfast. He was hardly inside the door when I began to pump him with questions. "Wong, what happened? Were many people hurt? What's going on now?"

Wong waved his hands about a few times and began to stammer out a reply in his limited English. "Soldiers run like crazy. Shoot all over, bang, bang. My house made of bamboo and four shots come through walls. We go outside and lie in ditch of water. Crazy people!"

Before breakfast was ready Joe came back from the hospital. I expected to see him looking tired and worried, but instead he seemed amused. "We really had a tremendous battle last night," he said. "All that shooting and there was one killed and one wounded. A few insurgents slipped into town and attacked the police station. There were two police officers asleep in the shack; one was shot through the head as he slept and the other jumped up and ran and was wounded in the shoulder. Apparently, small bands of insurgents placed on all sides of town opened fire to divert and frighten the soldiers at the camp. That's why we kept hearing shots from all directions. The soldiers came out of the camp shooting wildly at anything, everything, and nothing. Most of the shots we heard came from the army. It was a miracle no one was killed in the village, what with bullets whizzing through those bamboo houses. I spent a couple of hours patching up the policeman's shoulder, and that's all there was to it. The latest rumor is that the insurgents left a note at the police station saying they would be back on Saturday night."

By Saturday evening the rumors were flying that this was really the big night. I wasn't sure what to believe, but Saturday night came and went and all was quiet. Apparently the rebels had gone back into the jungle.

Various lesser incidents occurred soon. There never was any big military drive, but plenty of hit-and-run, bandit-type action. The army was not able to penetrate the hills and jungle, where the guerrillas thrived.

A few days after the Namkham skirmish, a convoy of soldiers was attacked in an isolated area along the Burma Road to the south of us and three wounded soldiers and three dead ones were brought into the hospital. From then on it became virtually impossible for trucks carrying rice and other commodities to get through the mountainous spots without being stopped and the food removed for insurgent use. It became necessary for such trucks to travel in convoys with soldiers going before and after for protection. Still, drivers continued to be killed or wounded by sharpshooters hidden in the trees. The army had no vehicles of its own, so when they had need of one they commandeered the truck of some poor fellow and made him do the driving for them. All too often he was the one who stopped a bullet during an ambush.

The rebels became so bold and attacked along the Burma Road so often that it was closed to traffic for about a week. During this time we received no rice or other commodities for sale at the bazaar, and no mail. That hit me hardest of all. I could do without rice for a while, but mail was all-important.

In spite of convoys, goods became increasingly scarce. For months the road to the north into the Kachin State had been cut off by insurgents, making Namkham the end of the line, and we got only what was left after the other towns along the road had been served. The price of rice went up at the bazaar. Wong Jack refused to buy that "no good lice" which was shipped in from south Burma, choosing rather to buy from local farmers at prices which were lower than the minimum set by the government. Cotton material was hard to find and wool disappeared altogether. The government screamed about black marketeers and exploiters of the people, and all the while they were incompetent to handle the many duties they had taken upon themselves. Rationing was practiced wherever possible, and there was much grumbling. There were no imported goods in the bazaar or in any of the shops in either Namkham or Rangoon. Previously, we had bought canned margarine or butter from Australia, but such things became a luxury to be enjoyed on rare occasions. The price of beef and pork went up, and chicken became almost prohibitive. Tiny eggs, all too often rotten, cost about seven cents apiece. Fortunately, we had been receiving large, fresh eggs by bus once a week from the National Christian School in Kutkai. The shelves in most shops were bare, and without the incentive of competition, shop clerks were unconcerned. After nationalization all shops were called People's Stores and given a number. For example, U Tin Tun's Clothing Store became People's Store No. 196. There was a common joke that they were called People's Stores because people were the only thing in them.

About ten one night we noticed a bright red illumination in the sky to the west of Namkham. As we watched it grew larger and brighter. In the morning a straggly bunch of Paloungs arrived carrying several wounded and burned villagers. Their small village had been attacked and burned by Shan insurgents because some of the Paloungs had acted as scouts and police for the army.

In the midst of the increased insurgent activity, Dr. and Mrs. Silgardo were making preparations to leave for India. Mrs. Silgardo had finally convinced her husband that they should leave

Namkham. In spite of the way he had been treated he felt an obligation to the hospital and to Dr. Seagrave, but he knew there was no future for himself or his family in Burma.

The nurses were saddened by the Silgardos' impending departure. A large dinner party was held in their honor, and many people came to bid them farewell. Songs were sung, a skit presented, and speeches made. Dr. Seagrave spoke for ten minutes, all about himself. He began by saying, "When I was on my way to jail," continued with, "After I got out of jail," and concluded with, "Dr. Silgardo told me he would stay here as long as I lived. But things have changed and now he feels it best to go. He is free to do as he wishes."

Dr. Silgardo responded with words of praise for "The Master" under whom he had worked for twelve years. "Master!" I groaned to myself. "What liars we all are. I know that's not what he's really thinking."

The Silgardo house and yard were filled with tearful nurses on the morning of their departure. The bulk of their household belongings had been sent ahead on the weapons carrier, but a mountain of baggage was being strapped to the top of the Rambler. Tun Shein was to drive the family to Lashio. He had been to the army camp to secure the necessary papers which would allow the Silgardos to travel, since no foreigners were allowed to travel outside their township without permission of the local army officer. "We can't go yet," said Tun Shein. "There has been some trouble just this side of Kutkai and the road is closed. The officer says it is not safe to travel."

This was too much for poor Irene Silgardo. The burden of packing plus all the strain had left her nerves ragged. She broke into loud wails. A sympathetic crowd gathered around and wept with her. Irene could no longer hold back all the frustrations of her seven years at Namkham. Just then the Old Man drove by on his way to class, and Irene sobbed, "See, there he goes. He will not come over here to tell us goodbye and he does not even look this way, and after all the good years my husband has given to this place. He is not having chapel this morning, probably because he does not want to pray for us. All of you please pray for us."

I wanted to say something comforting, but nothing seemed appropriate. The Old Man may have felt he had said his goodbyes the night of the supper, but he could have stopped for a last farewell. He hadn't even raised his hand to wave when he drove past. All of us felt it was wrong, but no one mentioned the incident again.

CHAPTER ELEVEN

RANGOON
VACATION

After Dr. Silgardo left, Tun Shein was anxious to find at least one other doctor to work at the hospital. However, the Burmese Government had made it clear that Americans would not be allowed to enter the country, and apparently there were no Burmese available. All of the younger physicians, and indeed most of the older ones, were in government service and posted at government hospitals. We were about to give up hope when Tun Shein hit upon the idea of searching for a retired Burmese doctor. He corresponded with a Dr. Lewis, formerly a professor at the University of Rangoon Medical School, and Dr. Lewis expressed a desire to come to Namkham. He would come alone and send for his wife at a later date.

Feverish plans were made for Dr. Lewis' arrival. The house begun eighteen months before for the American doctor who was to join us was still unfinished but could be occupied. Plumbing was hastily installed and the crude kitchen made ready.

I shall never forget my first glimpse of Dr. Lewis. He had come to chapel in order to be introduced formally to the staff and students. He was a small dark Indian with a bald head and beady black eyes. On this cold, foggy day he was wearing khaki pants and shirt and a heavy khaki army coat, all clean and neatly pressed. He looked like a college professor on an arctic field trip —and completely out of place at Namkham.

Still, we had great hopes that Dr. Lewis could adapt to country life and frontier hospital work. He was very congenial and I liked him immediately. Before long we discovered that he liked to talk almost as much as the Old Man did.

Joe showed him around the hospital and outlined his work. Dr. Lewis had never practiced, and any kind of clinical work was a little out of his line. During his active days he had spent most of his time lecturing to medical students. The bedlam in the admitting room baffled him, and he simply could not adjust to the routine of running fifty or more patients through the mill each day. Worse still, he hadn't the faintest notion how to treat the patients or which drug to use. He had never done surgery. He was seventy years old, too old to learn how to cope with the situation.

It looked as though Dr. Lewis was going to be a total loss, but Joe and Dr. Violet patiently worked around him as best they could. The one thing Dr. Lewis could do was talk and teach. He announced to Dr. Seagrave that he would take over most of the teaching duties. He thought the students should be getting more of certain subjects and less of others.

He might as well have advocated burning down the surgical building. The Old Man looked at him with fire in his eyes and told him that he had taught the nurses for forty-three years and would continue to do so. What they had always been taught was adequate, and Dr. Lewis should keep his big nose out of the matter. Dr. Seagrave reminded me of a little boy telling another to leave his toys alone.

As a result, Dr. Lewis spent most of his time drinking and

swapping stories with Dr. Violet's old father. He was accustomed to the heat of Rangoon and constantly complained that his old bones couldn't take the Namkham winter. He still wore the same khaki clothes, now not so clean and neatly pressed. Two weeks after he arrived, Dr. Lewis was on the bus headed back to Rangoon. He was gentlemanly enough to say that his reason for leaving was that he couldn't stand the weather, but we felt there was a much more important reason. The Old Man had run him off. It probably was best for all concerned.

Another problem arose at about that time. At first it seemed insignificant, but soon it had grown to gigantic proportions. The trouble began with a girl named Nang Tawng (Nang is the title for young women who are related to a Kachin chief or *sawbwa*). She was a unique girl in many ways. In the first place, she was fat, unlike most Kachins, who generally did not get enough food to add extra pounds. She was also boisterous and outspoken in contrast to her quiet and timid classmates in the nursing school.

I first noticed her at the softball games. She had a loud, deep voice which was constantly heard above the others. Once when the second baseman on the opposing team was guarding her base too closely, Nang Tawng ran squarely into the other girl and sent her sprawling. She was a fierce competitor.

In other ways Nang Tawng was not very considerate of her fellow students and, therefore, not popular. She was also noted for her ability to antagonize patients and staff nurses. However, her cardinal sin was that she irritated the Old Man.

And so at the end of her second year of training she was being expelled because of "bad character." Nang Tawng certainly was no favorite with the students or staff, but I did not know of anyone who really thought her character was bad except the Old Man. He had never liked her, mostly because she wouldn't roll over and play dead for him like the other girls did, and he was being kicked out mainly for that reason, I thought. Any other student nurse would have quietly folded her *longyis* and gone home, but not Nang Tawng. She wanted to finish her training and she wanted to stay at Namkham. Moreover, if she was being expelled for reasons of character, she felt that no other hospital would accept her. So she went to see the only man in the area who could override the Old Man, the captain at the army camp, and poured out her woes to him.

When the news leaked out, excitement and fear pervaded the hospital. The Old Man was so upset that he was in a state of near-collapse. At best he was not very strong physically, and the new shock kept him at home, where he refused to see anyone except Tun Shein and Pansy.

We were all afraid that the Burmese Government might seize this opportunity to take over the hospital. If it appeared that there was discrimination against a nurse, the government might announce that it was necessary for the hospital to be nationalized in order to protect the interests of all. Actually, we knew the official didn't need any excuse and could step in at any time without explanation, but they did like to make it appear that they were heroes stepping in to save a misused heroine.

As head of the local hospital committee, the captain of the army camp asked for a full-scale investigation. The committee decided to have a private interview with everyone on the staff and with each of the student nurses. That meant something like two hundred interviews. For a week the ancient hospital truck carried a few people at a time to and from town for interviews. Fortunately, Joe and I were not asked to "testify." As usual we were outsiders.

Many of the committee members had had private grievances against Dr. Seagrave for years, and the investigation gave them a chance to air their gripes. The girls were asked the most picayune questions, ranging from what they were given to eat, to whether money was subtracted from their small monthly stipend for incidentals such as toilet paper, to whether the Old Man acted in an improper manner when he gave them their physical exams.

After all the students were interviewed, it was the turn of the staff, and finally Tun Shein. Dr. Seagrave was not called, and during the entire investigation he remained at home.

When the investigation was completed, we waited for some official word, but none came. If the committee arrived at any conclusion, we never heard about it. The only visible result was that Nang Tawng stayed at the hospital. Her status was a little in doubt, but she was allowed to change her bright-red *longyi* for a green one, indicating promotion from a second-year trainee to a third-year student. She was more quiet and reserved, and stayed alone most of the time. Many of the students were sympathetic to her, but they were afraid to befriend her openly. In the past I had felt sorry for her, thinking her brashness a cover-up for loneliness, and now she most surely was lonely. Finally, at Joe's insistence, she returned to the ballgames and gradually she began to circulate again. The whole matter seemed to be forgotten, but it had brought the Old Man another step closer to a complete physical breakdown.

On other occasions I thought the Old Man dealt too harshly with the students. When one of them became ill, she was kept in the nurses' infirmary for a few days, and if there was no marked improvement she was sent home. Many of the girls contracted tuberculosis; most of them tried to hide their sickness as long as possible, hoping that a miracle would enable them to finish their training. Eventually, they would become too sick and would be placed in the infirmary. After a period of treatment, more chest x-rays would be taken, and if all evidence of the disease was not gone, the girl was sent home. Some of the girls would return after a few months, hoping they were well enough to resume their training. Dr. Seagrave rarely felt that any of them had recovered sufficiently to finish their work, and so he sent them home again with no regrets or words of encouragement. He had learned many lessons during his years at Namkham; perhaps one of them was that he did what he thought needed doing, and to hell with what anyone thought, or what the consequences were to others. Doubtless, he had also learned that once a girl had marked signs of tuberculosis, she rarely recovered enough to be able to carry on the rigorous life of a student nurse. Often it seemed to me that a girl should have been allowed to stay at the hospital for rest and treatment instead of being turned out. The Old Man was right, however, in maintaining that they were seldom able to withstand the hard work again.

For instance, there was Daisy, a thin Karen girl with a face scarred by smallpox. She wasn't particularly bright, but she tried hard and worked like a demon. As the winter days passed she became noticeably thinner and frailer, and finally she submitted to a chest x-ray. As we had feared, she had contracted tuberculosis, and it was reasonably far advanced. A few days later a very disheartened Daisy was boarding a bus for her home near Rangoon.

After six months Daisy returned to Namkham looking like a different person. She had been conscientious about resting and taking her medicine, and she had gained twenty pounds. She obviously felt well, and asked to be examined to see if she might not resume her nurse's training. Dr. Seagrave was skeptical, but he examined her superficially and sent her to the lab for a chest x-ray. The x-ray showed a good deal of improvement, though numerous cavities existed.

This was one of the few cases on which the Old Man asked Joe's opinion. "What do you think, Joe? She looks good, the x-ray looks better, but I've seen a hell of a lot of these cases turn sour. I say she goes. We can't have her around here infecting everyone in the nurses' home."

Joe felt differently. "It seems to me that there has been enough improvement so that her tuberculosis is arrested. She feels like working, so why not give her a chance? We can check her periodically to be sure she's doing okay."

"She can stay, but she'll never last."

In two months Daisy was back in the infirmary with a relapse. Joe had to agree that she was not strong enough to continue her training, and Daisy finally accepted the sad truth. When she left again it was for the last time.

The Old Man was becoming more and more unbearable. We all tried to stay out of his way as much as possible and to overlook his tirades. He was constantly upset over some incident or other, most of them trivial. For example, he blew his top because Joe preferred to write on the patients' charts in a single column instead of dividing the page into two columns. Joe liked his way and continued to use it. Then Dr. Violet started writing on the charts in a single column and there were more grumblings. The Old Man tried to coerce Dr. Violet into going back to the old way. He never mentioned this to Joe, since he never talked to Joe about anything. But several times, in my presence, he spoke about Joe to someone else in far from friendly terms. I was hurt, angry, and miserable, but I kept my mouth shut. I tried to convince myself that Dr. Seagrave was a very tired, sick old man who had never quite attained his great dream for his hospital, and now it was slowly slipping away from him. But I had heard enough from others to know that his disposition had never been much better and his heavy-handed methods had been practiced for years.

The last straw came at one of our softball games. Joe pitched a nice, slow ball to me and I hit it squarely. It was a beautiful high hit. The only trouble was that Plai Paw was standing squarely beneath where it came down and easily caught it to put me out. From his hunched position on the bench, Dr. Seagrave gave out with a loud string of profanity, the likes of which I had never heard, even from him. The game stopped as he continued to swear and rave at Plai Paw. So far as I could see, Plai Paw's only fault was his good fortune to be standing where he was when I hit the ball, but he was accused of everything from shoving aside all the players in the immediate vicinity to being a

"Goddamned s.o.b. whore hound." After about a minute of this ranting, the Old Man turned to me and demanded that I go back and bat again. I replied as calmly as I could, "No sir. I was out."

It took a few seconds for the gravity of my answer to strike me, and the other players as well. The Old Man didn't say a word as all eyes turned from me to him. Perhaps his silence was out of respect for me, or perhaps he was just too tired to object further. I took my seat on the grass and the next batter hesitantly approached the plate. The game went on in near silence.

Joe and I had been considering a vacation trip to Rangoon, and I decided that now was the time to go, the sooner the better. We consulted with Tun Shein about travel arrangements, and Joe asked Dr. Violet to care for his patients. We heard indirectly that the Old Man was furious because we had not asked his permission to leave.

At first we considered leaving our smaller children at Namkham with the nannies, but we abandoned that idea. The road might be closed at any time and our family would be separated. Traveling with five small boys was trying under the best of circumstances, and we were soon to find that travel in Burma with those same five small boys was nearly intolerable.

The Burma Airways had flights leaving Lashio twice a week, but I was too frightened to fly. They were using ancient DC-3 planes with no instruments, and I wasn't sure how they ever got up and over the mountains. The only alternative was the train.

Shortly after daybreak one February morning we loaded the seven members of our family, one of the nannies, Tun Shein, Hsu Aung the driver, and our baggage into the Rambler and headed for Lashio. We made a brief stop in Kutkai and arrived in Lashio by midafternoon. The train left for Mandalay at five-thirty the next morning, so Tun Shein had made arrangements for us to have dinner at the home of Martin Tan, a prominent Chinese businessman. After dinner we were to board the train, which was parked on a siding, and spend the night in our compartment.

We had met Martin Tan before. He was a handsome Chinese gentleman, probably in his late forties, who had owned and operated the Tin Tin Stores in Lashio before it was nationalized. Now he was reduced to being one of the poorly-paid employees of the store. However, he had his finger in numerous other pies—he was agent for the Burma Airways—so he had not suffered as much as many other businessmen.

As we drove into the yard of Martin's comfortable home, the sounds of rock-and-roll reverberated in my ears. I hadn't heard that maddening beat since leaving New York, and certainly hadn't expected it in the Northern Shan States of Burma. I could see several young people dancing to the music. Tun Shein explained that the Tans' had eight children and they were great American dance fans.

Seven of them, ranging in age from eight to eighteen, were at home between school terms. I was completely charmed by eighteen-year-old Valerie. Her dress, manner, speech—everything about her—showed the influence of Western culture. She must have thought me a real square for not knowing about the latest dance steps or hit tunes back in the States. She questioned me about the correct hemline, professed undying devotion to the memory of John F. Kennedy, and wanted to know about the intricacies of the United Nations.

"I have just taken my matriculation examination," she explained. "If I pass, I will go to Rangoon University soon, and I hope to study about politics. It fascinates me. My greatest dream is to work at the United Nations some day."

Later, she said, "I am very anxious to exchange letters with some young people in the United States. Can you give me the names of a boy and a girl about my age to whom I might write?"

I suggested my nephew, Mayes Scott. He was the same age, but I had not seen him for a number of years and had no idea whether or not he would enjoy corresponding with a strange girl. As it turned out, they struck up a pleasant correspondence.

Mrs. Tan was a short, round lady with a broad smile marred only by a top row of very crooked teeth. Like all the family, she wore American-style clothing. She had planned a delicious typical Chinese dinner for us.

The afternoon and evening passed quickly, and at nine-thirty we said goodbye and went to the railroad station. Our compartment comprised an entire tiny car. The seats had been made up into four single-size bunks, but with no linens. There was a lavatory with an Asian-type toilet. I soon found that I had to be in acute distress before going in to relieve myself, so pungent was the odor of urine which pervaded the small room. I played a kind of game to see if I could go in, conduct my business, and leave, all the time holding my breath. The whole compartment was filthy, and I had my first doubts about taking the train instead of a rickety DC-3. We managed to find room for the seven of us and the nanny to lie down on the four small beds. That was the ultimate in togetherness.

Many hours and a thousand tosses and turns later, the first streaks of light appeared in the east and the toy-sized train gave its first lurch. As I glanced out the dirty window, I saw Tun Shein standing on the platform waving farewell.

The motion of the train awakened the boys and our day had begun. We transformed the four miserable beds into two equally uncomfortable seats, and opened the food basket which Wong Jack had packed for us. I had wondered how my stomach would react to food in combination with the stinking restroom and the rocking motion of the train, but I need not have worried. One of the twins, though, lost his breakfast on the seat, thus adding his bit to the smell and confusion.

The mountain scenery was beautiful. Our train passed through places so narrow that our only view on both sides was sheer cliffs; then suddenly we would come into an open area with a waterfall in the distance and flowering trees all around. I was thankful for such vistas, for without them the day would have seemed interminable.

The train's top speed was about thirty-five miles an hour, and it made so many stops that it was rarely able to attain top speed before slowing down for the next village. At every stop there was great confusion on the outside. Hordes of curious villagers simply came to see the train, and many others were selling bananas, rice, pineapples, and curries to the passengers, who leaned from the windows and yelled to the vendor of their choice.

In the afternoon we entered a long tunnel, and after emerging, our train slowly and carefully made a turn and rolled across a bridge spanning a deep gorge at whose bottom was the Salween River. The bridge had been built in the 1920's by the Hoover Company in the United States, and was named the Hoover Bridge.

Toward evening we began to descend from the mountains into the lowlands. In many places the grade was too steep for the train. It was necessary for us to go forward a little and then back on switch tracks, and so we proceeded down the side of a mountain.

About dusk we arrived in Maymyo, where a number of army personnel boarded the train. After an army officer, his wife, and two small daughters were put into our compartment, there was not even standing room. By this time I had no doubt that we had made a mistake by taking the train. At one stop the officer, his wife, and oldest child got off and left the baby, who was fast asleep. When the train began to move, they still hadn't returned and we thought we had suddenly acquired another child. At least it was a girl. But at the next stop, the parents and sister returned out of breath. They had been riding in another car, where they were visiting when the train started up at the previous station.

At 8:30 we pulled into the Mandalay station. After traveling fifteen hours we had covered roughly 180 miles!

Our reservations for the night were at the Railway Hotel, just across from the terminal building. We were all so exhausted that we fell into bed and slept soundly in spite of the hardness of the beds and the heat. We were now in the lowlands and it was ten to fifteen degrees warmer than at Namkham.

The next morning Joe and I left the boys with Mu Nah, the nanny, and walked to the United States Information Service Office and Library. The assistant director, a Burmese, welcomed us into his office.

Joe said to him, "We had hoped to get several books to take back to Namkham with us, but we noticed a sign on the door of the library. Why is the library closed?"

"The Burmese Government has ordered us to make a list in triplicate of all our books and then give a short synopsis of each book. We have twenty thousand books and I am afraid our employees will never be able to complete such a task. Nevertheless, they are working on it now."

"It looks as though the government intends to put the U.S.I.S. out of business, or at least close down their libraries," Joe said. "Has the library in Rangoon been closed too?"

"Yes, and so has the one in Moulmein. I'm afraid you are right. This government seems to want to erase any influence another nation might have on our people. These libraries are well stocked with American volumes and our leaders do not want the people to read them."

Joe's prediction was correct, for the Burmese Government never allowed the U.S.I.S. Libraries to reopen, and thousands of books were lost.

After leaving the U.S.I.S. Office, Joe and I hired a driver with a ponycart so we could see the sights of Mandalay. Our final destination was the home of the American Consul, Donald Ellson. We had met Don at the Embassy in Rangoon upon our arrival. He and his wife, Fran, made us feel very welcome and invited our whole family to dinner that evening. The delicious dinner was served in grand style in the formal dining room of the consul's residence. I felt as though I had truly returned to civilization, but our five little boys did not fit into this grand atmosphere. The elegant tablecloth and carpet would never be the same.

The following morning we boarded the train for Rangoon. We had arranged for four seats in the first-class chair car, hoping that there would be vacant seats for our overflow of boys. For the first few miles we were lucky, but after that the car filled rapidly and we were forced to hold the four smaller boys on our laps. Actually, they spent most of their time running up and down the aisle. The lavatory was relatively clean, but always occupied, so we simply sat the boys down on their little pots in the aisle. At the next train stop we would pour the contents of the pot out the window. All this was of little interest to our fellow passengers, but they simply couldn't understand why two little Shan boys were traveling with an American family. They stared at Joe and me, then at the twins, trying to imagine if somehow . . . but then they would shake their heads and turn away.

At sundown we reached the outskirts of Rangoon. The tracks were lined with tiny hovels and everywhere people were making preparations for the evening meal as smoke rose from the rafters of the cook houses. Children were running and playing, and men squatted near their front doors. Though the people had only the basic necessities, they seemed happy. As compared to some parts of Southeast Asia, Burma was a rich country and there was plenty of rice for all. Here and there I noticed a man bathing (still in his *longyi*) in a small pool of water in front of his house. The *longyi* was indeed a versatile garment, for it not only served as clothing, but also provided a small measure of privacy. A Burmese could completely change his clothing beneath a *longyi* in a crowded place and never be without cover.

In the distance the last rays of sunshine were reflected brilliantly from the dome of the Shwe Dagon Pagoda, Rangoon's largest and most beautiful Buddhist shrine. The name Shwe means *golden* in Burmese, and the faithful worshippers of the Lord Buddha spend thousands of *kyats* each year for gold leaf to cover the large dome and many smaller spires of the pagoda.

Finally we pulled into the Rangoon station and were met by Bob and Eleanor Howard, Methodist missionaries whom we had met during our previous short stay in Rangoon. Eleanor looked just the same, though perhaps a few pounds heavier, but then so was I. Eleanor was about thirty-five and had spent most of her life in Burma. She had been born into a family of Baptist missionaries in Burma and had served as a nurse in the Baptist hospital in Moulmein.

Bob had been in Burma for only a few years, under the auspices of the Methodist Church. There he met and married Eleanor, and she transferred from the Baptist Foreign Mission Society to its Methodist counterpart to work with him.

Bob had changed since we last saw him. He was thinner, quieter, more detached, and seemed much older. During the ride home from the railroad station he said very little and we felt ill at ease, as though we might not be altogether welcome. Eleanor carried the conversation, in her smooth, easy manner. We had made previous arrangements to stay with the Howards during our two weeks in Rangoon. They had tried to visit us in Namkham but had been refused permission to travel in that area.

I hadn't been impressed with their compound several months before, but after living at Namkham their place took on a new grandeur. Entry to the Methodist Compound was through an iron gate from a busy street. The gate was left open during the day and early evening, but after eleven o'clock it was locked and a night watchman made regular rounds. We were locked out one night when we returned after midnight and had to call loudly for the watchman.

The grounds of the compound were immaculate. The frequent rains kept the grass thick and green, and flowers bloomed in profusion. There were large clumps of canna lilies, crotons, and other foliage with which I had been familiar in Florida.

The Howards' house was of brick, with a large screened porch across the front. To the side of the house and partially hidden by a screen of flowering bushes was a row of small wooden hovels, dwellings for the cook, the watchman, and the grounds-keeper.

In the rear of the house, across a chain fence, we saw a large three-story building which was well-lighted and bustling with activity.

"What's that building, Eleanor? I don't remember it," I asked.

"It's not a part of our compound. That's the Seventh Day Adventist Hospital," she told me. "It's the best hospital in Rangoon. Most of the Americans use it when they need a hospital."

After a delicious dinner we put the children to bed and took the nanny, Mu Nah, to the home of one of her relatives, where she was to sleep. Soon after we returned, Bob excused himself and went to his room. Eleanor, Joe, and I talked for an hour or two in the living room.

"We've had a change in plans," Eleanor told us. "There wasn't time to write to let you know before you left Namkham. Bob and I are going to leave tomorrow by train for Kalaw for two weeks. Bob hasn't been well and he needs to get away for a rest. It's very lovely at Kalaw. The Methodist Church has a school there. But you're very welcome to stay on here and use our home. The cook has agreed to shop and prepare meals for you."

I was sorry to hear that Bob was not well and relieved to know that we were not the reason for his coolness. It was a wonderful opportunity for us to have a whole house for our use, but I was a little hesitant to take over a strange place.

"We appreciate your making the arrangements for us. Are you sure the Methodist Mission will approve?"

"Oh, sure," Eleanor replied. "We often have guests here. Don't worry about that."

Shortly after the Howards left the next day, a Volkswagen bus drove into the Methodist Compound and stopped in front of our house. A businesslike-looking young American woman got out and walked briskly toward the door. "Hi, I'm Barb Winn," she said. "I live at Seminary Hill in Insein."

"Hello, I'm Sue Newhall. If you're looking for the Howards, they just left for Kalaw. We're from Namkham, and we'll be staying here while they're gone."

"Oh, I know who you are," she returned quickly, "and I've come to see you, not the Howards."

Her name was vaguely familiar to me, and suddenly I remembered hearing Eleanor Howard speak of Barbara Winn, a Baptist medical missionary.

Barbara was wearing a dress whose length and style plainly indicated that she had been out of the United States and away from the clutches of dress designers for several years. Her blonde hair was pulled straight back from her long face and fixed into a small bun in the back, and she wore Burmese *hpynats* on her feet. "No frills here," I thought, and instantly felt at ease with her.

Barbara came right to the point of her visit. "Bill—that's my husband—and I belong to the Kokine Swim Club, and I wondered if you and your children would like a swim today. Our four children dearly love the pool."

"Would we like a swim?" I almost shouted. It had been months since we had seen a pool, and the Rangoon heat and humidity had me practically melted into a puddle. "We'd love it!"

We hastily unpacked our swimsuits, rounded up the boys, and were on our way to the pool.

At first the twins were terrified of the water, but they slowly gained confidence and eventually were splashing about happily with the other boys. That trip was a real eye-opener for the twins from the very beginning. Although past two years old, they had never been off the compound at Namkham. The car ride and the long train rides had been both frightening and fascinating to them. The city of Rangoon held them spellbound, and they sat for hours and watched the cars and buses go roaring down the streets.

While the boys played, Joe and I got better acquainted with

Barbara. She told us that her husband Bill, who had completed most of his work toward a Ph.D., taught in the Baptist Seminary, and that she operated a small medical dispensary for the seminary students and schoolchildren, besides running a household and caring for their two girls and two boys. We also learned that the Winns were well overdue for a furlough to the United States but chose to go on with their work, knowing that if they left Burma the government would never allow them to re-enter.

That afternoon *The Guardian* reported that hundred- and fifty-kyat notes were no longer legal tender and must be turned in. The addresses of several places in Rangoon where the notes could be taken were listed. The reason given for the demonitization, as it was called, was that "certain exploiters, both national and foreign, have amassed great fortunes by cheating the people. Many of them have this money hoarded away in bills of large denomination, and by calling in all fifty- and hundred-kyat notes, such exploiters will be exposed."

One-hundred-kyat notes were worth approximately twenty dollars in U.S. money, which meant that there would be no bill larger that twenty kyats, the equivalent of five dollars in circulation. Anyone possessing bills as large as our ten and twenty dollars had to turn them in to the government, and if I knew anything about the workings of that government, it would be months before remuneration would be made, if ever.

"Do you have any 50- or 100-kyat bills?" I asked Joe.

He reached into his back pocket and pulled out his wallet. Inside were several bills, among them three fifty-kyat notes and one hundred note. "I would have more, but I spent two hundred-kyat bills yesterday in Mandalay to buy train tickets. Tomorrow I'll see if I can turn these in, though the newspaper says that the government won't be able to make remuneration until some later date. What will this lamebrained outfit think of next? Suddenly the money people have been saving isn't any good. Some of the folks at Namkham will be hit pretty hard. Grandma has been putting money aside so she can buy a little house in Taungyi and retire in a few years. And I wonder how this will affect Tun Shein and the hospital finances."

We stood to lose only about fifty dollars if remuneration was never made, but I really felt sorry for the Burmese people. Those who had been fortunate enough to earn a comfortable living by enterprise and initiative, and perhaps save a little, were automatically exploiters of the people. All foreigners were exploiters, of course. Why else would they be in Burma? Or so the government reasoned.

The next morning shortly after breakfast Joe left in one of the three-wheeled taxis to turn in his kyats. At eleven he returned with the money, thoroughly disgusted. "I went to that address on Signal Pagoda Road and there was a line two blocks long of people waiting to change their money. The place near the night market was the same, so I went to one of the banks and they didn't know what to do with me. Since I was from Namkham, they finally told me I would have to wait until we go back up country to turn in these bills. To heck with 'em, I'm going down to the U.S. Embassy this afternoon and see what they can do."

The trip to the Embassy proved well worth the effort. Arrangements had been made for Embassy personnel and their families to turn their money in together, for which remuneration in five- and ten-kyat notes was made immediately. We added our 250 kyats to the others at the Embassy and two days later a friend came by with the equivalent amount in smaller bills. Most of our Burmese friends were not so fortunate; it was several months before their money was returned, and only a few received the full amount in exchange. Most people were charged 40 to 65 per cent income tax on the money they had turned in whether or not they had already paid tax on their earnings.

We had corresponded with Elroy Thiel, the American Consul in Rangoon, and preparations were underway for our twins to receive U.S. visas. There had been endless forms to fill out, and we had written to Bradenton for copies of our birth certificates and marriage certificate. It took over a month for the various letters to go back and forth between Burma and Florida. Finally, all was in order and we had been promised a visa which would permit us to bring the twins into the U.S. However, we still had to secure permission from the Burmese so the boys could leave Burma with us. That was the problem we took to the present consul, Leo Reddy, soon after we arrived in Rangoon. Mr. Reddy listened attentively, then advised, "I think your best bet would be to secure a stateless passport for them. This is simply a paper, in lieu of a passport, which will allow the boys to travel. It will not allow them ever to reenter Burma, but since you expect to adopt them they will become American citizens and will not need to return to Burma."

He rummaged through a stack of papers on his desk and came up with what he wanted. "I'll give you the name of a local lawyer who can have these papers prepared for you. He's an old Chinese gentleman, perfectly honest, and he has helped us out in matters like this before. His name is Ben Leong. I'll have my secretary make an appointment for you, today if possible."

Fortunately, we were able to go directly to Mr. Leong's office. We gave him all the necessary information and he told us to return for the papers on the following day.

The next afternoon, the small booklets were ready. There was one for each twin containing a small picture and such information as name, age, and race. Then there was a short statement saying that this child had lost his citizenship and no longer was a citizen of any country. "This will enable you to travel with the boys," Mr. Leong stated. "But you know that they cannot use them as regular passports to reenter Burma at any time in the future, nor can I assure you positively that the Burmese immigration officials will let them out of the country. Most likely they will say nothing. I hope for your sake and theirs that this will be the case."

Mr. Leong's fee was fifteen kyats for each of the little booklets, or a total of about six dollars.

On our third day in Rangoon the telephone rang and a male voice asked, "Is this Mrs. Newhall?" When I answered in the affirmative, he said, "This is Roy Baden. I'm running for sheriff of Manatee County in Florida and I've come here to solicit your vote."

At first I was too stunned to answer. The name Roy Baden was certainly familiar to me. He is a real grass-roots politician who prides himself on knowing and being known by all the voters in Manatee County, but it was inconceivable—to say the least—that he would come all the way to Rangoon for two votes. "Now, come on, who is this?" I asked.

The caller at the other end of the line was obviously enjoying my bewilderment. He laughed merrily, then said, "Actually my name is John Hubbell, and I'm a major in the U.S. Army stationed here with Military Equipment Delivery Transfer. My wife and I call Bradenton our home, though we've been away for years. I ran into some folks at the Embassy yesterday who told me you were in town, and I thought I'd give you a ring."

We met Johnny and his wife, Sarah, that evening and had a pleasant visit. Knowing the Hubbells opened up a new world for us. Not only did we see them several times later, but through them we met many others who helped to make our Rangoon vacation a success.

On May 30, the American community in Rangoon held a Memorial Day service at the Methodist English Church on the compound where we were staying. As the service began, the American flag was brought to the front of the church and the organist struck the first notes of "The Star Spangled Banner." The congregation rose and lustily sang the first stanza of the anthem. I had not seen that flag nor heard that song in many months, and I was so overcome with emotion that tears came to my eyes. These were my people, and that song and flag represented my country, and I longed to be home.

Shortly after the service, a shiny black limousine with a small American flag flying from each of the front fenders stopped in front of our house. Joe, Tim, and I had been invited to lunch with Ambassador Byroade and his wife, and he had sent his driver for us.

When we arrived at the ambassador's home, Mr. Byroade himself opened the car door and greeted us. A handsome man in his early forties, he was dressed in slacks and a colorful sport shirt, as any man might have been on a holiday. Mrs. Byroade was so attractive that I immediately felt miserable. She was tall, slim, and immaculate in a casual dress, and she spoke in a soft voice with a slight Viennese accent. Soon my initial discomfort was forgotten as she charmingly put me at ease. We had learned earlier that Mr. Byroade had retired from the army at the age of thirty-five with the rank of brigadier general so that he might enter diplomatic service.

He was immensely interested in the Namkham Hospital and in Dr. Seagrave, and anxious to know if there was anything he could do to help in the work. We talked at length about the hospital, enjoyed a delicious meal, then Mr. Byroade drove us back to our home in a much smaller, less imposing vehicle. I was impressed with him because he seemed to be a man who knew his job and did it, and yet had not allowed the importance of his position to go to his head.

We also became better acquainted with several Baptist missionaries, since Rangoon was the headquarters of the Burma Baptist Convention. Brad and Marcia Allen were a hearty, happy couple about our age, also with a houseful of children. Brad a thoroughgoing extrovert, was pastor of the Immanuel Baptist Church in the heart of Rangoon. I never understood how he happened to find himself in missionary work, for he was as far from my original idea of a missionary as anyone could possibly be. His views on theology were ultra-liberal, and he was usually in hot water with more conservative missionaries and older members of his congregation. But he was a great favorite with the younger people of the church. We became good friends with Brad and Marcia, and on subsequent trips to Rangoon we stayed in their home. In fact, a year later we spent two weeks with them and Joe delivered their fifth child and second son.

One evening we joined Brad and Marcia, and Bill and Barb Winn, for dinner at the Inya Lake Hotel. The hotel had been built by the Russians a few years before and paid for by the Burmese in shipments of rice. The hotel offered the latest in comfort and convenience for the tourist, the only catch being that there were no tourists in Burma. The visas that were granted—and those grudgingly—were for twenty-four hours, with the proviso that the bearer not leave the confines of Rangoon. The few guests at the hotel were newly arrived personnel attached to the many foreign embassies, and they stayed only until more permanent quarters could be secured. The well landscaped grounds of the hotel had been allowed to grow weeds, the outside walls were covered with mildew from endless rains, but this was still the most elegant place to dine in Rangoon.

The six of us walked through the nearly deserted lobby and into the beautiful circular dining room. It contained at least a hundred tables, but only one was occupied. After we had seated ourselves, the headwaiter approached and politely informed Joe that he must wear a coat in the dining room. We all burst out laughing, not only because it seemed absurd to insist on formality in such a deserted place, but also because Joe had accidentally left the one bag containing most of his clothes in Lashio and it had not yet reached us. Joe told the waiter that he didn't have a coat. Master of the situation, the waiter disappeared, to reappear a few minutes later with a jacket over his arm. It was a few sizes too small for Joe, but it filled the bill, and we were free to order.

Joe and Barbara swapped medical stories, glad to find someone with mutual interests and concerns. We told our friends about Namkham, for none of them had been that far up-country due to government restrictions on travel. They told us about the perils and problems of missionary life, and after listening to a few of those tales, I decided that I preferred the kind of problems we had at Namkham.

It was on that first trip to Rangoon that we met May, the young Karen girl who went back to Namkham with us to help with the housework and take care of the children. She was about seventeen, so shy that I felt I had another child to take care of, but soon she proved her worth many times over.

The day before we were to return to Namkham I went to the Embassy Coop to shop for food to take with us. The store was in the basement of the Embassy and was small and crowded, but to me it looked like a great supermarket. Before I had covered two aisles my basket was full of cereals, cocoa, yeast, shortening, and an assortment of canned goods. It was hard to contain my enthusiasm, but I knew that there was a limit to what we could take back. As I stood pondering the matter, a well-groomed, gray-haired lady approached me. "Are you Mrs. Newhall from Namkham?" she asked.

"Yes, I am."

She then gave me her name and a good deal of her personal history, which included a period of association with Dr. Seagrave.

"Do you like it at Namkham?" she asked.

"Well, yes, I do," I answered, which was only a little bit untrue, but then I didn't have time to tell her all the reasons I didn't think Namkham was the greatest place on earth. Besides, I thought, few people were entirely happy anywhere.

"I know enough about Gordon Seagrave that I don't see how you stand it," was her reply. "I remember him as the world's greatest egotist and tyrant, and I mean every word of that."

"Well, he hasn't changed much." Then I felt compelled to say something in the Old Man's behalf. "But I suppose he has mellowed some through the years."

"At one time I admired Gordon a great deal," she told me.

"Then I got to know him better and saw how he treated people under him. Some people say the war changed him, but I say that it didn't change him, it just gave him a chance to express what he was really like all along."

Afterward, I was a bit ashamed that I had so eagerly listened to the derogatory things my acquaintance had said about the Old Man, but the truth of the matter was that I had enjoyed the conversation. Then I chuckled as I thought that the Old Man would probably have had a few choice things to say about this woman!

Remembering the seemingly endless train ride to Rangoon, Joe and I decided to brave the Burma Airways on the return trip. Two days before our departure we put Mu Nah and May on the slow train to Lashio so that they would be there when we arrived by plane. On the morning we were to leave we were up at 4:30. The embassy sent a Volkswagen bus and driver to take us to the airport, a courtesy we appreciated very much. Then, to our surprise, we found that instead of the usual broken-down DC-3 which made that run from Rangoon to Lashio, we were going to fly in a new German Fokker. New plane or not, the casual schedule still held, and we were about an hour late taking off. After four and a half hours and three stops, we landed at the Lashio airport. Tun Shein met us there, and with May and Mu Nah in the car, we began the bumpy 120-mile trip to Namkham.

CHAPTER TWELVE

THE OLD MAN'S DEATH

During the last months of 1964 we could see that Dr. Seagrave was failing fast. His coughing spells became frequent and more severe, and after each one he was forced to sit quietly for several minutes in order to catch his breath. There were mornings when he did not turn up for chapel or classes, and often he stayed home and rested instead of playing softball on Friday afternoons. He was not a man to break routine easily, and we knew that these were ominous signs.

One morning as we were eating breakfast, Tun Shein called to Joe from our back door. Joe went outside, and a few minutes later I saw the two of them disappear down the alley toward the Old Man's house.

When Joe returned later, he looked concerned, but not especially worried. "What's wrong?" I asked immediately.

"Dr. Seagrave passed out on the floor in his room. Actually, I think he fell out of bed. Pansy heard the thud, and she found him lying on the floor. She couldn't budge him, so she sent Augusta for Tun Shein, and by the time he got there, the Old Man had rallied enough to help them get him back into bed. Tun Shein wanted me to check him over, and everything seems to be okay. There are no bad bruises or broken bones. I don't know what happened to make him pass out, though I do have a pretty good idea. He takes about seven grains of phenobarbital every day to make himself sleep. That's about twice as much as I've ever given to a patient. He probably got too much and passed out as he was getting out of bed. You know how he's always complaining that he can't sleep, and never for more than four hours at a time."

"Is he going to be okay?"

"Well, as a long-range forecast I don't know, but he should get over this little episode without any trouble."

Sure enough, Dr. Seagrave was back at his same grind within two days. However, other setbacks occurred during the following weeks, and each time he bounced back a little more slowly. By winter Pansy did all his driving for him and waited on him hand and foot. When he walked he had to stop every few feet and catch his breath, and his feet and ankles had swollen so badly that he had to split the sides of his shoes to get them on. Pansy noted that he often fell asleep while eating or reading, and occasionally he dozed off in the middle of a sentence.

In November Joe suggested to Dr. Seagrave as tactfully as he could that there might be something seriously wrong. "Oh, hell, I'm all right," was the answer. Two weeks later Joe tried again, and Dr. Seagrave grudgingly agreed to have a physical exam. After going over him pretty thoroughly, Joe asked me to check his blood count. The next step was a chest X-ray, but here the Old Man drew the line. "I'm not going in that damned room and take off my clothes and freeze to death. Besides, this has gone far enough. As long as I can breathe and smoke my lungs are fine."

"We'll warm the room for you." Joe was determined.

"I can't take time out from my classes in the mornings and I have to sleep in the afternoons."

"Just pick your time and we'll have everything set up. All you'll have to do is walk in, have the X-ray taken, and leave."

Joe had an answer for each of the other objections that were raised, and finally the date and the hour for the X-ray were set.

Shortly after noon on the day in question, two student nurses put two large charcoal burners with bright-red, hot coals in the X-ray room. By four o'clock the room was fairly warm in spite of the concrete floor and stone walls. Esther and I were on hand to take the X-ray and Joe was there to help if necessary. Four o'clock came, then 4:15, and at 4:30 Pansy drove the black Rambler near the door of the building. Dr. Seagrave opened the door of the car, slowly got out, and shuffled into the room. "My God, what are you all waiting for, my funeral? Let's get on with this, I can't stand these damned charcoal fumes very long."

He sat down and Pansy helped him to remove his coat, two sweaters, a shirt, and undershirt. Then he stood in front of the machine, took a deep breath to expand his lungs, and Esther pushed the button. As fate would have it, something went wrong in the generator room and the electricity went off. I stood glued to the floor, expecting a verbal barrage, and I was not disappointed. When every last bit of his energy was spent, the old Man collapsed in a chair and Pansy helped him put on his undershirt, shirt, the two sweaters, and overcoat. By the time the last button was secured the electricity came back on. Glancing up at Joe, he said, "If you think I'm going to . . . oh hell, Pansy, take 'em off again." Slowly the many layers of clothing came off again.

That time the X-ray was taken successfully and we all breathed a sigh of relief. When his clothing was all back on, Dr. Seagrave got back into the car and Pansy drove him to his late afternoon clinic in the surgical building.

Esther developed the X-ray in the dark room and returned a few minutes later carrying the dripping film. "Dr. Joe, I am so scared. This is not a good X-ray and we do not dare ask the Old

Man to come back for another."

Joe took the film, walked to the window, and held it up to the light. For a moment he was silent as he studied it. Finally he said, "The X-ray is fine, at least the technical part of it. The trouble is with the Old Man."

Esther was sure that she had done something wrong. "See," she insisted. "It must be underdeveloped. Where the lungs should be there is only white."

"Yeah, usually the lungs are nearly transparent. His lungs are so congested they appear this way on the X-ray. Up here, near the top of the left lung, is a small clear area. That's the only part of his lungs he can breathe with."

Even I, who knew nothing about reading X-rays, could tell that this one was grossly abnormal. "What could have caused this?" I asked. "Could it be a malignancy?"

"We can't tell, though it might well be."

When the film was dry Joe carried it to Dr. Seagrave and handed it to him. With shaking hands, the Old Man held the X-ray to the light, and all too soon he saw the trouble. He probably had suspected all along what the X-ray would look like. His comment was, "I've seen thousands of these damned things, but never one just like this. I've been talking about dying for years, and now it looks like I can talk about it with some authority. Those are the sorriest-looking pair of lungs I've ever seen."

He was shaken, and very quiet. Virtually ignoring the Shan man who lay patiently on the examining table, he leaned back in his chair, lit a cigarette, and hooked his right arm over the back of his chair. For several minutes he sat that way, staring out the window.

Joe was the first to break the silence. "You need some therapy, you know. Would you consider going back to the U.S. to one of the medical centers where they can give you the best care? How about your old Alma Mater, Johns Hopkins? They have all the latest equipment and could probably clear up those lungs. At least, you could be made much more comfortable."

"Joe, I've vowed never to leave this place. I've spent most of my life here, and I want to die here. If I left this country Ne Win would see to it that I never got back in. And what would an old goat like me do in the U.S. for the rest of my life, even if it was just a short time? I'd be like all the missionaries who have retired and gone home. I'd buy my casket and sit on my ass until it was time for someone to put me in it."

"At least you should go down to Rangoon. The Seventh Day Adventists' Hospital is well equipped and has a good staff. You might be surprised what help you could get even from Rangoon General."

"That stinking hole of a Rangoon is the last place on earth I'd go. I spent enough months in jail there to last me the rest of this life, and some of the next. No, I'm going to stay here for whatever time I have left and work until the last minute. As soon as I kick off, tell the coolies to start digging a deep hole over yonder between Grace and Gordon Jr."

There seemed nothing more to say. The last thing Joe heard as he left the building was a loud bellow. "Damn it, Dorothy, get the hell in here and bring in the next patient!"

As Christmas of 1964 approached, we saw less and less of the Old Man. He missed chapel frequently and had given up the ballgames entirely. He didn't even watch them. But every morning, if he could possibly drag himself from his house, he was in his chair in the nurses' classroom teaching the girls; and almost without fail he continued to conduct the late afternoon clinics, when he examined all the patients admitted to the hospital since the previous afternoon. The student nurses carried patients on litters to the tiny examining room so the Old Man could poke around on their bellies, thump their chests, listen to their hearts, and read what the admitting physician had written on the charts. If he agreed with the diagnosis, he didn't add anything to the chart, but if he disagreed, he usually prefaced his remarks with,

"Any damned fool should be able to see that. . . ." The sicker he got, the sharper his comments became.

The older staff nurses who had been with Dr. Seagrave for so many years realized his time was short. Ngwe Nyunt, his adopted sister, said to me, "I saw his parents die, his sister Grace die, and now I see him dying a little more each day." She managed a smile and added, "Maybe after he goes I will be the next one to be buried in the little staff cemetery."

Pansy's face had a perpetual worried look, and she seemed to grow thinner day by day. She had numerous responsibilities in the hospital—she was in charge of linens and supplies, she was overseer of the student nurses as their dean, and she managed all of Dr. Seagrave's correspondence—but her most demanding chores were at home. She saw that Dr. Seagrave was dressed, his house kept clean, his meals cooked according to his specifications, that he had his weekly full-tub bath, and was chauffeured to and from his classes and clinics. In addition, she listened to his woes and wails, curses and complaints, abuses and threats, and never, to my knowledge, answered back. Her patience was a marvel and an inspiration to me. As Dr. Seagrave grew more ill, he demanded Pansy's full time. She slept poorly at night, always listening for his call.

In February, 1965, our family took a two-week trip to Rangoon. We had hesitated to leave Namkham, knowing the Old Man's condition, but he was still able to carry on his limited activities.

We returned to Namkham late one evening, and Joe went immediately to the Old Man's house. Pansy, obviously very distraught, met him at the door. "Oh, Dr. Joe, I'm so glad you are back," were her first words. "Daddy is very bad, and I cannot do a thing with him. He won't listen to me. He falls asleep in his chair and I am so worried that he might burn himself with his cigarettes. He has been making me drive him to his classes every day and it takes all my strength to help him in and out of the car.

This morning he just couldn't leave the house so he had all the students come here for classes. I tried to talk him out of it, but it was no use. When the classes were finally over he was exhausted and I helped him into his room, but he refuses to get into bed."

"Has he been taking any medication?"

"No, only the phenobarbital he always takes."

Joe followed Pansy into the Old Man's room, where he was hunched down in his padded chair. His massive head with its mop of shaggy white hair drooped on his chest, and he appeared to be asleep. His ankles were grotesquely swollen. His large abdomen heaved with each labored breath. Suddenly he gave a gasp and a shudder and opened his eyes. Without raising his head he turned his eyes to Joe and said, "Oh, so you finally decided to come back, did you? Why don't you go on back to Rangoon and play around a little bit more? I can die in peace without you."

"We had a nice trip," Joe replied politely, "but we're back now, and I'd like to help you if I can."

"Just get out of here. Did Pansy sic you onto me? She tries to boss me around. I'll get along fine without any of you Goddamned s.o.b.'s. Just let me alone."

Joe was unmoved. He decided that now was the time for plain speaking. "Now, you listen to me for a change. Call me what you like, but leave Pansy out of it. You'd have been dead a long time ago if it wasn't for her. I want you to get into bed so I can examine you."

No one had given orders to Gordon S. Seagrave, M.D., for many years. He sat perfectly still for a few seconds, as though he were contemplating his next move. Then he turned his eyes to Pansy and said, "Okay, you heard the man, let's get on with it."

Pansy helped him to remove his trousers and shirt and slip into his pajamas. Together, Joe and Pansy were able to get him to his small bed. Joe found his breathing shallow and labored due to the massive consolidation in his lungs, and the edema—extra fluid in his tissues—was causing heart distress.

Later, in the living room, Joe and Pansy made their plans. "He needs oxygen," Joe said, "and needs it badly. Somehow we're going to have to make an oxygen tent. Susie has some plastic sheeting, and the carpenters can make us a frame. The biggest problem is the oxygen. Maybe Tun Shein knows where he can get a few tanks. Right now I'm going to start him on a diuretic to see if we can't get rid of the edema, and large intramuscular doses of penicillin and streptomycin."

Within the hour Tun Shein and PoZo were at our house with a crude wooden frame over which we stretched heavy plastic sheeting (my sister had sent this so I could make waterproof pants for the little boys). There was one tank of oxygen at the truck garage. With Tun Shein and Joe supervising, various odd bits of material were put together to form a reasonably performing oxygen tent. The plastic-covered frame was placed over the top half of the Old Man's bed and a small hole made in the side of the plastic through which a tube led from the oxygen tank.

Early the next morning Tun Shein bounced down the hill in the ambulance to scour the countryside for tanks of oxygen. He traveled as far as Lashio, stopping at every machine shop or welding shop. By nightfall he had gleaned six tanks.

The next problem was how to administer an inhalant mist to help loosen up the lung consolidation. We had the mist, but no apparatus for dispensing it. Joe searched until he found a spray gun which had been used to kill mosquitos. He washed and scrubbed it inside and out and filled it with the Turgimist spray. The rest was simple. Periodically one of the nurses raised the tent and sprayed generously. This always brought forth loud rumblings and grumblings from the patient, who insisted he was being drowned.

During the next few days the hospital work went on as usual, but everyone waited anxiously to see if the Old Man would rally. Joe spent as much time as possible with Dr. Seagrave, in order to be ready for any emergency.

Trouble developed with the oxygen tent almost immediately. The problem lay not so much with the tent itself as with the Old Man. He insisted on smoking constantly, and it was extremely dangerous to keep him in the tent. Besides, he had such difficulty breathing while lying down that it was better for him to sit in his large padded chair most of the time.

Finally we attached a long piece of tubing to the tank, and to the end of this secured an adaptor which the Old Man could insert in his mouth when he needed oxygen. Thus he sat for hours, hunched down in his chair, his feet propped up and his head dropped on his chest while he held the oxygen tube. When he wanted to smoke, one of the nurses sat by to hold his cigarette for him. He dozed a good deal, awakening for a few drags on his cigarette, then a drag from the oxygen tube, before drifting back to sleep. When he tried to talk his words were mumbled and spaced so far apart that it was difficult to follow him.

Pansy decided it was time to notify his family. In early March, she sent cablegrams to his sons John and Sterling telling them of their father's grave condition.

A team of three nurses were placed on duty day and night so Pansy could get some rest, but still she continued to be on hand at all hours. The Old Man cursed if anyone but Pansy tried to feed him, and it seemed that no one else could change his clothes or make his bed or give his injections. And yet his tongue had no mercy even for her.

Late one evening a Jeep pulled up in front of the surgical building. Out stepped three rather impressive-looking gentlemen, two of them dressed in traditional Burmese *longyis* and the third in a Western suit. They were, respectively, the head of the Shan State Government, his assistant, and a government doctor, all from Taungyi in the Southern Shan States. With them were two Burmese soldiers. Their arrival was a complete surprise, but Tun Shein hastily appeared to welcome them. Joe was called, and the group retired to the small library on the second floor of the surgical building. After the usual amenities and a cup of Shan tea, the doctor, a man in his mid-thirties, spoke. "We have heard that Dr. Seagrave is very ill. General Ne Win and his Revolutionary Council send their best wishes, and have directed us, as their personal emissaries, to do all we can for him. I am sure that your good doctor," and he indicated Joe, "has done well, but with his permission, I would like to examine Dr. Seagrave."

Most of the conversation had been in Burmese, between the officials and Tun Shein. Now, however, the doctor spoke in English, and Joe answered, "As far as I'm concerned, you're welcome to examine Dr. Seagrave." To himself he thought, "But the Old Man might have a few things to say about it."

He wondered what to make of these strangers. They were Shans, which meant that they were token officials. What little authority they might have had depended on the whim of General Ne Win and his Burmese underlings. Undoubtedly they had come to Namkham not because they wanted to or because they felt any real concern for Dr. Seagrave, but because General Ne Win had ordered them to. Did the General sincerely want to help, or was he simply checking to see whether the Old Man was seriously ill?

Tun Shein escorted the officials to Dr. Seagrave's house. When they arrived, the Old Man was propped up in bed holding his oxygen tube and raising hell with the student nurse who had just given him an injection. He was dressed in several pairs of pajamas and his tousled white hair stood out in all directions.

Tun Shein said, "Doc, these men have come from Taungyi to see you at General Ne Win's order. They flew as far as Lashio and drove the rest of the way in an army Jeep with a government convoy."

The Old Man said nothing, but looked from one to the other of the men with glowering eyes beneath droopy lids. Once again, the doctor was spokesman, since he spoke English well. Smiling, he reiterated that General Ne Win had ordered the group to come to Namkham to see to the welfare of Dr. Seagrave, and to help in any way possible. "I should like to examine you, sir, and to urge you to travel to Rangoon, where all of the services of the Rangoon General Hospital will be at your disposal. The General wishes it."

When there was still no answer from the patient, the doctor hastened on, somewhat ill at ease. "General Ne Win would even send a helicopter to Namkham for you so there would be no long trip to tire you."

The Old Man examined his visitors, moving only his eyes. Finally he spoke in his slow manner, which was even more accentuated since his illness. "Why did you *really* come here? General Ne Win couldn't care less whether I live or die. Correction: he'd rather I was dead. He probably sent you to find out if I was about ready to kick off so he'd know if it was time to start celebrating."

It had taken a supreme effort for him to say that many words, and he burst into a paroxysm of coughing which left him gasping for breath and exhausted. One of the nurses on duty came hurrying into the room, turned on the oxygen valve, and placed the adapter in his mouth. Joe stepped to his bedside, reached for his wrist, and began to count pulsebeats. The three visitors looked nervously at one another and shifted about in their chairs.

In a few minutes Dr. Seagrave was calm. Tun Shein said quietly, "We'll go now, Doc. These men will be here tonight and we can continue this conversation in the morning when you feel better. I do wish you would consider what the doctor has told you. You could get better care in Rangoon than you can here."

"Hell, what better care could I possibly get in Rangoon? I have three good nurses on duty all the time, and I have as good a doctor as can be found." Then he stopped short, as though he had said something of a highly secret nature. Cutting his eyes in Joe's direction, he continued, "Dammit Joe, I didn't mean to say that in

your presence. I don't want that head of yours to get any bigger."
To the three strangers he said, "You tell General Ne Win I am not
going anywhere except to the little cemetery. I know what he
wants. He wants me to leave Namkham so he can dream up some
excuse to keep me from coming back. Why can't you all get it
through your heads that I am going to die right here, nowhere
else? If you really want to help me, let my sons come to see me."
Then he closed his eyes and was asleep.

Tun Shein made arrangements for the group to spend the night
in the partially finished house intended for another American
doctor, and then for Dr. Lewis.

That evening we invited the doctor to have dinner with us. He
was a pleasant enough fellow, and we were always starved for
company. Joe enjoyed discussing general medical problems with
him, and the Old Man's case in particular. After talking for a
while, we felt that the doctor was sincere in wanting to help the
Old Man, and that General Ne Win had sent the officials in good
faith.

The next morning the three made their way back to Dr. Seagrave's house. He was no more cordial than he had been before,
but he did consent to a quick examination by the visiting physician. When the examination was completed the visitors repeated
General Ne Win's offer of treatment in Rangoon. Then they
climbed into their Jeep and drove off to catch the returning convoy to Lashio. That was the last we saw or heard of them.

There were times when the Old Man seemed to rally. His respiration was more normal and his pulse approached regularity.
The diuretics had been partially successful and he had less
edema, though his ankles were still markedly swollen. But sometimes his condition would worsen, and each time he slipped back
a little further. His disposition never changed. It ranged from terrible to more terrible. He was miserable and seemed to want
everyone else to be miserable too.

I felt like a fifth wheel during those trying days. There was so little that I could do to help. Nobody could take Pansy's place, and she was the one who needed relief most. Often I went to the Old Man's house and just sat, either in his small room or in the living room. There were more nurses than were needed, and all other chores were well handled.

Dr. Violet carried the terrific hospital load. Joe spent most of his day at the Old Man's bedside, checking his pulse and respiration, giving an injection when necessary. As soon as he left the house, one of the nurses would come looking for him. Every night he was awakened by one of the girls at our bedroom window, calling, "Dr. Joe, please come. Daddy's heartbeat very irregular." Finally, in desperation, Joe took an air mattress and slept on the floor in the Old Man's living room.

One morning a cablegram arrived stating that Sterling, Dr. Seagrave's youngest son, was in Bangkok awaiting an entry visa to Burma. Though he made little response, the Old Man seemed cheered by the news. The big question was, how long would it take? Under ordinary circumstances the Burmese Government granted visas for twenty-four hours to people stopping over in Rangoon. But these were no ordinary circumstances, and we could only hope that out of respect for his father's many years of service to the people of Burma, the Revolutionary Council would allow Sterling into the country. The next hurdle was to get permission for him to travel to Namkham, which was in a restricted area. Our friend Leo Reddy, the vice-consul at the U.S. Embassy, was working on this, as were many others, including the ambassador, Henry Byroade.

The day after Sterling's cablegram arrived, I was in the Old Man's room. Joe had gone to check on a medication, and I was alone with Dr. Seagrave. I realized how very small the room was. Just large enough for the Old Man's single bed, a night table—on which sat a kerosene lamp, a package of cigarettes, several books, and a pair of glasses—a dresser, his padded chair, and a large bookcase filled with his favorite books. The Old Man claimed he couldn't sleep for more than four hours at a time and spent many nights reading by the light of his kerosene lamp after the generator had been turned off. He read his favorite books over and over, everything from historical novels to light reading to downright trash.

Another bookcase in the living room held two or three times as many books. The Old Man had read them all and had decided views about each one. I remembered once noticing a volume containing the three short books written by Dr. Tom Dooley. I asked Dr. Seagrave if I might read them, and he replied, "You can read that damn thing if you want to, but it's a waste of time. Tom Dooley wasn't really a doctor, he was a great showman. All he did was run around through the backwoods of Laos and Vietnam and set up worthless little medical dispensaries and turn them over to the natives to run. A lot they knew about treating sick people. The only way to do any good medically in these countries is to set up the best hospital you can in one place and stick with it like I've done here." I had recognized the old Seagrave ego coming through, but what he said made sense.

Now I went to examine the books more closely, and realized that Dr. Seagrave was watching me. I turned and rather foolishly asked, "How do you feel?"

He looked like some large white grizzly bear propped up in bed. His chin touched his chest, and his eyes were staring straight at me. He had eaten very little since his illness and his face was slack and gaunt. His toothless mouth hung open. Finally he dragged out the words, "Like hell, thank you." There was a long pause and then he drawled, "You're pregnant, aren't you?"

I was, in fact, about three months pregnant, but had kept the news within our family. My condition was becoming difficult to conceal, and yet I had kept quiet. I was enjoying my secret. So the Old Man's question surprised me somewhat, though I should have known better than to be surprised at anything he said.

"How did you know?" I asked meekly.

He took a few drags from his oxygen tube. "Oh, you can't fool me on something like that, even when I'm three-quarters dead. I can tell by the way you walk, how you look, and you can't hide everything under those *longyis*. I guess I have enough of the devil in me to see things other people can't. I don't know why it is, but all the American females who come here have felt it necessary to get pregnant. Maybe it's the long, cold winter nights. They seem to do wonders for the human production business."

I listened intently, for he didn't always speak clearly. Now his words were well spaced, although it had taken him several minutes to complete that short speech.

He went on, "I'm glad Sterling is on his way here. God knows, he'll make it if the Burmese Government will cooperate. Sterling is a writer and a funny guy. We never could get along well. He's too much like me, I guess. I hope John can come. John's a fine, sensitive boy, and he'll go far in this old world. He's a graduate of M.I.T. A man can't be a fool and walk off from there with a diploma. His wife is a Swiss girl. He was in Europe a few years ago, and when this girl waited on him in a restaurant he knew right away that she was for him. He wouldn't leave for the U.S. until she had promised to marry him. She took him to meet her parents, and right away they started calling him 'son' and he knew he had it made. They have a little girl and an infant son. Regi, that's my Swiss daughter-in-law, writes to me and always sends pictures of the children. I've never met her, but I can tell she's just what John needs. And she calls me Daddy, too." With that he closed his eyes and was asleep again.

I began to reassess my thinking about this man who lay there so desperately ill. There had been times when I had despised him for his egotism and hated him for his profanity and what I considered his misuse of other people. Had I misjudged him? Now he was like any old man who loved a daughter-in-law he had never seen because she wrote to him and called him Daddy. Half lying and half sitting on his deathbed, he didn't seem the tyrant

I had often thought, and instead of hate I felt pity.

He was dying from a combination of diseases and would probably never leave that room until he was carried out for the last time. He had devoted his life to a dream, his hospital, and it was now a question of which would collapse first, he or his dream. He was fully aware of the problem. That's probably what was killing him.

The next day we received a telegram from Sterling. After a delay of eight days in Bangkok he had finally reached Rangoon. He was to take the Friday morning plane to Lashio and asked that someone meet him. Tun Shein rarely left the Old Man's house— night after night he slept there, either sitting up in a chair or sprawled on the living room floor—so Chuck drove the ambulance to meet Sterling.

Lulu, Tun Shein's wife, said sadly, "Sterling not here sixteen years now. Now he come for a very sad reason."

When I met Sterling I was startled by his resemblance to the Old Man. He looked exactly as his father must have looked years before. He was perhaps thirty years old and about six feet tall, with a shock of hair hanging over his forehead and a rakish mustache. He came into the lab with Pansy and Augusta, and Augusta clung to his hand. She had never met him, but evidently he represented to her all that was good; now that "Uncle Sterling" was with them, she felt "Grandy" would be all right. Sterling introduced himself to me and extended his hand. I noticed that he had a decided tremor, unusual in one so young. He was very likable, and I got the impression that he was a man who had been places and done things.

The Burmese Government had not permitted Sterling to travel alone. An official from the foreign office in Rangoon was with him, and in Lashio they had been joined by an intelligence officer. Sterling's visa was for two weeks. The two men were to watch and protect him, and see that he left promptly when his time was up.

March 18th was Dr. Seagrave's sixty-eighth birthday. In the evening, the entire group of student nurses stood in the yard beneath his window and serenaded him. Their final song was one of the Old Man's favorites, "Going Home" from Dvorak's "New World Symphony." There were tears in the eyes of many of the girls because they knew how appropriate the song really was.

A few days after Sterling's arrival, word was received that John, his wife, and their two small children were on their way. No one knew exactly where they were or when they would arrive at Namkham, but the Old Man was excited by the news. He seemed to be holding death at arm's length, as though he was determined with every stubborn ounce of strength to live to see John and his family.

Then we heard that John had arrived in Rangoon. It was expected that the family would take the same Friday flight to Lashio that Sterling had taken the week before. This time Tun Shein made the drive. He returned just before dusk, grim-faced and with an empty Jeep. The Seagraves had not been on the plane.

This was a shock to everyone, especially to the Old Man. He was despondent and felt he couldn't hang on any longer. He begged Joe to give him an overdose of a sedative. "You know I can't do that, Doc," was Joe's reply. "I couldn't live with myself. If I did that, I'd have to go along with you."

The Old Man reached out, took hold of Joe's hand, and said quietly, "Let's go."

Abruptly, Joe asked one of the nurses to prepare the usual sedative so the patient could rest, and the Old Man was soon asleep.

John had indeed arrived in Rangoon, but permission for the family to travel up-country had been delayed, causing them to miss the Friday plane. There was no plane until the following Tuesday. Their only alternative was to take a train to Mandalay. Tun Shein met them there on Saturday. When they finally reached Namkham late that night the Old Man was in a coma and was not aware of their presence until the next day.

John and Sterling immediately wired Ambassador Byroade in Rangoon, urgently requesting a special respirator. Mr. Byroade and his staff not only secured a respirator from a U.S. military hospital in Bangkok, but also enlisted the services of Burma's best known heart and lung specialist, Dr. Ronald Lwin.

Since U.S. military aircraft were forbidden to fly over Burma, Embassy officials rented a Burmese plane to make the flight. Originally the plane was to land on a small airstrip at Muse, a town just twenty miles from Namkham. But during the flight, word was received over the plane's radio that they would have to land at Lashio (a much longer drive for Tun Shein, who was to pick up the respirator and Dr. Lwin). Since Muse was situated directly on the Burma-China border, it would have been necessary for the plane to pass over a small area of Chinese territory in making its landing approach. And this might have touched off an international incident which neither Burma nor the United States wanted.

At first, I was furious at the grand plans of Dr. Seagrave's sons. Pansy, Tun Shein, Joe, and the nursing staff at Namkham had given unstintingly of their time for almost a month, taking care of the Old Man and putting up with his hell-raising. They had done for him everything that they could—and much more than he willingly permitted. He had been offered the medical services of the Burmese Government and had been urged to go to Rangoon for treatment, all of which he had refused. Well, if Mohammed would not go to the mountain, these two sons were determined to bring the mountain to Mohammed, and were doing rather well at it.

However, I soon changed my mind, especially with regard to John. He felt a deep responsibility to insure that everything possible was done for his father's comfort and recovery. John appeared to have all the good qualities the Old Man had attributed to him. He was a little older than Sterling and apparently of a much more gentle disposition. He resembled his father and brother, but he had no mustache and very little hair.

The nurses responded immediately to Regi and loved her dearly. She was young and slim, wore her golden blonde hair in a short bob, and walked barefoot about the compound. She looked extremely attractive in a *longyi* and *engyi*. As for the children, the nurses could not get enough of carrying them about and entertaining them.

John and his family also had been required to travel with an officer from the foreign office and an intelligence officer. Our Namkham population was growing by leaps and bounds.

The Old Man, genuinely pleased to see John, rallied enough to talk a bit and to admire his grandchildren. I felt it was a great shame that he had deliberately deprived himself of such pleasures for most of his life. But he had told us many times that his hospital meant more to him than anything else, including his family, and he had sacrificed all for it.

Dr. Lwin, the Burmese specialist, was a man in his fifties with an expanding waistline, thinning hair, glasses, and an air of self-importance. He was a fish out of water at Namkham. His professional career had been spent in the city and he didn't seem to care for the rural life with its inconveniences and potential dangers. He spent one day examining the patient and touring the compound, and left the following morning. His only suggestion was to change the type of diuretic being used.

On Saturday, March 27, the Old Man seemed better than he had been in over a month. John and Sterling even considered going home and returning in the near future, when their father might be strong enough to visit with them.

Then, on Sunday morning, March 28, Joe went to the Old Man's house to make his morning call. He was at the front gate when he heard a frantic voice: "Dr. Joe, come quickly!"

Joe had heard that call dozens of times over the past month, but this time it seemed more urgent. He brushed passed the family standing in the narrow hallway, and entered the small room. The nurses were attempting to connect the special breathing apparatus, but it was too late. The Old Man had breathed his last.

I had been sitting at the desk in our living room writing my biweekly letter to my family when Tim came to my side and said quietly, "Mom, Dad told me to come tell you that Dr. Seagrave is dead."

I couldn't believe it. He had passed crisis after crisis and had clung to life. He had even begun to improve ever so slightly. This was the time I least expected to hear the words "Dr. Seagrave is dead."

I hurried down the familiar alley past the truck barn, through the gate, and into the flower-filled yard. When I got there, I wondered what my hurry had been, for there was nothing I could do. Pansy and one or two nurses were in the Old Man's room behind closed doors. I had no words for the members of the family, huddled together in stunned silence in the living room. Joe passed me and didn't even notice me.

Slowly I retraced my steps and returned home. In the distance the clang of the iron bar against the tire rim announced that church services would soon begin, but I didn't feel like sitting still. The nanny was about to take the boys for a walk, so I dismissed her and took them myself. We went down the hill from our house, up the next hill to the cluster of hospital buildings, past the surgical ward and nurses' home, and started down again toward town. There, in one of our favorite spots, I sat beside the road while the boys threw rocks into the rice paddies far below. People were bathing and doing their laundry in the little stream that ran through the paddies, as they did every morning. Now and then an ancient vehicle struggled toward us, or a plodding oxcart or a Shan pushing his bicycle up the steep grade. In the tiny bamboo sheds beside the stream, Shan women pounded out the wet pulp which they stretched on frames to dry in the sun.

Later it would be sold as coarse brown paper.

I heard the sound of a truck, and I recognized the old weapons carrier grinding up the hill with a load of lumber. It was the Shan teak which had been ordered and carefully set aside for the Old Man's casket. Now it was on the way to the carpenter's shop.

I began to wonder why I was so disturbed at the Old Man's death. We had expected it for weeks. He had been no one special to me. I had never wished him dead, heaven forbid, but sometimes I had been so angry with him that I had felt that the world in general—and Namkham in particular—would be better off without him.

Then, as I looked over the broad expanse of the Shweli Valley, I knew that no one had lived and died in that valley over the past forty-three years without coming into contact with Gordon Seagrave. He had treated their ills, excised their tumors, and cursed their backwardness. He had renounced a more comfortable way of life to work in that far corner of the earth. Undoubtedly he had been lonely many times, but there was no indication that he had ever regretted his decision. He had constructed his own kingdom on the hill, and in that small spot of earth—if in no other— he had been the final authority. Perhaps the adjustments and sacrifices he had made were not because of a deepseated drive to be a humanitarian, but because that way of life nourished his ego. The more I thought about it, the more I was convinced that this was not necessarily in his disfavor. After all, very few people are pure humanitarians, suffering privation solely for the benefit of others. In the Old Man's case, the end result had been good. Whether they loved him or not, thousands of people throughout the Union of Burma were better off because of his work.

CHAPTER THIRTEEN

THE FUNERAL

The news of the Old Man's death spread rapidly throughout the valley. Women crouching amidst the confusion and filth of the bazaar whispered to one another, "The old American doctor on the hill has died." Men standing in the rice paddies, thrusting young seedlings into the ground, said to one another, "The Old Man is dead." And so it went. As far away as Lashio the Old Man's passing was soon common knowledge.

The curious from Namkham began to file slowly up the steep clay hill, still slippery from a recent rain. Dressed in their black skirts and white blouses, towels wrapped about their heads, the women carried their black umbrellas to shield them against the sun. The men, in their brown baggy pants and gray-tinged shirts and headwraps, followed. Before noon on the day the Old Man died, the compound was crowded with curious onlookers who milled about, strolled past the Old Man's house, and then squatted in the shade nearby.

217

Work was begun on the coffin immediately. From our house I could hear the incessant sawing and hammering in the carpenter shop. The sound depressed me, and I spent most of that day, March 28th, 1965, walking with the children about the compound, away from the carpenter shop. But there was no letup. At dusk, lights were strung about the open shop and the work continued.

That night a service was held at the Old Man's house. Every inch of floor space was covered; all the people who came to the regular Sunday night service were there, and many more. Scriptures were read, the Old Man's favorite hymns were sung, and many words were spoken. The service dragged on and was very solemn indeed. Finally an elderly Karen, dressed in a uniform left over from the days of the Karen Rebellion, rose to his feet. He had a straggly gray beard and smelled heavily of cheap liquor. As he began to speak in perfect English, many smiled uneasily and shifted about, wondering what this unpredictable one might say or do. His first words were, "I have known Gordon Seagrave for many years, and I am going to miss him. Now, if you will excuse me, I am going to say goodby to my good friend."

With that, he tottered off across the room, weaving among the silent people sitting on the floor, and headed toward the door which led into the hall. Tun Shein and Pansy looked anxious. Many of the onlookers hid snickers behind their hands. Since his death that morning, the Old Man's body had lain in his bed behind closed doors. Later that evening following the service, Joe and Dr. Violet were to prepare it, although they had no real means of embalming. There was no hurry, for the coffin was still far from complete. I watched as the old fellow disappeared behind the curtain which hung over the doorway, wondering what would happen next. After a few minutes he returned quietly, apparently satisfied, and the meeting came to a close.

Joe was very late returning home. He had not had enough rest for weeks and after this trying day he was exhausted. He and Dr.

Violet had closed themselves in the small poorly lit morgue with the Old Man's body, and worked for hours, accomplishing what preservation they could. After their work was done, the nurses who had been with Dr. Seagrave for many years dressed him in the one suit he owned. I had heard him say that he did not intend to wear it again until he was buried.

By now it was long past midnight. The coffin still was not ready, so the Old Man's body was laid out on the bed in the guestroom. The last sound I heard, when I finally closed my eyes, was the screech of the electric saw.

After the carpenters had completed the coffin, the women took over. The interior was lined with gleaming white satin, and the outside was covered with a rich black velveteen carefully tacked in place. The finished product was beautiful. It was a very large coffin, and shaped in the old-fashioned way, tapering toward the foot. It was probably no longer than an American coffin, but much deeper. Once the body was placed inside, the lid was sealed, but a rectangular glass window had been placed directly above the Old Man's head, so that all could view him for the last time. As I gazed into the depth of the coffin, I had the odd illusion that the body was a dozen feet below me.

The U.S. Embassy in Rangoon had been notified of the Old Man's death, and permission was granted by the Burmese Government for Donald Ellson, the consul at Mandalay, and Bob Mount, the press attache from Rangoon, to attend the funeral as official representatives of the United States Government. The funeral was scheduled for Wednesday afternoon, March 31.

We knew Mr. Ellson and had met Mr. Mount, so it was arranged that they should stay at our house during their two days at Namkham. It was a rare experience for them to be allowed in that restricted area, and they were eager to see and photograph the hospital about which they had heard so much.

An Anglo-Burman by the name of Peter Boog, the Associated Press representative in Burma, arrived with a Burmese photographer on Monday. Thus, the American newspapers were soon flooded with material about the Old Man's death. I learned about this weeks later from my family, who anxiously read every news item they could find. For some reason, my letters to them at that time were greatly delayed, and they were fearful that some trouble had befallen us.

The Burmese Government seemed to take no notice of the Old Man's passing. They sent no message of condolence, nor did they send an official representative to the funeral. That was a sore point with John and Sterling, who felt that their father's long hard years of service entitled him to some recognition. But it was a different government, and times had changed. No matter what a person had accomplished in Burma or for the Burmese people, if he carried another nationality he was a foreigner and had no business in Burma any longer. This was mute testimony to the lesson I had been learning during the past year and a half: the governments of small countries of the world did not appreciate help from well-meaning people, whether individuals or countries. They wanted money and more money, and they exchanged dollars for contempt when the fancy struck them.

Don Ellson and Bob Mount were eager to see the countryside around Namkham, but they were placed under such tight restrictions by the government that they could not even leave the hospital compound. Finally, Tun Shein arranged for them to take a trip to the suspension bridge over the Shweli River. I decided to go along, expecting that the two men and I, and perhaps a driver, would go to the bridge, take a few pictures, and return. My first surprise came when our driver turned the Jeep in the direction of the army camp instead of toward town. Heading straight for the gate of the camp, he drove inside and stopped before one of the crude buildings.

Amazed, I asked Don Ellson, "What on earth are we doing here?"

"Well, it seems that the Burmese officials don't want to take any chances with Bob and me since we're official representatives of the U.S. Government. They're sending along an armed escort to protect us."

There had been occasional insurgent uprisings outside of Namkham, and particularly near the bridge, but the thought that any harm would come to us had never occurred to me. Joe and I and the children had driven to the bridge before and no one had stopped us. But perhaps that had been because we never informed anyone that we were going!

After a short wait, six armed soldiers in full battle dress climbed into the jeep parked near us, and indicated that we were to follow them. In Namkham we stopped and picked up the town officer, who looked and acted bored as we bounced off down the narrow road.

Due to the condition of the road we always drove slowly, but that day we were really traveling at a snail's pace as the soldiers ahead scanned the hillsides. About six miles out of town, as we were nearing the bridge, our escort stopped and directed our driver to park beside the road. While two soldiers stood guard, the other four took off and began to climb a rather steep hill near which we would soon pass. A few minutes later they emerged on the road about a half mile away. It was later explained that the hill was a favorite spot from which snipers could prey on unsuspecting motorists.

After the brief delay, we proceeded to the bridge. From a small outpost nearby soldiers guarded the bridge and checked each vehicle before it was allowed to cross.

The scene was a familiar one to me, but I viewed it now with great interest. The bridge itself, perhaps a hundred yards long, was suspended on large cables buried in the rocks on either side. The river flowed by with a slow, steady current some fifty feet below, but during the rainy season it was a raging torrent. On either side of the river, disappearing down into the water, was the twisted wreckage of the original bridge, destroyed by American bombs during the Japanese occupation.

While the two men snapped pictures, I sat in the back of the Jeep and watched the flow of traffic to and from the Kachin State, whose boundary was a short distance across the bridge. On the way home the soldiers stopped again to scout the same hill, and then we proceeded to the hospital compound. After the soldiers escorted us sagely to our back door they drove away, obviously glad to be rid of us.

The morning of March 31, 1965, dawned bright and clear. With the coming of the dawn the people gathered, for few had watches, and they simply rose with the dawn and went to bed when it was dark. There were Shans, Kachins, Karens, Paloungs, Chinese, and others, most of them dressed colorfully in their native costumes. They came by oxcart, bus, and bicycle, and some walked from their villages in the hills. From early morning until afternoon people streamed up the hill, into the Old Man's house, to the room where he lay. There they paused to look down into the coffin for a last glimpse of the stubborn old man. Then they shuffled out the front door and squatted in the shade to wait. Some of them placed floral pieces near the huge black coffin. There were Easter lilies and Canna lilies in profusion, and many other spring flowers.

At two that afternoon there was a short service at the house. People sat on the floor in every room. After the service, the line began to form for the procession to the church. At the head of the group were the three ministers: Donald Crider, a missionary from Kutkai, Saya Daniel Tun Baw, the pastor of the Namkham church, and an aged Shan minister from Muse, Saya Kham Maung, who had known Dr. Seagrave since his early days in the Shan States.

Father Cadei from Kutkai had been asked to read the scripture in the church and at the graveside. At first he had agreed, then he changed his mind and would not participate formally in the service. He realized that the funeral would receive wide publicity, and he confided to me that he was afraid of criticism from his superiors if he took part in a Protestant service.

Immediately behind the ministers came the casket, draped with an American flag and carried by eight Burmese soldiers. Since there were no handles on the huge casket, four heavy cloth straps were placed under it and over the shoulders of the soldiers.

The family walked behind the casket. First, John and Regi, then Sterling with Pansy and Augusta. Father Cadei walked beside Regi and John, the Roman Catholic members of the family.

Behind the family was the long line of nurses. Two by two they came. First the staff, followed by the fourth-year, third-year, second-year, and first-year students. Each nurse carried a floral piece to the church, making a most colorful and beautiful procession.

Joe and I chose to walk behind the last of the nurses, and behind us was the public.

The route from the house to the church was hardly a quarter of a mile, but that day it seemed much longer. The sun beat down mercilessly, and the dust from the road filled our nostrils and throats. Many of the girls covered their faces with handkerchiefs, giving an impression of deep grief, but they may have been only trying to filter out the dust. Whether or not they were genuinely mourning was hard to tell, for it was their custom to hide emotion. People crowded both sides of the road, pushing this way and that, and obstructing the progress of the procession. The casket was so heavy that the pallbearers were forced to stop every few feet and set down their burden. When they were tired, eight others would step up to take their places.

When we finally reached the church we found it already filled with people who had been sitting there for hours in order to be sure of a seat. The front rows had been reserved for the family and staff nurses, but the rest of us were left standing outside. Joe directed the students to sit in the aisles, and he and I found standing room in the rear.

The service was short. Each of the three ministers read from the scripture and said a prayer; an obituary was read, and a choir of nurses sang two of Dr. Seagrave's favorite hymns.

The long procession formed again and we moved toward the small cemetery a few yards from the church. There were grunts and groans as the pallbearers struggled to lift the casket up and over the stile which crossed the fence around the church.

The grave had been dug in the exact spot the Old Man had specified. On one side was the massive rock tomb of Dr. Grace Seagrave, on the other a smaller version where seven-year-old Gordon, Jr., was buried. The new grave had been lined with cement blocks, and into that small spot in the earth were laid the remains of Gordon Stifler Seagrave.

That night a brief service was held in the living room of the Seagrave home. Tun Shein ably summarized the feelings of most of us. In fact, there were times when I thought he must be talking directly to me. He said, "Many of you were often angry with Dr. Seagrave and harbored ill feelings toward him. You felt that he treated you unfairly and dealt harshly with you. I have felt that way. But I think that he did those things to make us do our very best. He was not a lazy man and he could not stand to have lazy people around him, or people who did not do the very best work of which they were capable. Dr. Seagrave did many fine, unselfish things in his lifetime, and I do not know about you, but it is for these things I will remember him, and nothing else. He will live on because of them."

Early the following morning John and his family and Sterling left Namkham to return to America. Their time had run out and the Burmese Government refused to let them stay. They must have left with heavy hearts, not only because of the loss of their father, but because of the great uncertainty about the future of the hospital. I'm sure they realized that probably they would never again be allowed to return to the spot where they had spent their early years.

We learned later that as they were winding down from the hills on the most treacherous part of the road into Lashio, the unmarked car in which Sterling and the Burmese escorts were traveling was fired upon by rebels or bandits. They escaped unhurt, and the Namkham ambulance in which John and his family rode was not bothered when it passed the same spot a few minutes later.

CHAPTER FOURTEEN

FINAL
DEPORTATION
ORDERS

After the Old Man's funeral, our life resumed its routine. Joe and Dr. Violet continued to handle surgery and patient care. The only major adjustment was in the nurses' training school, where the Old Man had done almost all the teaching. Joe met with Tun Shein and the senior staff nurses, and the responsibility for the courses then underway was delegated to various people. Pansy was well qualified to teach, and Emily could handle the chores of midwifery, with the help of Grandma and others. Government exams for the first- and third-year students in preliminary and final sick nursing were due within a month, so review classes were begun. Joe taught a group, and I started a class to review the phases of laboratory work.

We also had the assistance of a delightful young Chinese, Matthew Yang, who lived in Namkham. He had just completed his second year at the medical school in Mandalay, and since his education was being paid for by the A.M.C.B. at the recommendation of Dr. Seagrave, he spent his free time doing odd jobs at the hospital. He worked in the lab and the office, observed in the operating room, and cooperated wherever he could. I was especially grateful for his services as interpreter in my review class. Even if the girls understood English fairly well, they absorbed so little the first time around, and I hoped they might learn more if the information was repeated in Burmese.

We were of help to Matthew, too. His problem was a critical need for clothing. He was due to return to school in Mandalay in a few weeks and his entire wardrobe consisted of one pair of trousers, a few shirts, and several *longyis*. Like most students, he wore western clothes, but often fell back on the comfortable *longyis* because they were readily available and much less expensive.

I rummaged through Joe's clothes, most of them unworn since we had left Bradenton, and discovered two suits still in good condition, and some new white shirts. But alas, when Matthew tried on the suits, they were much too big for him and he looked like Charlie Chaplin in his early movies. It was impossible to cut the suits to fit, so I showed Matthew an old Sears Roebuck catalog and let him wish a while. He had never seen pictures of so many beautiful clothes, and was surprised to know that Americans could go into one store containing all those items of clothing, and make a choice. I assured him that this was so, except for paying the bill. If he would select some things, I would see if Fanny Ellison in New York would have them sent to him. It was hard for him to decide, but he finally chose a suit, a sport coat, two pairs of trousers, three white shirts, a belt, and some ties. I took his measurements, filled out the order blank, and sent it to Fanny with a letter.

Fanny was most cooperative, but since our catalog was two years out of date she had to make all sorts of changes. When the large bundle reached Matthew about three months later, none of the items were exactly what he had picked out, but he thought they were the most magnificent clothes he had ever seen, and, indeed, they probably were.

In addition to Matthew, there was a young man from Namkham, known to me as Robin, who came to the hospital every day to learn lab work. He had finished high school, or the Burmese equivalent, and had taken the matriculation exam. If he passed that, he would be allowed to go to college, after which he hoped to study medicine. But he couldn't be sure that he would be allowed to do this, for the government was the final authority. While he waited to hear the results of the matric, as the exam was called, he was spending his time profitably at the hospital. He was a very bright boy, and once he had learned the basic tests he took a responsible part in the running of the lab. Since he was not a paid employee, he could have coasted along, but he took his work seriously. Robin's family had been supporters of the hospital and its allied school for many years. His aunt had been one of the earliest graduates of the school of nursing, and his two sisters, Rose and Colleen, had both taught at the Shweli Valley School. It was a pleasure for me to know all of them.

One morning while brushing my teeth, I looked in the small bathroom mirror and noticed that my face seemed lopsided. The right side was very swollen and there was a big lump just in front of the ear. By that time I had a fair-sized lump in my abdomen, but I had never known pregnancy to affect my face too. When I took my first bite of breakfast and was struck with excruciating pains on the right side of my face, the awful truth dawned. I had mumps. Most of our boys had had mumps a few weeks before, but having escaped the disease for thirty-six years, I felt secure in my immunity. The year before I had blossomed out with German measles during an epidemic. Now it seemed to me that I had entered my second childhood.

I managed to get along very well with my mumps. The only time I was really bothered was at mealtime, but I persevered through the torture. Another person might have given up eating temporarily and thereby lost a few pounds, but not I. I have rarely been so sick that eating was not a pleasure.

My pregnancy was progressing and gave me no special trouble. I had the usual petty discomforts, but I had learned to live with those long ago and would have felt lost without an occasional bout of heartburn or swollen ankles. I was enjoying myself and looking forward to having another baby. Joe was the one who was anxious, though he managed to conceal it. He was going to deliver the baby, and whereas he had performed thousands of deliveries, I was a unique patient. I wasn't worried, for to me he was not only the best obstetrician in Burma, he was the best anywhere. I looked forward to sharing this experience with him.

We had made all our plans, though the big event was still months away. The delivery room at the hospital was nothing more than a small unpainted room with a homemade wooden table, so we decided that my baby was going to be born in the operating room. It had a professional look, at least, and there were facilities for administering an anesthetic. I didn't consider myself a sissy, but I wasn't a nature woman either.

The only thing that concerned me was the possibility of a premature baby or one which needed particular attention. Our method of protecting premature babies was simply to wrap an extra blanket around them to keep them nice and warm. There was no special equipment of any kind. But the possibility that my baby would be born early was so remote that it held no great anxiety for me.

We did, however, have other, more acute problems. First of all, Joe did not look well to me. Soon after our arrival at Namkham, he had contracted two or three respiratory illnesses from patients. None of them had been severe and he had recovered in due time, but they had taken their toll. He had begun to lose weight, and he had continued to do so. By early 1965 he was thirty pounds lighter than when we had left Bradenton. His appetite was poor, principally because he didn't care for our predominately rice diet.

I had been raised on a rice farm in southwest Louisiana, so rice was almost as important to me as to the Burmese, but Joe regarded it as a tasteless, vitaminless mass of starch. Perhaps my concern for him was mixed with envy that he was so slim and trim while I was growing steadily in the opposite direction.

Our biggest headache was how to keep the hospital in operation. We had had no shipment of drugs from the United States in over two years, since the Burmese Government had decided to demand an exorbitant duty. We were able to obtain small amounts of certain things from the Burma Pharmaceutical Company, but our supply of usable drugs was dwindling daily. Joe was rarely able to order the drug of his choice for a disease. Instead, he had to search through the drug room for a substitute, often of doubtful therapeutic value.

Each day he came home from the hospital a little more discouraged. Finally, one afternoon he flopped down on the bed and said, "Susie, I know where this thing is going to end, but I'd be much happier if I knew when. We're gradually being squeezed to death. This morning we had three new suspected cases of typhoid from Monwing, and I couldn't treat them. Yesterday a patient had a ruptured amebic abscess and all I could do was give him a triple dose of an antibiotic that had been out of date for two years. It's getting so I don't feel I am doing enough good to justify our being here."

"What did you mean by saying that you know where it's going to end?"

"I guess I don't even know that exactly. Eventually the government is going to take over the hospital. They're bound to. The big question is whether they are going to run us out before we run out of drugs, or before they nationalize the hospital."

Just then I heard the sound of a man clearing his throat, and looked up to find Tun Shein at the door of the bedroom. I never did adjust to having people suddenly appear in the house that way, but it was the custom to leave one's slippers at the door and pad noiselessly in without knocking. With the traffic in our house, I found it safe always to be fully clothed.

Tun Shein came into the room and sat down on the edge of the bed beside Joe. Evidently he had heard the last of our conversation and he said, "I know you are discouraged. We all are. But God will see us through somehow. Pansy and I have decided to drive to Rangoon in a few days. We must see about securing a headstone for the Old Man's grave which the U.S. Embassy has promised to give, and while we are there I will pay a call on the Burmese Minister of Health. It is possible, now that the Old Man is gone, that the government may allow another American doctor to take over that visa."

I felt a surge of enthusiasm and hope. "Do you really think they might? I mean, is there any chance another American doctor may be able to come here?"

"Well," Tun Shein replied, and he slurred the words in his usual way, "there's a chance. Up to now, we have tried to be as quiet as possible and not attract attention from the government. That's the way the Old Man wanted it, and it was probably the best policy. But now, I feel that we have nothing to lose by asking for a few things. They can only say no." To Joe, he added, "Why don't you and Violet make out a list of drugs you feel are absolutely necessary? While I am in Rangoon I will send the list on to Fanny and she can have them sent to us. Order the bare minimum, because we'll have to pay duty."

Joe seemed to brighten. He and Violet made their list, and I added a few things that were sorely needed in the lab. The instrument on which we determined hemoglobins had been broken, so I ordered two new ones, and some white cell pipettes, plus a few essential reagents. Then, with prayerful hearts, we saw Tun Shein and Pansy off to Rangoon.

They were gone for two weeks, and during that time my thoughts were constantly with them. Had they been able to see the Minister of Health? If so, what had been his reaction to Tun

Shein's suggestions? What was in store for us?

The first evening Tun Shein was back at Namkham, he came to our house after supper. He looked tired and discouraged, and I could tell instantly that all had not gone well. He slouched down in the big chair in our living room and said, "Well, I saw the Minister of Health. When I suggested that another American doctor be allowed to come to Namkham, he laughed. His very words were, 'There will be no more American doctors in Burma, and since all Burmese doctors are in government service, you will have to do without them as well. I cannot help you, but I will not interfere at this time, so you are free to do the best you can with what you have. The health of the people is the business of the government, and we will attend to it in our way.'"

I was too crushed to answer, and Joe too said nothing. We sat in silence, and I was aware of Wong Jack washing dishes in the kitchen. Tun Shein added, "I didn't bother to send the list of drugs on to Fanny."

I felt like crying. Fighting to keep my voice steady, I said, "But it's not fair. They aren't ready to take the hospital and run it, and they won't let us have the things we need to do it ourselves. They're slowly squeezing us to death. And what about us, Joe and me? How long are we going to have to stay here? We've been here almost two years now, and I'm getting anxious to know when we can go home. If we knew we were going to be at Namkham six months longer, we could begin to make plans. As it is, we can't. Joe can't leave Violet alone with all this work, and there isn't any hope of getting anyone else up here. We're trapped."

I was instantly sorry that I had spoken so harshly. I *did* feel trapped, but one look at Tun Shein and I remembered that the future he faced was much less bright than ours. If and when the hospital was taken over, he would be without a job, and he didn't have a comfortable life waiting for him back in America. He looked very tired, and more discouraged than I had ever seen him.

Joe, shifted in his chair, and said, "I've been so disgusted these last few weeks that it wouldn't have taken much for me to pack up and head for home. The only thing that's saved me has been your faithfulness and optimism. Now those people in Rangoon have got me so mad that I'll stay here and rot unless they run me out first. They really want us to throw up our hands and give in so they can say they had to take over the hospital because we weren't able to run it. I'll be damned if I'll let them say that."

"You're already beginning to sound like the Old Man," I muttered.

Tun Shein rose wearily from his chair. "We must go on as long as we are allowed to do so. We must live each day for itself, not worrying about tomorrow." Then turning to me he added, "Please be patient. God will see us through."

We went on, day by day, always wondering if it might be the last day. Drugs were getting more scarce and equipment was wearing out. Nothing was wasted. Surgical sponges were washed and resterilized over and over until they were mere shreds. Our white cell pipettes in the lab were chipped, but there were no replacements, so we used them anyway.

Everywhere there were signs that the government was flexing its muscles. One hundred and forty private schools throughout the country were taken over in one sweep, most of them Baptist and Catholic mission schools. The largest schools were appropriated first, the smaller ones left for another day. There were not enough government teachers to carry the load of the extra schools, and in many schools the children in the higher grades were placed in charge of the younger children. Nuns were told that they would not be allowed to teach unless they removed their robes. Some of the Burmese nuns stayed on at the schools doing odd jobs, but many of the missionary nuns returned to their home countries.

We had no inkling of what they intended to do about the few

private hospitals. Rumors flew thick and fast. The most persistent
one was that the government was waiting until the next class of
medical students graduated so there would be doctors to staff the
hospitals. That time was months away.

To keep up morale and provide entertainment for the nurses,
Chuck planned a gigantic athletic tournament. It gave us our
brightest moments during that spring of 1965. There was competition between the classes in softball and volleyball, as well as
singles, doubles, and mixed doubles in badminton. Probably the
most hard-fought games were in softball. Various members of the
staff were parceled out to the student nurse teams, and Joe and I
were placed with the fourth-year students. I was really too pregnant to be cavorting around a softball diamond, but I needed the
exercise, and my doctor gave his okay. I did my own batting but
had one of the girls run for me. I played first base since I could
catch pretty well, and it didn't require much moving about. Joe
pitched for our team, and with him scooping up the short
grounders and firing them over to me on first base, we shaped up
as the team to beat. Actually, we did win that tournament.

In our first game against the second-year girls, one of their run-
ners bumped into me, sending us both sprawling. I wasn't hurt
but the poor girl was so embarrassed that she ran off the field.
After that episode, the opposing team players were so afraid of
hurting me that they scarcely ran after batting. Our team was accused of taking unfair advantage!

I also entered the badminton singles competition, not realizing
how strenuous it was going to be. In my first match I was paired
against a second-year student named Mumu, and without half
trying, Mumu turned me every way but loose. I comforted myself
with the thought that she was twenty years younger, twenty-five
pounds lighter, and not pregnant.

The second-year class emerged as the over-all winner, and an
awards presentation ceremony was held on the softball field. Individual winners were given small gifts and a huge plaque was

presented to the second-year girls. It was planned to have the tournament each year and to have the plaque engraved with the winning class. I had the pleasure of giving out the awards, since the money to pay for them came from our home church. Months before, the Junior High group at Westminster Presbyterian in Bradenton had raised seventy dollars selling Christmas cards and had sent the money to us. I had suggested that half the money should go to the church on the compound and half should be used to entertain the student nurses in some way. The thirty-five dollars set aside for the nurses took care of the awards. It couldn't have been better spent.

I presented the other thirty-five-dollar-check to Pastor Tun Baw for the church. After much deliberation, it was decided to buy a bell to replace the tire rim used to announce the services. There was a belfry over the church, but it had been without a bell since the days of the Japanese occupation, when it had been taken down and melted for bullets. Now we found that there was not a bell to be had in all of Burma, and I do not know into whose pocket the money finally came to rest.

June 5, 1965, began like any other day. The rainy season was just getting underway and by ten in the morning we had had a quick shower. The rice seedlings in the paddies had long since been transplanted and were growing well in their soft water bed. This meant that the farmers had time to visit the hospital to be treated for general backache, or to have abscesses drained, or for any number of major or minor ills. As a result, the hospital was jammed with patients of all ages with a wide variety of medical and surgical disorders.

When the patient load was greatest our lab work was also at its peak. I was busy at my small table by the window helping some of the students set up Kahn tests when I saw Chuck run up the back steps of our building. He was carrying a brown envelope, and as he reached the top step he caught my eye and smiled before hurrying on. Tun Shein had been sick for several days, which meant that Chuck had taken over the administrative chores in the office.

Later, I wondered why I had particularly noticed Chuck that morning, or why the brown envelope had left an impression on me. It was not uncommon to see him hurrying to and from the office with papers. But I remembered that when he smiled, he looked as though he had been caught off guard and wished I had not seen him.

Shortly after lunch, when Joe was relaxing before treating the hordes in the outpatient clinic and I was preparing Timmy's lessons for the afternoon, Chuck quietly appeared. In his hand was the same brown envelope. Indicating the letter, he told us immediately why he had come. "This came for you this morning from the Burmese Immigration Office. It is only a form letter and it is written in Burmese. I have read it over several times, and so has Uncle Tun Shein. It is very difficult to translate directly into English and be sure we are getting the exact meaning."

As he talked he removed the letter from the envelope and handed it to Joe. I could see that it was only one page, a printed form with certain blank spaces filled in by typewriter. Other than that, I understood nothing.

"What do you and Tun Shein think it means?" Joe asked as he returned the paper to Chuck.

Chuck said hesitantly, "In essence it says that your visa will be extended to August 12th of this year, and after that time you must be out of the country, under penalty of the law."

It was strange how this news affected me. I couldn't have felt less concerned if Chuck had said that another rain shower was expected at two p.m. A year and a half before we had waited daily for some word from the Immigration Department, and as the weeks and months slipped by I had almost forgotten that we might hear from them. Now that the letter had come, I felt completely detached.

Outwardly, Joe seemed unmoved as well. Slowly and deliberately, he filled his pipe, lit it, and settled himself more comfortably on the couch before answering. "But why do they say that our visa will be extended until August 12th when we have never had a visa to extend? Could this be good news in a strange sort of way? Are we being given a visa until August, after which we can apply for another one?"

"Maybe, but I don't think so. Uncle Tun Shein thinks this is an answer to the appeal he took to Rangoon in December of 1963. He says it has taken them one and a half years to act, and their answer is no. They are giving you two months to get out. It is very hard to translate and get the exact meaning, but there is no mistaking that August 12th is the date printed here, by which time it says you must be out of Burma."

"If we can trust my ability to keep records, August 12th is also the date our baby is due to arrive." That, of course, was my comment.

"Looks like they hit the nail right on the head there," Joe commented. "But I still wonder if we're being too pessimistic. Susie and I have gotten to be almost as good as the Burmese about stalling and dragging our feet. Why don't we wait until August and then reapply? We can always say we misunderstood, and who knows, it might be another year and a half before they discover we're still here. I could help Dr. Violet a few more months, at least, and we could have the baby here as planned. By the first of next year he'd be old enough to travel."

I agreed, though somewhat hesitantly. Neither of us feared that physical harm would come to us if we stayed on. It would simply be a matter of pulling out later, at a time more convenient to us and to the hospital, if real pressure were put on us. But I couldn't help remembering how we had felt trapped at Namkham, not able to leave because there was no one to replace us. Now we were actually being ordered to leave and we were finding excuses not to go. I guess our reaction was to rebel, just as we did when we were ordered out the first time. We simply didn't like being told that we had to leave.

As he knocked the ashes from his pipe, Joe said, "If you have a few minutes Chuck, let's go over to Tun Shein's house."

With that, the two men walked out. I called Timmy in from the yard to start his lessons. He was unhappy because I had interrupted his play, and my mind was definitely not on third-grade arithmetic, so after a half hour of quarreling I adjourned school for the rest of the day.

After what seemed like an eternity, although my watch insisted that only an hour had passed, Joe returned. "Tun Shein thinks we should go," he said. "By the way, he looks terrible. He has a urinary tract infection and is running a pretty high fever. Maybe his poor health accounts for his pessimism, but he insists that this letter is a negative answer to our old appeal, and that we should go now. Since the baby is due about that time, he's probably right. Tun Shein's afraid that if the hospital is nationalized while we're still here, we might have a lot of trouble getting away. If they take over all the hospital trucks and jeeps we couldn't even get to Lashio. I trust Tun Shein's opinions and I think we should take his advice."

And so, with mixed emotions, we began to pack. We set Monday, June 14th, as our deadline for leaving Namkham, and began to work feverishly to be ready within the remaining eight days. In two years we had collected an unbelievable number of things. Friends and patients had given us many gifts which we treasured, and we packed them carefully for the trip home. Much more important than material things were the many memories and the friends we had made. The thought that we would never see those friends again saddened me. Our main purpose in going to Namkham had been to help people, and in many cases they had been more helpful to us than we had been to them. When I was discouraged I had only to look at the faces of the Christians about me who trusted God for their every need and were satisfied with infinitely less of this world's goods than I felt I needed. We had done our best to heal the tuberculous patients, cure the ones with syphilis, get rid of the thousands of intestinal parasites, and give vitamins to the malnourished, but all too often when patients returned to their villages and to the conditions which had caused their diseases, they became ill again. Our help had been temporary at best, but the inner good and happiness we had acquired would have lasting value.

I was worried about Wong Jack. He had been a cook for most of his life. When we left who would need the services of a cook who specialized in Western-style dishes?

What of E Poi, Wong's wife? She could stay at home as she had for many years before coming to us, but she had grown accustomed to the extra money and needed it for the education of their seven children.

And there was May, our little Karen nanny who worked so faithfully. I had arranged for her to go to school on the compound so that she might finish her basic studies. She had decided to return to Rangoon with us when we left, for that was her home. I wanted very much to have her enrolled in school there and to leave her enough money to see her through the rest of the year.

I could hardly bear to think of leaving Pansy, who had become like a sister to me. Then there were Esther and Ja Naw, Chuck and Violet, Tun Shein, and endless others. We would soon be half a world apart, with little chance of meeting again. I tried to comfort myself with the fact that we still had our Shan twins, James and John, and by adopting them we were taking home a small part of the Burmese to keep with us forever.

Boxes began to litter the floor in all our rooms. I gave away as many of our clothes as I could and packed the rest. We had to carry some things with us, the remainder were to be packed in trunks and crates to be sent by ship. My mind fairly whirled as I tried to decide what should go where.

A farewell party was planned for our last Saturday night at

Namkham. There would be a dinner, songs, and farewell speeches. I knew that I would be asked to say a few words, and I decided to make a short speech in Burmese if possible. My Burmese had not progressed much farther than the "How are you, I am fine," stage, so I enlisted Chuck's help. I wrote a short paragraph in English and Chuck translated it for me. Then I memorized it.

Everyone was looking and feeling glum the night of the party. The nurses sang in different languages, following the pattern of our welcoming party. However, this time there were no smiles and the songs were slow and sad. I was completely overwhelmed by the farewell gifts we received. For me there was a handwoven Kachin outfit, a Karen dress, and a Shan outfit. I had longed for these things but had not been able to have them made. A silver *dah*, a long knife beautifully handcrafted by Shan silversmiths, was presented to Joe along with articles of Shan, Kachin, and Karen clothing. There were gifts for the children as well.

Finally it was time for the speechmaking. Chuck, Tun Shein, and Joe gave short talks, all of them depressing, I thought. When it was my turn, I couldn't have been more frightened than if I had been asked to address the General Assembly of the United Nations. I said that I was preparing to give my first and last speech in Burmese, and then in a faltering voice I started my memorized speech. Smiles began to appear on faces which had been entirely expressionless throughout the evening. The mood of the audience lightened, and soon everyone was smiling or laughing out loud. Halfway through the speech I shouted, "Na: leh la:" meaning, "Do you understand?" From all corners of the room came the answer: "Yes!" Thus encouraged, I finished my speech and sat down to applause. My face was flushed with pleasure, and the meeting closed on a happy note.

The next day was our last, and the following morning we made our final departure from the place that had been our home for two years. As we were having an early breakfast, Pansy and

Augusta came to say goodbye. The leavetaking was brief, and they left with tears in their eyes. During the next hour and a half, many of the nurses and staff members came to the house. Confusion reigned as our living room literally overflowed with people and baggage. Finally, all the baggage was loaded onto a large truck and it was time for us to climb into the ambulance. As usual, Tun Shein was driving, and on this occasion Fred Taw went along to help expedite matters in Rangoon.

A slight rain was falling as we drove away. I turned to look back and saw dozens of the nurses moving down the hill toward the hospital. They carried large black umbrellas, and on this grey day their *longyis* seemed unusually bright and colorful.

When we reached the highway, I stole one last backward glance. Several of the girls were waving from the balcony above the entrance to the surgical building. Then I saw Yogi, the big spotted dog we had raised from a pup. He was running wildly toward us, trying to catch up. Huckleberry was with us, of course, but we had had to leave Yogi and our two cats, hoping that they would adopt a new family. One of my saddest memories of that morning was watching the poor dog grow smaller and smaller as we left him behind, still running as hard as he could go.

Our immediate destination was Lashio. We were to spend the night there, meet with the District Internal Revenue Officer the next morning, and then take the noon flight to Rangoon. We reached Lashio by mid-afternoon, stopping only once when we were flagged down by two soldiers who recognized the hospital ambulance. One of their friends in a small army outpost was in the throes of malarial chills and fever and needed medicine. Joe reached into his bag and handed them some chloriquine, and we continued on our way.

At the Internal Revenue Office our records were carefully studied by the officer in charge to be sure that we did not owe the Revolutionary Government one kyat. If we would now sign some papers we would be officially released from the district. The officer spoke excellent English and was most cordial. Toward the end of our visit he said, "I understand there is only one doctor left at the Namkham Hospital. I have also heard that your supply of drugs is very low. Perhaps the Revolutionary Government will have to take over the hospital soon to see that the people get needed care."

At that moment, Joe was signing one of the papers. His pen paused, and I would not have been surprised if smoke had come from his ears. He completed his signature and asked in a voice that was much too calm, "Are we finished now?"

With the help of two men from the Lashio hospital we were able to get our baggage and ourselves aboard the plane for Rangoon. Tun Shein and Fred Taw had already left in the ambulance and were to meet us there.

We ran into a blinding rain storm just outside Rangoon. It was dark by that time, and the old DC-3 shuddered and shook and bounced about the sky. I literally held my breath until the wheels of the plane finally touched the airport runway. It was still raining, and as we ran toward the terminal we were joined by the pilot, who said, "That was a bad storm. My windshield wipers would not work. I had to guess where the runway was." No instruments and no windshield wipers! I thanked God that we had made our last trip from Lashio with the Burma Airways.

Two long, hot weeks passed in Rangoon before everything was completed and we were allowed to leave the country. That was record time, for we had heard of missionaries who had been delayed for months. Without the help of Tun Shein and Fred we might have suffered the same fate, for those two spent hours each day going from one government office to another, handling an exhausting number of details for us.

We discovered first that we had to have a Stay Permit. That important document, of course, was the one we had never been able to get. However, now that we were on our way out of the country the Immigration Office issued us a Stay Permit so that it could be officially revoked!

Next we had to make several trips to the Internal Revenue Office to be thoroughly investigated. Fortunately, they found no fault for we had paid and paid and paid. Burmese tax rates were even higher than the rates we had paid Uncle Sam.

Our last task was to receive final clearance from the Immigration Office. The whole family had to present themselves, and we waited for hours on a hard bench. The large, dirty room was filled with people, most of them Burmese nationals trying to get out of the country. Our children became restless, and fought and cried before it was our turn to talk with the officer who sat behind a long wooden table. He examined our papers and asked a few questions. All went well until he noticed the twins. He spoke to them in Burmese and looked very surprised when they failed to understand. He called another officer, and the two held an animated conversation in Burmese, pointing first to our papers, then to the twins. One of the twins said, "Daddy, I want to go home." The officer said to the boy in English, "Where is your Daddy?" The answer was "Over dere!" and a small finger was pointed in Joe's direction. The officer shrugged his shoulders, stamped the papers *cleared,* and we were free to leave.

Now all we had to do was to purchase our plane tickets. I was a bit apprehensive because the airlines had a ruling that no woman more than thirty weeks pregnant could ride a plane. However, in our case, no questions were asked because we had to leave Burma. Also, if there was an emergency, I was fortunate enough to be traveling with my obstetrician!

The night before our departure I was completely exhausted, physically and emotionally. We were staying at the Baptist Guest House, and after the children were tucked in bed I stepped outside for a breath of air and a chance to be alone. The street was deserted. A few street lamps glimmered in the damp, intense darkness. Suddenly, I was overcome with a great sadness to be leaving this country which had once seemed so strange and forbidding. Already I longed for the familiar faces at Namkham. Most of all, I wondered what kind of person I had become during the past two years. I felt I had acquired a new sense of values and had strengthened some old ones. Could I return to our former life with ease? At that particular moment I had a fleeting scorn for the comforts and rewards which seemed so important in our American society. What next, I wondered, and burst into tears.

Inside the guest house a child cried, and then I heard the anxious call, "Mommy!" One of our sons had awakened in a strange dark room and was calling for me. My concern and weariness lifted, and I knew where my future course lay. Whatever else life offered, I had five children—there would soon be six—who needed me, and I would devote myself, with God's help, to seeing that they became strong, honest young men. What better work could there be, and what higher reward?

We were driven to the airport in the guest house Volkswagen before daylight the next morning. I was touched by the number of friends who came to see us off at that early hour: Tun Shein and Fred, three Namkham nurses who were in Rangoon on vacation, Brad Allen, our nanny May, and Sergeant and Mrs. Johnson from the Embassy. We said our tearful farewells before going into the customs check, an ordeal I dreaded. I had heard stories of customs inspectors who had searched the baggage of departing foreigners and taken jewelry and other items. But the first person we met, wearing a stiff white uniform, was the Anglo-Burman from Mongyu who had been Joe's patient. He had been promoted to chief customs inspector at the airport. He greeted us courteously, and was so kind that what might have been a difficult process passed quickly and pleasantly.

With customs inspection out of the way, we went into a lounge to await the call of our flight to Bangkok. A light rain was falling, but our two older boys went outside to watch the planes. We found them there later, nonchalantly urinating before the large crowd gathered on the balcony above. No one paid the slightest attention. It occurred to me that we would all have some adjustments to make when we arrived home.

When we were settled aboard the comfortable jet-prop plane which Burma Airways operated between Rangoon and Bangkok, it occurred to me that the company might do well to update the crates on their Lashio route as well. Soon we were taxiing to the end of the runway, and with a mighty surge we sped away and rose into the leaden skies. I could see the airport terminal already shrinking to miniature size in the distance. Below us the city of Rangoon sprawled in the early hours of the morning. A single ray of sunlight pierced the rain clouds and shone brightly on the golden dome of the Shwe Dagon Pagoda. Surrounding the city on all sides were thousands of rice paddies. From the air they looked like an endless patchwork quilt.

Our plane gained altitude swiftly and the clouds closed below us, a fleecy white blanket forever blotting out our view of Burmese soil. I turned to look at Joe, who seemed deep in his own thoughts. He reached out and closed his hand over mine.

Tomorrow? Let it come!

Epilogue

About 7:30 a.m. on July 5, 1965, just six days after our family had left Burma, a truck bearing some fifteen soldiers in full battle dress drove onto the Namkham Hospital Compound. The soldiers jumped from the truck and scattered to various positions about the hospital buildings. Shortly thereafter a Jeep appeared with several army officers and a major in command. The gong had just sounded for chapel, and since the officers said nothing, the staff and students gathered for worship. The air was electric with suspense and anticipation. During chapel service, the officers—still silent—waited in the nurses' home. In the meantime, the soldiers on guard padlocked the doors to every building and sealed the locks with red tape.

After chapel, the major asked everyone to remain seated. He reached into his pocket and drew out an official document which he read aloud. In substance, the document stated that the hospital was now officially nationalized and belonged to the Revolutionary Government of Burma. The name was to be changed from the Namkham Hospital to Civil Hospital. All staff members would remain on duty and would continue their work. An inventory would be made of everything belonging to the hospital, and those in charge of the various departments were to be held accountable. The major's final words were that he expected full cooperation from the staff during the critical changeover period. He anticipated that all arrangements would be completed within one week.

There was little visible reaction from the staff. They had expected nationalization, but not so soon and not without warning. The nurses on duty in the wards showed more emotion. Some wept openly, some cursed, but still they had to obey every command of the nationalization committee. Among the patients there were sudden, inexplicable rises in temperature, suspected heart attacks, and a general undercurrent of fear and uncertainty.

Tun Shein and Fred Taw were still in Rangoon attending to the shipment of our baggage. When they heard of the nationalization they turned over all responsibility for our belongings to Ambassador Byroade and began the long, hard drive back to Namkham. They arrived three days later, and the take-over was well underway.

Each staff member responsible for a particular inventory was accompanied by an officer on the nationalization committee. It was Pansy's duty to count every sheet, blanket, pillow, and rag in the linen room. A soldier was posted at the gate to her house, Dr. Seagrave's old home, and she was not allowed to return there until the major in charge gave special permission.

Every pill had to be counted. The officers did not trust Chit Tin, who was usually in charge of the drug room, so they ordered two men from town to do the counting. When these two were discovered with a generous supply of vitamins and drugs in their pockets, they were relieved of their job and Chit Tin was reinstated.

All medicines and equipment had to be accounted for and added to the inventory. Everything in the house where we had lived was listed. Pansy's house was scrutinized carefully. Many of the furnishings belonged to her or had been possessions of Dr. Seagrave; in each case, Pansy had to prove that they did not belong to the hospital. She had to produce the bill of sale for the old refrigerator and other appliances, to keep these items from being turned over to the government. The Burmese Government was not about to let anything slip through its grasp without a struggle.

Money was of utmost interest to the nationalization committee. They removed the donation box from the outpatient department, and placed a padlock on the safe in the office. Later, when the safe was opened, all the money was counted and the financial records studied in detail. Since there were no banks in the immediate area, Tun Shein often kept money for staff members in the hospital safe. Several hundred kyats of such savings were taken from the safe at the time of nationalization. Tun Shein was responsible for the money and had to borrow from Pansy to repay it. The A.M.C.B. subsequently reimbursed him.

Three government doctors were sent to Namkham to begin work. One acted as medical superintendent and the others carried out the medical and surgical work. Dr. Violet was kept on the staff, for she too had become a government servant.

The nurses were ranked in accordance with other government hospitals, and their uniforms changed. Grandma Naomi was designated matron, or chief nurse, and Esther, Emily, and Say Paw became nursing sisters. All other nurses held the title of staff nurse. Pansy was told that henceforth there would be no such post as dean of nursing; the nursing school would be discontinued. She would be expected to do general nursing and help out wherever necessary. She was directed to move from the house where she and Dr. Seagrave had lived, in order to make room for the medical superintendent.

Three staff members discovered that they would no longer be needed. One was PoZo, whose job as chief engineer was abolished. I have often wondered if his job as chief cow-chaser was abolished, too. Chuck was now without a job, and, of course, so was Tun Shein. Their jobs had been administrative, and would be handled by the medical superintendent, a government doctor.

The changeover period, instead of being completed in a week, dragged on for months. A hospital which had been almost fifty years in the building could not change hands in a few days. The Old Man's empire was not easily dissolved.

We first heard of the nationalization when we stopped overnight in Okinawa on our way back to the States. A Burmese who worked with the U.S. Government monitoring Burmese broadcasts had heard the newscast reporting the hospital takeover. Four other hospitals, the only remaining private institutions in Burma, were nationalized at the same time. They had been operated by the Baptists, Roman Catholics, and Seventh Day Adventists.

The first information we could get was scanty and unreliable. Our friends from Namkham could not write freely because their letters might be censored and they dared not speak unfavorably of the government. We feared for the safety of friends who had served the Namkham Hospital so faithfully. There was almost no news from Burma in our papers, and what little we read we knew was farcical. For instance, one Associated Press release from Rangoon, written by Peter Boog in 1966, stated, " . . . At Namkham service is still free and, while Seagrave's American assistants have been replaced by Burmese, his famed nurses are still there.

"The hospital previously operated with a $10,000 yearly government grant and about $20,000 in private contributions from the United States, mostly in the form of medicines.

"Now the Burmese Government provides approximately $60,000 annually to help the hospital service a wider area than it did during Seagrave's time. Funds were never sufficient and medicine was scarce."

We had heard enough from Burma to know that the services provided by the hospital had been greatly curtailed. Most of the old Seagrave nurses were still there because they were not allowed to leave, or else they were old and had no other place to go. As for money and drugs, the A.M.C.B. had provided much more money than the article stated and could have given infinitely more in drugs had the Burmese Government allowed the

Board to do so.

In a carefully written letter from Tun Shein, we learned that he had moved his large family and meager possessions to Rangoon, where he was working with the Burma Baptist Convention. During the summer of 1966 all missionaries were expelled from Burma, and much of the responsibility for the changeover of property from the American Foreign Mission Society to the Burma Baptist Convention fell to Tun Shein. He continued to house and feed from twenty to twenty-five people: family, students, teachers, and transients who had no place to stay.

Soon after the hospital was nationalized the A.M.C.B. disbanded. Their funds, over $200,000, were turned over to the American Korean Foundation to establish a Gordon S. Seagrave Memorial Hospital and School of Nursing in Korea. The site for the memorial was chosen by the A.K.F. after a search which led to the small township of Kaejong in the North Cholla Province, near the Yellow Sea port of Kunsan and 110 miles south of Seoul. There, since 1948, Dr. Lee Young Choon had labored to build the Institute for Rural Health to care for the medical needs of some 800,000 poor farmers and fishermen. The similarity between the lives and work of Drs. Seagrave and Lee first attracted the American Korean Foundation to the Institute for Rural Health, and so it was chosen as the hospital to receive American aid under the aegis of the Seagrave Memorial. It is hoped that funds will be available to send American doctors and nurses to join Dr. Lee and his staff, and to give them the modern equipment they have always needed. Someday soon, perhaps, the Gordon Seagrave Memorial Hospital will act as a model for the solution of the health problems of rural Asia, and a lasting tribute to international cooperation.

On August 19, 1965, one month after we returned to the States, Judson Joseph Newhall was born. He was not the girl, Karen Shan, we anticipated, but I welcomed another son. After all, few ladies are fortunate enough to be the sweetheart of seven handsome men.

Our family is happily resettled in Bradenton. Joe practices obstetrics and gynecology with the same partners and I am busy with housewifely chores. The boys, except Judson, are in school. Joe and I have formally adopted the twins, James and John, and they are naturalized citizens of the United States.

Pansy and Augusta have also joined our large family. Pansy was released from the hospital in August, 1966, and stayed with Tun Shein in Rangoon while waiting to be released from Burma. We had easily completed all necessary paperwork from the U.S. side, but she could get nothing but frustration from the Burmese. After thirteen anxious months she was given papers allowing her to travel—but not an official passport—and five days later she was flying across Europe and the Atlantic.

It was Pansy who furnished me with most of the information about the hospital nationalization. She is completely disheartened by the changes that have taken place in Burma and at the hospital. The hospital provides almost no surgery, and since the last students have completed their nursing course the training school no longer exists. Medicines are scarce and fewer patients come for treatment.

The internal situation in Burma is generally bad. Food is rationed, expensive, and in meager supply. The same is true of clothing, piece goods, shoes, and all other commodities. The people are restless, the Black Market flourishes, and insurgent activity has reached a new height. Everyone is careful not to be accused of actions contrary to government policy, lest they be jailed and forgotten. Pansy told us that one staff nurse at Namkham had been accused of aiding the insurgents and was sentenced to ten years in jail. Another friend was suspected of rebel connections and was jailed in Lashio. He was released nine months later, after nothing could be proved.

Pansy has made the tremendous adjustment to life in America.

She works as office nurse in Joe's office, sings in our church choir, and has many new friends. Augusta has made equally good progress.

I do not believe in ghosts, but sometimes I wish I did. It would be easy to imagine a flurry of spirit activity in a certain small plot of ground near the Civil Hospital in Namkham, Burma. A shaggy, gray-haired old specter is ranting and raving in several languages. During the sixty-eight years that he lived in the body of Gordon S. Seagrave, he was never quiet or at peace with himself or the world. Now all that he worked for and dreamed about has been reduced to an ill-functioning instrument of the Burmese Government, and he still can't rest.

"Those Goddamned s.o.b.'s are against me," I can hear him say. "They hate me, but I'll haunt them to the bitter end."